Fundamentals of the Bond Market

Fundamentals of the Bond Market

Esmé Faerber

McGraw-Hill

New York • Chicago • San Francisco • Lisbon
London • Madrid • Mexico City • Milan • New Delhi
San Juan • Seoul • Singapore • Sydney • Toronto

Library of Congress Cataloging-in-Publication Data

Faerber, Esmé.
    Fundamentals of the bond market / by Esmé Faerber.
       p.   cm.
    ISBN 0-07-136251-7
    1. Bond market--United States.   2. Bonds--United States.   I. Title

    HG4910.F26 2000
    332.63'23'0973--dc21   00-053703

McGraw-Hill

A Division of The McGraw·Hill Companies

1 2 3 4 5 6 7 8 9 0 DOC/DOC 9 0 2 1 0 9 8 7

ISBN 0-07-136251-7

Printed and bound by R. R. Donnelley & Sons Company.

McGraw-Hill books are available at special quantity discounts to use as premiums and sales promotions, or for use in corporate training programs. For more information, please write to Director of Special Sales, McGraw-Hill, 11 West 19th Street, New York, NY 10011. Or contact your local bookstore.

 This book is printed on recycled, acid-free paper containing a minimum of 50 percent recycled de-inked fiber.

Contents

Preface

Fixed income investments are difficult for most beginning investment professionals and investors to understand. This is partly due to the greater focus given to stock investments and their management in college courses. As a result, many beginning investment professionals and individual investors are not as comfortable with bond investments as they are with their stock investments. The intent of this book is to build an understanding of the different types of bond products, the factors that affect their performance, and how they fit into investors' portfolios. Many of the chapters include discussions with regard to the different strategies and how investors can take advantage of changing conditions in the bond markets.

Several themes are consistent throughout the chapters in the book. These are as follows:

1. A discussion of the basic concepts in each chapter.
2. An integration of the theory discussed with practical applications.
3. Exercises and worksheets to familiarize the readers with the theoretical and practical concepts discussed in each chapter.
4. The term *investor* is used in a broader context to include entry level professionals along with individual investors.
5. References to the Internet are made whenever it is perceived to be helpful to investors. These references are current. However, due to the rapid growth of the Internet, these references over time may change due to new Internet sites. The purpose of introducing the use of the Internet is to familiarize investors with this medium so that they can become more accomplished in their usage and exploration of this tool.

Chapter 1, "Origins: The Markets and Their Beginnings," begins with a discussion of the bond markets and how bonds are used in investors' portfolios. The rest of the chapter focuses on the different types of investments and how the components of an investment plan determine the choices of investments.

Chapter 2, "Basics: Terms, Definitions, Trends, and Policies," explains what bonds are, their characteristics, and terminology. The differences between stocks and bonds are emphasized so that investors can choose the right mix of these investments for their portfolios. The latter part of the chapter includes an overview of the economic influences, which have a bearing on bond prices. Understanding the relationship between the economy and the bond markets is of great significance for bond investors.

Chapter 3, "Beginnings: What Affects Prices?" investigates the factors that directly affect bond prices. These direct factors are interest rates, length of time to maturity, risk and coupon yields, and the yield to maturity. An analysis of bond quotations is a starting point to this discussion. The indirect factors, which provide floor and ceiling prices on bonds, are the different features that bonds might have in their indentures such as call, put, sinking fund, and conversion features.

Chapter 4, "Categories: Types of Bonds," discusses the different bond securities individually, namely short-term fixed income securities (which include money market mutual funds, Treasury bills, certificates of deposit), Treasury notes and bonds, Treasury inflation-indexed securities, government agency and pass-through securities, corporate bonds, municipal bonds, convertible bonds, and zero-coupon bonds. These can be read in any order in the chapter.

Chapter 5, "Trading: Buying and Selling Bonds," discusses the practical aspects of buying and selling bonds. It starts with an analysis of the different types of bonds, a discussion of the risks and returns in order to determine which bonds to purchase within the framework of an asset allocation plan. The latter part of the chapter shows the route of an order from the origination by the investor to the confirmation.

Chapter 6, "Analysis: Evaluating Bond Characteristics," evaluates the different characteristics of bonds in order to enable investors to make better choices in the bonds they purchase and hold. Ratings, yield, duration and convexity are discussed to assist investors in the management of their bond portfolios.

Chapter 7, "Risk versus Return: Enhancing Investment Performance," focuses on the techniques for balancing risk and return, including a discussion of the yield curve and how to use it. This is followed by the practical aspects of developing an investment plan, determining acceptable levels of risk, selecting the appropriate investments, and managing the portfolio taking into account risk and return.

Chapter 8, "Diversifying: Bond Mutual Funds," includes information on bond mutual funds, starting with what they are, how they work, risks, returns, how to buy and sell, the tax ramifications, the advantages, disadvantages, and caveats. The chapter ends with a discussion of whether investors should consider bond mutual funds or individual bonds.

Chapter 9, "Managing a Bond Portfolio," concentrates on the strategies for managing bond portfolios, and Chapter 10, "Brokers: Investment Companies and Services," discusses the different types of financial assistance available.

Bonds are not riskless investments. By understanding the factors that affect their valuation, investors will be more comfortable investing and holding these securities.

Esmé Faerber

Acknowledgments

The preparation of this book was greatly facilitated by many people. I am grateful for their help and I would like to thank the following people for their assistance: Kelli Christiansen, at McGraw-Hill Publishing Company for her superb editorial assistance; Michael A. Faerber and Jennifer A. Faerber for their computer assistance; Tisha Findeison and James H. Gately at the Vanguard Group, and Bruce Fryer, at Morgan Stanley Dean Witter for their investment materials.

A special note of thanks goes to my husband Eric, and our children, Jennifer and Michael, for their patience and continued support.

Chapter 1

Origins: The Markets and Their Beginnings

Origins: The Markets and Their Beginnings

The U.S. bond market is both large and diverse and presents important investment opportunities to individual investors. Figure 1-1 gives a sense of how large the U.S. bond market was in comparison to the stock market and investments in bank assets for 1999 (Economist, 1999). Investment in the U.S. bond market accounted for almost 50 percent of total investments. Stock investments accounted for 30 percent of the total, leaving the balance of investments in bank accounts. It is not surprising to find that investments in bonds outstrip stocks and that the bond markets are much larger than the stock market. This is due to several reasons. Both governments and companies issue bonds, whereas only companies issue stocks. Secondly, when companies do raise cash in the capital markets, their preferred form of financing is through debt, namely bonds and notes. Thus, more bonds than stocks are issued. A historical perspective of the growth in the bond markets will clarify this point.

Historical Growth of the U.S. Bond Markets

In 1998, the U.S. bond market was around $13 trillion and the Bond Market Association's Research Quarterly estimated growth of two percent into the first quarter of 1999 (Research Quarterly Press Release, June 3, 1999). This includes the debt from all the bond sectors: corporate, asset, and mortgage-backed securities, municipal, federal agency and government sponsored debt, and money market securities. Figure 1-2 exhibits a breakdown of the U.S. debt market for the second quarter

Figure 1-1   How Assets are Held in the USA (1999)

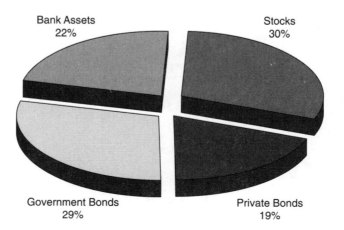

Bank Assets
22%

Stocks
30%

Government Bonds
29%

Private Bonds
19%

of 1999, and Table 1-1 shows the make-up and growth of the U.S. bond markets from 1990 to1998.

Treasury Market

Treasury securities account for the largest segment of the U.S. market, which has grown by 52.8 percent over the eight-year period. This sector is composed of non-interest bearing Treasury bills, Treasury notes and bonds, and the new Treasury inflation indexed securities.

Corporate Bond Market

The second largest segment of the U.S. bond market is corporate debt, which has grown by 84 percent in the period from 1990 to 1998. The corporate bond sector is subdivided into different segments: industrial, utility, financial, and transportation securities. Industrial and utility

Figure 1-2   U.S. Debt Market, Second Quarter, 1999

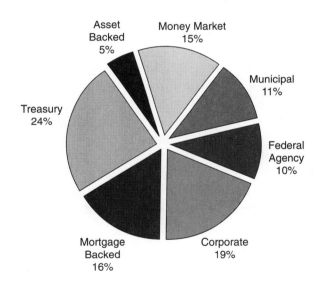

Table 1–1   Make-up of the U.S. Bond Markets 1990-1998 ($ billions)

	Municipal	Treasury	Agency-Mortgage Backed	Corporate	Federal Agency	Money Market
1990	1,184.4	2,195.8	1,024.4	1,333.7	434.7	1,156
1991	1,272.2	2,471.6	1,160.5	1,440.0	442.8	1,054
1992	1,302.8	2,754.1	1,273.5	1,542.7	484.0	994
1993	1,377.5	2,989.5	1,349.6	1,662.1	570.7	971
1994	1,341.7	3,126.0	1,441.9	1,746.6	738.9	1,034
1995	1,293.5	3,307.2	1,570.4	1,912.6	844.6	1,177
1996	1,296.0	3,459.7	1,711.2	2,055.0	925.8	1,393
1997	1,367.5	3,456.8	1,825.8	2,213.6	1,022.6	1,692
1998	1,464.3	3,355.5	2,018.4	2,462.0	1,296.5	1,978

Source: www.bondmarkets.com/research/osdebt.shtml

companies issue most of the U.S. corporate debt securities. Corporate debt differs from Treasury securities because a wide range exists in the types of debt and the quality of the issues. Treasury securities are backed by the full faith and credit of the U.S. government, which means that no risk of default exists on the interest payments and repayment of principal. Corporate debt can be issued by investment grade companies such as Ford Motor Company or Exxon Corporation (two examples of the highest investment grade companies), or at the other extreme, by high-risk, speculative grade companies that may be heading toward bankruptcy. In the latter example, a company has a good chance of defaulting on either the interest payments and/or the repayment of the principal.

Not only is there a range of credit quality, but also many different types of corporate bonds exist. *Debenture* issues are unsecured bonds backed only by the promise of the issuer to pay timely interest payments and the repayment of principal. *Subordinated debenture* bonds are junior unsecured bonds, and the bondholders' claims are subordinated to those of the regular debenture issues of the issuer.

A growing segment of the unsecured corporate debt market is the high yield or junk bond market. These bonds are rated below investment grade by the ratings' organizations (Standard & Poor's, Moody's), and are typically issued by small companies or companies using the debt to finance leveraged buy-outs of other companies.

Secured bonds are senior bonds, and their claim to interest payments and the repayment of principal are backed by the assets of the issuer. *Equipment trust certificates,* issued by transportation companies such as the airlines and railroads, are used to purchase airplanes and railroad cars, which also serve as collateral for the bonds. Other examples of secured type bonds are *collateral trust bonds,* which use financial assets as collateral for the bonds. Also, within the corporate bond market are *zero-coupon* and *convertible bonds,* which have different characteristics to regular coupon corporate bonds.   .

Federal Agency and Mortgage-Backed Bond Markets

The markets for Federal agency and agency mortgage-backed bonds have grown by 300 percent and 50 percent respectively over the eight-year period of 1990 to 1998. *Agency securities* are obligations issued by U.S. government agencies and U.S.-sponsored corporations. In general, the characteristics of agency bonds are similar. The different agency bonds make their interest payments semi-annually or annually and are issued in minimum denominations ranging between $1,000 and $10,000. Some issues are exempt from state and local taxes, and others are not.

Agency mortgage-backed bonds are also referred to as pass-through securities. This is because these bonds represent an undivided interest in a pool of mortgages. The mortgage-backed bondholders receive interest and principal payments, which are the pass-through mortgage payments of the mortgagees (borrowers) to the government agency. The different agency mortgage-backed bonds may differ considerably in their minimum issue denominations, the rate of interest, and principal repayments. In addition, the payment amounts are not fixed. Also, the payment amounts include a return of principal, whereas with regular agency bonds, the principal is repaid at maturity (when the bonds mature).

Municipal Bond Market

The municipal bond market has not grown as rapidly as the aforementioned bond markets during the same eight-year period of 1990 to 1998, but it still accounts for a large percentage of the total U.S. bond market (16.09 percent in Figure 1-2). States, counties, and local governments issue municipal bonds. The distinctive feature of municipal bonds is that the interest payments are exempt from federal income taxes. The interest income is also exempt from state and local taxes if the investors live in the state and county issuing the bonds.

Two types of municipal bonds exist: general obligation bonds and revenue bonds. *General obligation bonds* are usually secured by the taxing power of the issuer. In other words, the interest and principal payments are backed by the taxing power of the state, county, city, school, or special district, and its ability to raise more taxes. *Revenue bonds* are issued by specific revenue producing projects of municipal governments such as hospitals, toll roads, bridges, public water works, and the like. The revenues generated by these projects or enterprises are used to pay the interest and principal repayments on the debt. Some municipal bonds are sold with guarantees by third parties. The issuing municipality will buy insurance from a third party who guarantees the interest payments over the life of the bond. This lowers not only the risk of default for investors of the bond issue, but also the coupon rate that the issuer would have to pay to attract investors to invest in the issue.

Money Market

The size of the U.S. money market has grown by 71 percent from 1990 to 1998. This market consists of short-term securities with maturities of one year or less. Treasury bills, commercial paper, bankers' acceptances, repurchase agreements, and negotiable certificates of deposit are examples of money market securities.

What Investors Should Know About the Bond Markets

Investors should understand how the different bond markets work because this is where the price of the bond is determined. The bond markets do not work exactly like the stock markets; some distinguishing differences exist. The bond markets are fragmented; without a centralized trading floor, fresh bond prices are hard to come by. The Internet has brought individual investors accessibility to online stock trading. However, the advent of online bond trading is much slower and not as widespread for various reasons.

New issues of bonds are sold in the *primary* market, whereby the issuer of the bonds receives the proceeds through the selling intermediary, the investment banker. Investors who have acquired bonds at issue could sell them before maturity, which can be done in the *secondary* markets. In other words, the buying and selling of publicly traded bonds take place in the secondary markets. These markets are important because they provide varying degrees of liquidity, which also determines the pricing of the issues.

Treasury and U.S. Government Markets

In the secondary market, Treasury securities are sold through 38 primary dealers, which include some of the large investment banks and large banks in the major U.S. cities. These large institutions also make markets for U.S. agency securities. Dealers quote bid and asked prices for Treasuries and U.S. agency securities. However, the availability of price quotations differs considerably within the different bond markets and from the pricing transparency of the stock market.

With online trading, investors receive current prices on all listed traded stocks. However, not all bonds follow this rubric. The Treasury market is the most liquid of the bond markets and the spreads between the bid and asked prices are the smallest. They are rarely larger than one-eighth of a point. Therefore, Treasury securities are much more conducive for on-line trading because they possess more price transparency than most other types of bonds. Treasury security prices are quoted in the daily financial newspapers, and investors can obtain fresh bid and asked price quotes on these securities. The San Francisco-based Bond Exchange provides users with these current prices.

In contrast, U.S. agency securities are not as liquid, and spreads are much greater than those of Treasury securities. A number of factors contribute to this difference such as credit risk, the volume of bonds traded, the coupon yield, the length of time to maturity, and market rates of interest. Prices of the different government agency securities are not quoted in the daily newspapers, and investors cannot obtain the latest dealer-to-dealer or dealer-to-customer trades during the day. Several on-line brokerage firms are tapping into the Bond Exchange to provide both sides with prices of agency securities.

Corporate Bond Market

Corporate bonds may either be listed on the exchanges (New York and American Stock Exchanges), or unlisted, whereby bond dealers trade them in the over-the-counter market. Only a small number of corporate bonds are listed. The majority of trades, particularly large trades, take place in the over-the-counter market.

Information on the closing prices of listed bonds on the New York and American Stock Exchanges can be found in the daily newspapers, but it is somewhat limited. These prices do not include the bid and asked spreads (the prices at which dealers are willing to buy and sell securities). Thus, a bond investor can never be sure of the brokerage markup. Investors currently interested in buying listed bonds would have to compare prices of the same issues at different brokerage firms in order to ascertain the best price.

Because the majority of corporate bonds are traded in the over-the-counter markets, currently even less price transparency exists than for listed bonds. In the-over-the-counter market, the broker/dealer trades the buy and sell orders for the bonds held in their inventory, making profits from the spread in the buy and sell orders. The spreads for these unlisted corporate bonds may be quite large, particularly for junk bonds and thinly traded corporate issues. Investors may have little to no access to these spreads.

Dealers generally keep prices of their trades to themselves for a number of reasons. First, dealers own their trading information and cannot be expected to hand this over to others who could potentially profit from disseminating their information, particularly in the case of stock prices where the stock exchanges make money by disseminating price quotes. Secondly, corporate bonds are not nearly as liquid as stocks. Most corporate bonds bought are held for long periods of time. The Bond Market Association estimates that only one out of 25 corporate bonds is traded once in a given year (Patterson, November 5, 1999).

The *National Association of Securities Dealers* (NASD) is attempting to put together a corporate bond trading system that will address the lack of pricing transparency. In the NASD proposal, dealers would report all their trades to Nasdaq and this information would be distributed to the public. Bond dealers are not happy about the proposal, and problems in the price quotes' ownership would have to be worked out in order for this proposal to be implemented. Another alternative mentioned would be to have all price quotes of corporate bonds traded go through the Bond Market Association's own trading information system called Corporate Trades (Doherty, November 29, 1999, p.MW10).

Municipal Bond Market

The large investment banks underwrite municipal bonds and, consequently, are actively involved in the secondary municipal bond market. Banks are also involved because of their large investment portfolios in municipal bonds.

Municipal bonds suffer from the same lack of pricing transparency as corporate bonds because the municipal bond market is so fragmented and these bonds are traded in the over-the-counter market. Broker/dealers trade the municipal bonds held in their inventories for profit.

The Bond Market Association provides wholesale prices on municipal bonds traded on the previous day (Patterson, November 12,1999). Online brokers such as E*Trade and DLJ Direct provide investors with bid and asked spreads for municipal bonds.

If more dealers add their inventories of bonds to the Bond Exchange system, the spreads will narrow with more competitive pricing. With more broker/dealers listing their bonds on the Internet, investors not only have a wider selection of bonds available for purchase, but they can also compare the commissions or markups charged to trade municipal bonds.

Money Market

Money market securities are those with maturities of one year or less. The money market does not have a specific location like the New York Stock Exchange, for example. Instead, it consists of a collection of markets in different locations such as New York, Tokyo, London, and other financial capitals around the world. The major participants in the money markets are as follows:

- The primary dealers (about 38 in number) in U.S. Treasury bills
- Large money center banks in the financial capitals around the world
- Commercial paper and bankers' acceptance dealers
- Other money market brokers

The secondary market for U.S. Treasury bills is active and spreads are narrow, even though dealers buy and sell these securities from their own inventories. Individual investors with relatively small investments in commercial paper and bankers' acceptances may find difficulty in liquidating their positions before maturity. Money market mutual funds offer investors liquidity, instant access to their money, and similar rates of return as the individual money market, without having to enter the secondary markets to withdraw their funds.

An Investment Plan that Includes Bonds for the 21st Century

The investor's investments and investment strategy can have a significant impact on his or her current and future lifestyle. The returns on investments can make the difference between living comfortably or struggling, both now and in the future. This is partly due to increasing costs of education, health care, and taxation, as well as the fact that Americans are living longer.

HMOs and health insurance companies have been reducing the amounts paid to healthcare providers in order to boost their earnings. As a result, both premiums paid to HMOs and insurance companies, and out-of-pocket payments from subscribers will increase to consume greater percentages of disposable income. Educational costs have doubled in this past decade, and if this trend continues, it will cost a quarter of a million dollars for an undergraduate degree from a private college by the end of the first decade of the 21st century.

Many people may disagree with my premise on taxation, citing that the top marginal Federal tax rates have fallen from over 50 percent to

---

Worksheet 1–1

How to Reduce Transaction Costs When Buying Bonds

The Internet is changing the way bonds are bought and sold, by making prices more available to individual investors. With greater access to more offerings, investors can receive better prices and reduce their commission/markup costs.

1. Shop around at the following Web sites first, before buying:

www.bondsonline.com	Information on bonds
www.publicdebt.treas.gov	Treasury securities
www.investinginbonds.com	Previous day's prices on bond trades
www.tradebonds.com	Bond prices
www.munidirect.com	Munibond prices
www.etrade.com	Broker's inventory of bonds
www.dljdirect.com	Broker's inventory of bonds
www.schwab.com	Broker's inventory of bonds
www.bondagent.com	Broker's inventory of bonds

2. Open accounts at several brokerage firms.
3. Compare the bid/asked spreads and commissions.
4. Use the bond research tools available on the different Web sites.

---

the 39.6 percent over the last quarter of the 20th century. However, Americans pay many other taxes besides federal taxes such as state and local income taxes, payroll taxes, real estate taxes, and sales taxes on the consumption of certain goods, as well as gift and estate taxes. When all these taxes are added up, the amount left for savings and investments may be much lower than anticipated. Life expectancy is increasing, which will require a more sophisticated approach to investing in order to fund longer periods of retirement.

The key to success for the 21st century is two-fold:

• To save more; and
• To invest it wisely.

Worksheet 1-2 outlines a strategy for putting more money towards savings. Most of us wait for an increase in salary to put money aside, but most often it is too late to build a nest egg for retirement. The choices of how to spend disposable income are infinite, but investors should not short-change their savings. Retirement is so distant for many people that the urgency to save does not present itself until it is too late. Many other reasons exist for saving besides retirement:

Worksheet 1–2

How to Save More

Rule 1. Investors should pay themselves first at the beginning of every month.

Waiting to see how much money is left over at the end of the month never works as well as deciding what amount can be saved at the beginning of the month. This is because most investors spend whatever is available, leaving little to nothing for savings. See Worksheet 1–3 to determine the amount to save at the beginning of each month. The compelling reasons to save are often replaced by our desires for instant gratification, which comes from spending to satisfy the latest wants. Another reason to save at the beginning of the month is the power of compounding. A dollar invested today is worth more than a dollar in the future. Figure 1–3 illustrates the benefits of saving at the beginning of the period rather than at the end of the period. A hundred dollars saved at the beginning of every month instead of at the end of the month results in $16,470 instead of $16,388. The larger the amounts saved, the longer the time period and the higher the rate of interest, and the more significant the difference will be. This rule can be applied to an investor's IRA payments. Instead of waiting until the end of the tax year to deposit an IRA payment, the investor makes it at the beginning of each tax year.

Figure 1-3   Timing of Amounts Saved

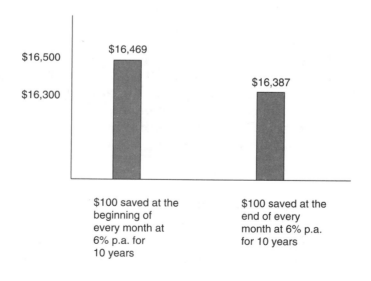

Rule 2. Investors should save as often as they can.

Whenever additional amounts of money are received, investors should save it before they have the chance to spend it. Small additional amounts of as little as $25 per deposit can make a difference, thanks to the compounding of interest.

Rule 3. Start saving now.

The earlier the savings program is begun, the longer the compounding period and the greater the future earnings power. Figure 1–4 illustrates this process showing the growth of a $5,000 deposit invested for 5 years, 10 years, 15 years, and 20 years at 6 percent p.a. The benefits of longer investing periods should prompt many young people to invest when they are young and not wait until they are older.

Figure 1-4   The Effects of Time on Compounded Amounts

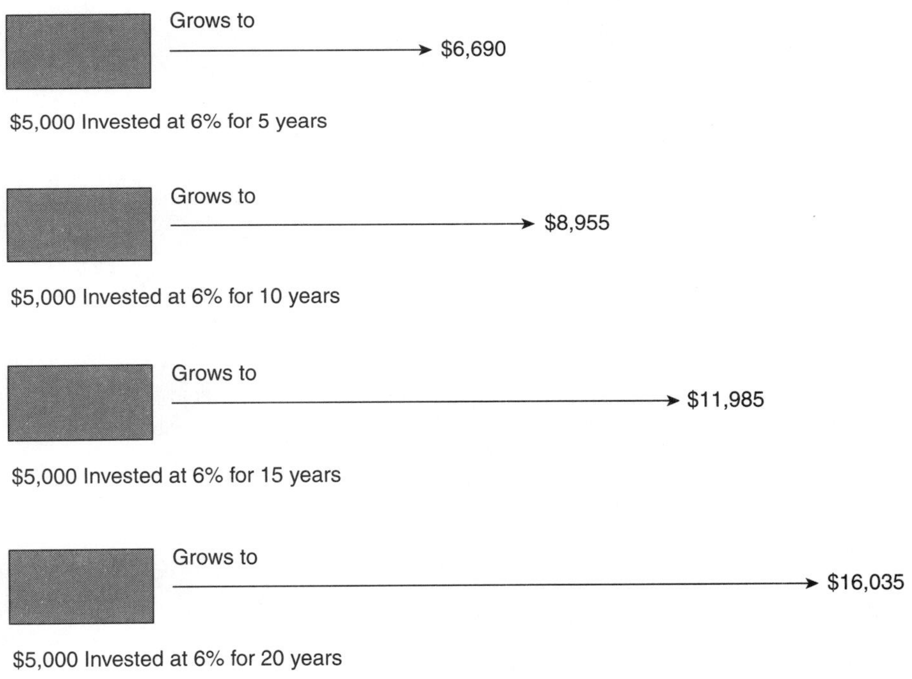

Grows to
→ $6,690

$5,000 Invested at 6% for 5 years

Grows to
→ $8,955

$5,000 Invested at 6% for 10 years

Grows to
→ $11,985

$5,000 Invested at 6% for 15 years

Grows to
→ $16,035

$5,000 Invested at 6% for 20 years

Worksheet 1–3

Use a Budget to Determine the Monthly Savings Amount

Monthly Budget

Inflows/Receipts
Salary   _____
Partnership Profits   _____
Interest/Dividends   _____
Rental Income   _____
Gain on Sale of Assets   _____
Tax Refund   _____
Other   _____
Total Inflows   _____

Outflows/Expenditures

Mortgage/Rent   _____
Food   _____
Clothing   _____
Utilities   _____
Medical/Dental   _____
Home Insurance   _____
Auto Insurance   _____
Life Insurance   _____
Disability Insurance   _____
Auto Loan   _____
Auto Expenses   _____
Real Estate Taxes   _____
Estimated Taxes   _____
Contributions   _____
Child Care Payments   _____
Recreation   _____
Other   _____
Total Outflows   _____

Surplus/Deficit of Cash Flows

Inflows Minus Outflows   _____
Savings from Surplus   _____

Three steps to constructing this budget are as follows:

1. List all sources of estimated monthly income.
2. List all the expenses for the month.
3. If expected revenues exceed expected expenditures for the month; a surplus will result (a deficit is when expenditures exceed revenues). If a projected surplus is available, the

investor can determine how much to put into savings at the beginning of the month. This leads to a more disciplined approach to savings than waiting to see how much is available at the end of the month. The temptation to spend money is much greater if it is sitting in a checking account than if it is not there. A word of caution: Before all the surplus is put into a savings account, the investor should review the projected future months' surplus/deficits to even out any unusually large expenditures such as annual insurance premiums, quarterly tax payments, semiannual real estate taxes, among others.

- To buy a house
- To set up a college education fund
- For financial security
- For emergencies

The second part of the successful strategy is to invest one's savings wisely. Investments are made to generate future purchasing power that will keep well ahead of inflation. In other words, rates of return need to exceed not only the rate of inflation, but also any investment expenses and taxes paid on earnings, in order to generate future purchasing power. The amount of the premium over and above these costs (inflation, investment expenses, and taxes) will vary considerably for the different types of investments over time as economic and financial circumstances change. If the rates of return on investments do not exceed these costs, the investments earn negative real rates of return and lose future purchasing power.

What Are the Investment Choices?

People have a wide array of investments to choose from, ranging from bank savings accounts and money market mutual funds, to individual stocks and bonds, and equity and fixed income mutual funds. These investments are all very different and investors need to be aware of their characteristics to determine if they are suitable for their needs.

Many investors are not rational in their thinking about their investments. After buying a house, the average investor's funds go into low-yielding bank savings accounts, money market funds, and certificates of deposit. This strategy results in low real returns after the costs of inflation, investment expenses, and taxes are deducted. Yet many investors persist with these investments, partly because they find the complexities of stocks and bonds to be overwhelming. Additionally, the stock and bond markets have increased volatility, which can result in a loss of their principal. Therefore, these investors are paralyzed into keeping their money invested in low yielding accounts.

The record stock market of the large capitalized stocks over the past four years through November 1999 enticed many investors who had never previously invested in stocks to jump into the market. This shift became apparent by the frenzy to invest in Internet stocks, *initial public offerings* (IPOs), and other risky plays, which have defied gravity in their meteoric ascent to dangerously high valuations. The incredibly high returns earned in relatively short periods of time from Internet stocks prompted many investors to disregard the risks of investing in these expensive stocks. Euphoria arises when stocks have the potential to go up 25 to 50 points in one day, but the downside is that these stocks have the potential to go down by that margin and more on a bad day. Ignoring the volatility of these stocks in the market in pursuit of higher returns may be disastrous for investors who do not weigh the overall risks of these investments.

Rapid sell-offs in the stock market such as the one in the weeks of August 1998, emphasize the short-term volatility of stock prices, driving many investors, who react to the news headlines, back to the safety of their low-yielding investments in bank accounts, money market funds, and certificates of deposit. This myopic look at the stock and the bond markets makes investors feel secure with their low-yielding investments. The lack of understanding of how stocks and bonds perform perpetuates investors' fears of loss and promotes the safety of the different low yielding savings options.

Understanding the characteristics of the different types of investments will help investors to determine which investments are right for their needs. Figure 1-5 illustrates the characteristics and some of the advantages of money market investments. Figure 1-6 lists the characteristics of stocks and bonds.

Which Investments Are Best?

It becomes apparent from Figures 1-5 and 1-6 that money market investments are temporary parking places for funds, and the real returns that keep ahead of inflation, investment expenses, and taxes, are earned from stocks and bonds. Astute investors might even wonder why they should consider bonds when stocks provide the greatest returns over long periods of time and have consistently outperformed bonds over long periods of time. A number of reasons support why bonds should be a part of a portfolio of investments.

Despite the fact that stocks have historically outperformed bonds over long periods of time, they are volatile. Bond investments offer less variability in returns than common stocks (8.4 percent for long-term corporate bonds versus 20.5 percent for common stocks in the Ibbotson study [1994], refer to Figure 1-7). However, if there is a long investment period, the higher variability risks for common stocks can be averaged, resulting in higher returns for stocks.

Figure 1–5 Characteristics of Money Market Investments

Money Market Equivalents		
Investments	**Objectives**	**Advantages**
Bank Savings Accounts	Preserve Capital	• Instant access to money • FDIC Insured
Money Market Mutual Funds	Preserve Capital/ Earn Income	• Access to funds within 3 days or less • Overnight electronic transfer of funds • Check writing privileges with some limitations • Rates of return slightly higher than savings accounts
Certificates of Deposit	Preserve Capital/ Earn Income	• Access to funds at maturity (available before but with an early withdrawal penalty) • Rates of return slightly higher than money market funds • Bank CDs may be FDIC insured
Treasury Bills	Preserve Capital/ Earn Income	• Safe investment with no risk of default on principal and interest • Short-term investment with maturities of 13-52 weeks • May be sold before maturity (with a risk of loss of maturity) • Rates of return similar to money market mutual funds

Common stocks represent ownership in a corporation, whereas bonds are IOUs and bondholders function as debt-holders or creditors. Investors in common stocks are the owners of a corporation and are entitled to voting rights, claims on income, and assets. As for the latter, common stockholders stand last in line for their right to share in the income and assets. Shareholders are only entitled to receive dividends after the bondholders and preferred stockholders have been paid. Similarly, in bankruptcy, the claims of bondholders are settled first, while common stockholders are the last to receive the collection of any remaining proceeds from the liquidation of assets.

Figure 1–6 Characteristics of Stocks and Bonds

Investments	Objectives	Advantages
Stocks	Provides Capital Growth	• Provides long-term growth (also the possibility of capital loss) • Possibility of income as some stocks pay dividends • Provide a store of value over long periods of time • Overall rates of return from stocks are greater than over bonds and money market investments over long periods of time • Reduces the amount of taxes paid through the emphasis of long-term capital gains over current income
Bonds	Provides Income	• Provides regular streams of income • Provides greater rates of return than money market investments • Provides the possibility of capital gains (also the possibility of capital losses) • May lower the amount of taxes by investing in municipal bonds • Can choose bonds with different maturities to suit the investor's needs

Bonds have a maturity date, at which time the bond is paid back at par value, $1,000 per bond. For longer maturity bonds, the risks increase. Thirty-year corporate bonds, for example, are riskier than 30-year U.S. Treasury bonds because the U.S. Treasury backs the interest and principal payments for the Treasury bonds. Anything could happen within a 30 year period to force a corporation into bankruptcy before the bonds are redeemed. However, in the event of a default, corporate bondholders still have a priority claim over the common stockholders, and the bondholders' claims would have to be paid before any proceeds are paid to the common stockholders.

Figure 1-7 Historical Returns 1926-1993. (Ibbotson and Sinquefield Study 1994)

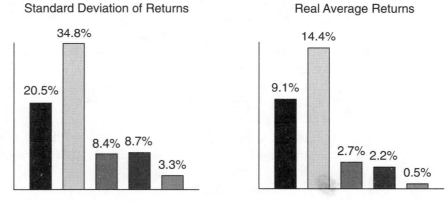

Source: Ibbotson, R.G. and Sinquefield, *R.A. Stocks, Bonds, Bills and Inflation: Historical Return 1926-1933.* Chicago, IL: Dow Jones-Irwin, 1994, page 32.

Investors in common stocks are not guaranteed dividends. Dividends on common stocks are declared at the discretion of the company's board of directors. If the board decides to use the money for alternate purposes or earnings go down, dividends may be reduced or may not be declared. By contrast, investors in bonds can count on a steady stream of interest income. Investors who are reliant on current income should buy bonds over common stock.

Investors are greatly attracted to common stocks for their ability to provide capital growth over long periods of time as confirmed by the Ibbotson study. Bonds also offer the potential for capital appreciation (an increase in the selling price of the bond/stock over the purchase price), but investors invest in bonds primarily for current income.

The following comparison of the characteristics of stocks and bonds highlights some reasons why investors should also consider investing some of their portfolio in bonds:

- Due to the higher volatility of stocks over bonds, investors might not want to be 100 percent invested in stocks. According to an earlier Ibbotson study, stocks were three times more volatile than bonds in the 64 years since 1926. The worst year for U.S. intermediate-term bonds was 1994 where they fell 5.1 percent in value. The worst year for stocks was 1991 where stocks prices fell by 43.3 percent (Zuckerman, May 8, 1998, C1). By diversifying and investing some of their portfolios in bonds, investors may lower their risks of loss due to a stock market downturn.
- In the current economic climate, bonds offer positive real rates of return. Bonds offer a steady stream of income, whereas stockholders are not guaranteed the receipt of dividends. If inflation remains low, around the current 1.5 percent annual rate, and bonds continue to yield nominal returns between five and six percent, bonds can still provide positive real rates of return of around four percent, which exceed those of bank accounts and Treasury bills. The S & P dividend yield for stocks is currently around 1.5 percent, which means that bond returns exceed those of common stocks with regard to income. Stocks of small companies and growth companies generally do not pay dividends.
- Investors, who are risk averse and/or have shorter investment horizons, might shun stocks in favor of bonds to protect against possible downturns in the stock market, which would cause losses in principal when stocks are sold.
- With the recent excessively high valuations in the stock market, it may be a good time to take some profits of some of these stocks and put the money into bonds if a short-term need exists for part of this money.
- Investors in high tax brackets can reduce their federal, state, and/or local taxes by investing in municipal bonds and government bonds.
- With the growth of the Internet, investing in individual bonds is becoming easier for small investors.

However, for long periods, investing in common stocks offers the following advantages over bonds:

- The potential for greater average rates of return.
- The ability to reduce federal, state, and local income taxes. Capital gains on common stocks are only taxed when the stocks are sold (at lower marginal rates than ordinary income such as interest and dividends), whereas interest income from bonds (and dividends from common stocks) are taxed when they are earned.

- The potential for keeping ahead of the rate of inflation and providing growth to a portfolio.

Worksheet 1-4 provides a summary of the reasons to consider bonds. Investing in the stock market supplies the long-term growth to a portfolio. Investors who have a long time horizon (longer than five to 10 years), and do not need the income from the investments, should stick with stocks. Investing in the bond markets provide for current income. These investments are more suitable for investors who are risk-averse and have shorter time horizons for the money.

Other factors should be considered. If an investor has a long time horizon, but has difficulty sleeping at night when the stock market goes down, stocks may not be a suitable investment for that person.

Selecting the right investments will also depend on the investor's circumstances. For example, an investment in stocks for a college fund in three year's time may turn out to be a poor investment if the stock market and the stocks chosen decline in price when the money is needed. In contrast, a Treasury note or bond with a maturity of three years provides a guaranteed return of the principal amount invested plus regular payments of interest every six months for that period of time. An investment in 30-year corporate bonds for retirement in thirty years may not grow as much as an investment in a diversified group of stocks for that same period of time. For this long time horizon, the variability in the potential returns from stocks may be evened out. With an investment plan, the investor will be able to determine the right mix of investments to suit his/her circumstances.

Worksheet 1–4

Use a Budget to Determine the Monthly Savings Amount

1. Provide current income

2. Require a shorter time horizon than stocks

3. Are more suited to the risk-averse investor

4. Municipal bonds and government bonds can lower federal, state and local taxes

5. Provide real rates of return when inflation rates are low

Determine an Investment Plan

The first step in any investment plan is for the investor to determine his/her financial net worth (what is owned minus what is owed) because then the investor will know how much he can afford to invest (see Worksheet 1-5). A portion of these funds should be kept in liquid investments such as bank money market accounts, money market mutual funds, Treasury bills, and other money market securities for living expenses and for any emergencies. The amount to keep in these liquid investments for an emergency/living expense fund will vary according to the investor's circumstances. An examination of personal assets will determine how much to keep. A conservative rule of thumb is to keep three to six months' worth of expenses in liquid investments. Keeping too much in these liquid investments is not a good idea because this may result in a loss of current and future purchasing power (see Figure 1-7 for the historic returns on Treasury bills, which is a money market equivalent).

Premiums for life, health, and disability insurance should be included in monthly expenses. It is especially important for the breadwinner of the family to have adequate life and disability insurance. Health insurance is important for all members of the family. Similarly, home and auto insurance premiums should be included in the monthly expenses.

Once an emergency fund has been created, an investment program should be started for the medium and long-term future. Even on a modest starting salary, setting aside small consistent savings can make a difference over time. The secret is for investors to pay themselves first. At the beginning of the month, investors should write a check to their investment accounts rather than waiting until the end of the month to see what is left for savings. Certain mutual funds enable investors to deposit amounts as small as $25 per month on a regular monthly basis. Refer to Figure 1-8 for the steps in the investment planning process.

List Objectives

List the goals and objectives for a medium and long-term future investment plan. This will determine how much is needed to invest to reach these goals and the appropriate types of investments to make. For example, the following objectives have a time horizon:

- Buy a car in two years.
- Save for a down payment on a house in five years.
- Fund a college education in 10 years.
- Accumulate a retirement fund in 25 years.

Worksheet 1–5

Determine Net Worth

Personal Balance Sheet

Date _____

ASSETS		LIABILITIES	
FINANCIAL		CURRENT	
Checking Accounts	_____	Credit Card Balances	_____
Savings Accounts	_____	Department Store Charges	_____
Money market funds	_____	Other	_____
Stock and Bond mutual funds	_____		
Individual Stocks	_____	**Total Current Liabilities**	_____
Individual Bonds	_____		
Annuities	_____		
Cash Surrender Value of			
Life Insurance Policies	_____	LONG TERM LIABILITIES	
Pension accounts	_____	Auto Loan(s)	_____
IRAs, Keoghs	_____	Mortgages:	
Other	_____	Home	_____
		Vacation Home	_____
Total Financial Assets	_____	Other	_____
NON FINANCIAL ASSETS			
Home	_____	**Total Long-Term Liabilities**	_____
Condominium	_____		
Other Real Estate	_____	**TOTAL LIABILITIES**	_____
Automobiles	_____		
Computers,TVs, Stereo	_____	**NET WORTH**	
Furniture/Antiques	_____		
Paintings/Art	_____		
Jewelry	_____		
Other	_____	Total Assets	_____
		Minus Total Liabilities	_____
Total NonFinancial Assets	_____		
TOTAL ASSETS	_____	**NET WORTH**	_____

Figure 1-8 Investment Plan

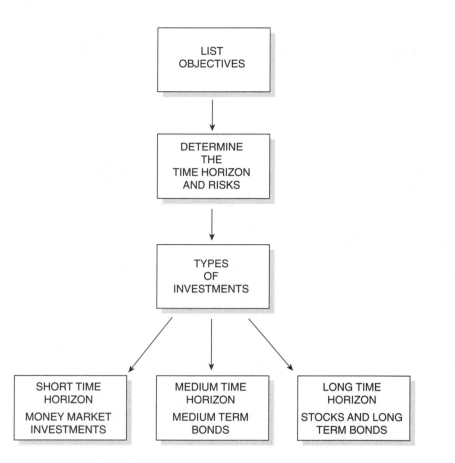

Determine the Time Horizon and Risks

Next, the types of investments can be geared to the time horizons of these objectives. The first two objectives are short- to medium-term time horizons, which means that the investments chosen should focus on generating income and preserving the principal. Investing the money set aside for the purchase of a car in two years in the stock market is risky, because over a short period of time, the risks of losing money in the stock market are quite high and diminish over longer periods of time.

Types of Investments

Investments in an emergency fund should be *liquid*, which is the ability to convert them into cash without losing very much of the principal in the conversion. Examples of these are U.S. Treasury bills, commercial paper, bankers' acceptances, money market mutual funds, short-term (six month) certificates of deposit, money market bank deposits, savings, and checking accounts.

Investments for short- and medium-term horizons should produce higher yields than money market investments and the maturities should match the time period for which the money invested is needed. Investments in two year and five year U.S. Treasury notes, for example, provide current income with virtually no risk of default on the interest and principal amount invested. Other options for these shorter maturities are U.S. government agency notes, short-term U.S. Treasury bonds, and short-term bond mutual funds.

Investing options to fund a college education in 10 years are greater and could include a mixture of common stock and bonds. With a 25 year time horizon, the mix of investments should be weighed more heavily towards stocks than bonds. This is because over long periods of time, stocks have outperformed bonds and most other investments, which means that if the past is a reflection of the future, investors could expect average yearly returns of seven percent for stocks versus four to five percent for bonds. Investors who are nervous about stock market corrections or crashes might consider investing some of their retirement savings in 30-year U.S. Treasury bonds. Bonds are not securities without risk. They also suffer from changes in interest rates, economic changes, and the risks that affect the markets, the types of bonds, and their quality. Before investing in bonds, stocks, or mutual funds, investors should be aware of their risks and characteristics. These are explored in later chapters. Worksheet 1-6 provides a framework for investors to list their objectives and time frame in order to select the investments that would fit their circumstances.

The key to building a large portfolio is for investors to get their finances in order. Table 1-2 provides some guidelines.

End Notes

Doherty, Jacqueline. "Nasdaq is Moving Into the Bond Market and Bond Dealers Aren't One Bit Happy." *Barron's*. November 29,1999. p. MW10.

Ibbotson, R.G. and R.A. Sinquefield. *Stocks, Bonds and Inflation: Historical Return (1926-1993)*. Dow Jones-Irwin: Chicago, IL., 1994, p. 32.

Patterson, Dean. "Corporate Pricing Not as Simple as it Sounds," November 5, 1999. www.cnbc.com

Patterson, Dean. "Muni Direct CEO says Muni Revolt Begins." November 12, 1999. www.cnbc.com

The *World in 1999*. Economist Publications.

Zuckerman, Gregory: "Bonds Pitched as Alternative to Wild Stocks," *The Wall Street Journal*, May 8, 1998, p. C1.

Worksheet 1–6   Create an Investment Plan

List Investment Objectives and Time Horizon

Less than 12 Months	**One to Five Years**	**Greater than Five Years**
1. Emergency Fund	1.	1.
2.	2.	2.
3.	3.	3.
4.	4.	4.
5.	5.	5.
6.	6.	6.

Investment Choices

Money Market Securities	**One to Five Year Bonds**	**Stocks and Bonds**
1. Money Market Fund	1. Treasury Notes & Bonds	1. Common Stocks
2. Treasury Bills	2. Municipal Bonds	2. Bonds with maturities longer than 5 years
3. CDs (1 year or less)	3. Corporate Bonds	3. Stock and Bond Mutual Funds
4. Savings Accounts	4. Agency Bonds	
	5. Short-term Bond Mutual Funds	

List Investments

Table 1-2 Guidelines to Building an Investment Portfolio

1. Pay off all high interest credit card debts first and then make extra payments to a mortgage account.
2. Cut all frivolous spending to increase amounts saved.
3. Save amounts at the beginning of the month.
4. Open an automatic investment plan to encourage regular savings.
5. Contribute to a retirement plan.
6. Map out an investment plan, listing all objectives.
7. Determine the acceptable level of risk that is comfortable for the investment types.
8. Increase the rates of return on these investments within comfortable levels of risk.
9. Review the investment strategy with regard to taxes. High tax bracket investors should increase their municipal bond holdings.
10. Review the investment plan once or twice a year.

Excercises

1. How can an investor increase the amounts that they save?

    (a)

    (b)

    (c)

2. How can investors benefit from the compounding of interest (time value of money)?

3. What are the objectives and advantages of

    (a) Stocks?

(b) Bonds?

(c) Money Market Investments?

4. Match the objectives to the different types of investment groups (money market securities, bonds and stocks).

Chapter 2

Basics: Terms, Definitions, Trends, and Policies

This chapter begins with a discussion of the basics of bonds, which include definitions, bond characteristics, and terminology, and is followed by a comparison of bonds and stocks. The last section focuses on the relationships between bonds and the different economic statistics.

Bond Basics

A bond is an IOU. Bonds bear certain similarities to *certificates of deposit* (CD) and savings accounts. When an investor deposits money in a CD (or savings account), the investor is in effect lending money to the bank. The bank pays the investor interest on the deposit and returns the principal when the CD matures. Similarly, investors in bonds make loans to the issuer (corporation or government). This makes them creditors, and not owners, as in the case of common stock investors. In return, the issuer pays a specified amount of interest on a regular basis until the date of maturity. Virtually all bonds have a maturity date, at which time the issuer returns the face value of each bond ($1,000) to investors. Figure 2-1 illustrates the payment flows of a bond graphically.

The major difference between savings accounts, CDs, and bonds is that investors can sell their bonds to others before they mature. Savings accounts and CDs cannot be sold to other investors. Bear in mind that certificates of deposit in amounts over $100,000 can be sold before maturity and are negotiable. Therefore, bonds are negotiable IOUs, unlike savings accounts and CDs below $100,000.

Bond Terminology

An understanding of the basic terminology is a precursor to investing in bonds.

Par (Face) Value   The par value, also known as the face value of the bond, is the amount returned to the investor when the bond matures. For example, if a bond is bought at issuance for $1,000, the investor bought the bond at its par value. At the maturity date, the investor will regain the $1,000. The par value of bonds is usually $1,000, despite a few exceptions.

Discount   Bonds do not necessarily trade at their par values. They may trade above or below their par values. Any bond trading below $1,000 is said to be trading at a discount.

For example, at the time of this writing, AT&T bonds, with a coupon rate of six 1/2 percent, maturing in the year 2029, are trading at a discount of $870 per bond.

Premium   Bonds may also trade at a premium, which is more than $1,000 (par value). IBM's seven 1/2 percent bonds, maturing in the year 2013, are trading at $1,030 per bond at the time of this writing. This is a $30 premium per bond.

Figure 2-1   How a Bond Works

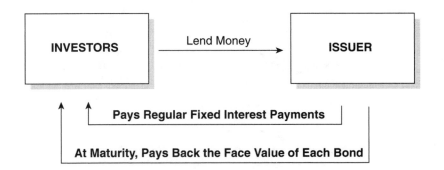

Coupon Interest Rate   The coupon rate is the interest rate that the issuer of the bond promises to pay the bondholder. If the coupon rate is five percent, the issuer of these bonds promises to pay $50 (five percent x $1,000) in interest on each bond per year.

Many bonds pay interest semi-annually. If the issuer pays a five percent coupon, semi-annually, the bondholder receives $25 per bond every six months. Some bonds have adjustable or floating interest rates, which are tied to a particular index. In other words, the coupon payments fluctuate based on the underlying index.

Maturity   The maturity of a bond is the length of time until the bond comes due, at which time the bondholder receives the par value of the bond.

Market Rates of Interest   Market rates of interest affect bond prices. The following example illustrates this point. Suppose an investor purchased a bond last year with a coupon rate of five percent, when market rates of interest were five percent, and the investor paid $1,000 per bond. This year, market rates of interest rise to six percent.

What price would the investor receive if he or she tried to sell this bond? Obviously, new investors would not pay $1,000 for a bond yielding five percent when they could buy new bonds with current coupon rates of six percent for $1,000. The new investor would expect to get at least six percent, which means that this bond would sell at a discount (less than $1,000) in order to be competitive with current bonds.

Conversely, if market rates of interest fall below the coupon rate, investors would be willing to pay a premium (above $1,000) for the bond. Thus, bond prices are vulnerable to market rates of interest as well as other factors, which are discussed in later chapters.

Call Provision   Many bonds have call provisions. This means that the issuer of the bonds can call or redeem the bonds at a specified price before their scheduled maturity.

Issuers exercise the call provision when market rates of interest fall well below the coupon rate of the bonds. A bond with a coupon rate of eight percent, maturing in twenty years, might have a call provision which enables the issuer to call in the bonds if market rates of interest fall well below their rate at issuance. This is advantageous for the issuer who can call in these bonds with a coupon of eight percent and issue new bonds with a lower coupon rate.

Put Option   A bond with a put option enables bondholders to resell their bonds to the issuer at par (face) value, $1000 per bond. The put option is the opposite of the call provision of a bond because the bondholder has the decision whether or not to exercise the put option.

Bid Price   Bonds are quoted on a bid and ask price. The bid price is the highest price buyers will pay for the bonds. For example, a bond might be quoted at a bid of $94 1/2, which means that when selling this bond, the most buyers will offer is $945.00 per bond.

Ask Price   The ask price is the lowest price offered by sellers of the issue. For example, if a bond has a bid of $94 1/2 and an asked price of $94 5/8, an investor buying this issue would pay $946.25 per bond (the lowest price sellers of this issue will accept).

Spread   The spread is the difference between the bid and the ask price of the bond, part of which is a commission that goes to the broker/dealer. A large spread indicates that the bonds are inactively traded.

Price Quotes   Bonds are quoted in hundreds, but trade in denominations of thousands. A bond with a price quote of $86 3/4 means that the bond is not trading at $86.75, but at $867.50 per bond.

Basis Point   A basis point is one-hundredth of a percentage point. For example, if the yield on a bond falls from 5.25 percent to 5.20 percent, then the yield has declined by five basis points. Basis points are used to measure the differences in bond yields.

Common Characteristics of Bonds

All bond securities have the following similar characteristics, which are summarized here:

- *A maturity date*, which is the date when the bond is paid off.
- *Interest payments*, which the issuer promises to pay in return for the use of the money loaned.
- *Repayment of principal*, which the issuer promises to pay back at the maturity date.

All bond issues have a master loan agreement, called a *bond indenture*, which contains the information for the issue. The following terms of a bond issue are included in the indenture:

- The amount of the bond issue.
- The coupon rate.
- Frequency of interest payments (annual or semi-annual).
- Maturity date.
- Call provision, if any. This provision allows the issuer of the bonds to call them in and repay them before maturity.
- Refunding provision, if any. This provision allows the issuer to obtain the proceeds with which to repay the bondholders when the issue matures by issuing new securities.
- Sinking fund provision, if any. This provision offers bondholders greater security in that the issuer sets aside earnings to retire the issue.
- Put option, if any. This provision allows the bondholders to sell the bonds back to the issuer at par value.

Rules of Bonds

The astute reader will be able to put together certain rules or axioms from the information presented so far in Chapter One, "Origins: The Markets and their Beginnings," and this chapter. These are summarized in Table 2-1.

The regular fixed interest payments of bonds make them more suitable for investors seeking income rather than growth. The discussion on the shortfalls of pricing transparency of bonds in Chapter 1 points out the difficulties of using bonds as trading vehicles. They are unlike stocks, which have readily available fresh prices and narrow bid-ask spreads, enabling investors to trade them actively. In addition to the lack of fresh price availability on bonds, commissions on bonds are much greater than those for stocks. Thus, bonds should be bought and held to maturity. Another reason for holding bonds to maturity is that bondholders will receive the face value of their bonds. This is a return of their principal investment.

Table 2-1 The Rules of Bonds

- Bonds provide regular payments of income.
- Bonds are not conducive to being actively traded like stocks.
- Bonds are more conducive to being bought and held to maturity.
- Bonds mature at par value, $1000.
- Bonds return the principal invested if held to maturity.
- Bond prices react inversely to changes in market rates of interest.
- When market rates of interest rise, bond prices of existing issues fall.
- When market rates of interest decline, bond prices of existing issues increase.

Bonds are sensitive to changes in market rates of interest. Rising interest rates have a depressing effect on prices of existing bond issues. Similarly, with declining interest rates, prices of existing bond issues rise. This is due largely to the relationship between the coupon rate of a bond and market rates of interest. Theoretically, when market rates of interest are the same as the coupon rate, the bond will trade at its par value, $1000. When market interest rates are greater than the coupon rate, the bond will trade at a discount (below $1000). When market rates of interest fall below the coupon rate, the bond will generally trade at a premium (above $1000).

Bonds Versus Common Stocks

Historically, common stocks have outperformed bonds over long periods of time. Most notably, the returns on a small number of Internet and technology stocks, such as CMGI, AOL, Yahoo, Oracle and Sun Microsystems, have more than doubled within several months in 1999. When this is contrasted with the negative returns received on bonds in 1999, investors might wonder why they should even consider bonds. Some compelling reasons for investing in bonds were presented in Chapter 1.

Bonds are very different from stocks. Table 2-2 summarizes these differences. Stocks provide the growth to a portfolio in the form of capital gains (when stock prices increase above their purchase prices), whereas bonds provide regular fixed income payments and the return of the principal at maturity. The returns received from stocks for long periods of time far outweigh those from bonds (refer to Figure 1-7). This

Table 2-2   Stocks versus Bonds

STOCKS	BONDS
1. Provide long-term growth. 2. Need a long time horizon. 3. Require investors who do not need the income from the stock investments to live on. 4. Require investors who can withstand the volatility of the stock markets. 5. Provide potential for capital gains, which are taxed at lower tax rates than current income. 6. Provide a store of value.	1. Provide current income. 2. Have a shorter time horizon. 3. Require low current and future inflation rates. 4. Favor risk-averse investors. 5. Municipal bonds and government bonds. lower federal and state taxes respectively.

Worksheet 2-1

Determine the Cash Flow Payments of Bonds

Fill in the cash flows for the following bond:
An investor buys a corporate bond for $970 with a coupon of five percent, maturing in five years.

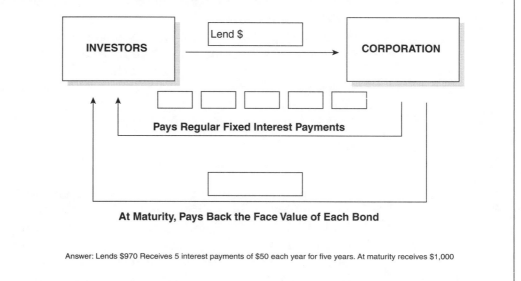

Pays Regular Fixed Interest Payments

At Maturity, Pays Back the Face Value of Each Bond

Answer: Lends $970 Receives 5 interest payments of $50 each year for five years. At maturity receives $1,000

---

was true even for the shorter period from 1994 through 1999. The stock markets had meteoric rises as measured by the Dow Jones Industrial average, the Standard & Poor's 500 Index, and the NASDAQ Index, whereas a 30-year Treasury bond investment in 1994 and 1999 would have returned negative returns for both years. These phenomenal returns in the stock markets have fueled more money to flow into stocks from bonds. As money leaves the bond markets to go into the stock market, pressure is put on bond yields which are driven up to attract money. This is why, since 1997, anytime the stock market rallied, the bond market declined. In other words, when stock prices rose, prices of existing bonds fell. This relationship seems to be a reversal of the general trend that the bond and stock markets rally in tandem. So why should investors even consider bond investments?

Stocks are volatile. If investments are made in stocks that appreciate in price, no problem exists. However, without hindsight, one can never be sure that the stocks chosen will be the winners. Many stocks have had negative returns, so investors can lose money on stocks if they are forced to sell when their stocks are trading below their purchase prices. Bonds are less volatile than stocks, but bond investors can also lose money in bonds if they have to sell their bonds when they are trading below their acquisition prices. However, this risk is reduced if bondholders hold their bonds through maturity when they will regain the face value of their bonds.

Volatility is also related to the length of time of the holding period for securities. The longer the holding period lasts, the less chance one has of losing money on both stocks and bonds. This is illustrated in Table 2-3 as compiled by the Vanguard Group (1998). The risk of loss from holding stocks and bonds for a one-year period is 43.1 percent and 8.1 percent, respectively, during the period 1926 to1998. For the holding period 1960 to1998, the worst year for stocks was in 1974 with a negative return of 26.3 percent, and 1969 for bonds with a negative return of 8.1 percent. By increasing the holding period, the risk of loss is reduced because the negative returns in the bad years even out with the positive returns in the good years. With a longer time horizon, investors will not be forced to sell when the markets are down.

The question then is not whether to consider investing in bonds or stocks, but to have an appropriate mix of stock and bond investments. This mix of investments depends on the total assets, age, risk tolerance, and investment horizon of the investor.

Determine the Right Mix of Stocks and Bonds

The aim of investing in both stocks and bonds is to reduce the overall risk of loss by protecting against any negative developments within these markets. The bond and stock markets do not always rise and fall in tandem. If the stock market goes down, the bond and money markets can sometimes protect against losses to the portfolio value by preserving capital. This is because there appears to be a weak relationship be-

Table 2-3   Range of Returns for Stocks, Bonds, and Cash

RANGE OF ANNUALIZED TOTAL RETURNS ON COMMON STOCKS, BONDS, CASH: 1926-1998

	Holding Period (Years)															
	1				3		5		10		15		20		25	
	HIGH	YEAR	LOW	YEAR	HIGH	LOW	HIGH	LOW	HIGH	LOW	HIGH	LOW	HIGH	LOW	HIGH	LOW
STOCKS	54.2%	1933	-43.1%	1931	31.2%	-26.9%	24.1%	-12.4%	19.9%	-0.8%	18.1%	0.6%	17.7%	3.1%	14.9%	5.9%
BONDS	45.5%	1982	-8.1%	1969	21.9%	-3.5%	22.5%	-2.0%	16.4%	0.2%	13.6%	0.7%	10.8%	0.9%	9.8%	1.2%
CASH	15.1%	1981	0.0%	1939,1940	12.7%	0.0%	11.5%	0.1%	9.5%	0.2%	8.6%	0.3%	7.9%	0.5%	7.5%	0.7%

RANGE OF ANNUALIZED TOTAL RETURNS ON COMMON STOCKS, BONDS, CASH: 1960-1998

	Holding Period (Years)															
	1				3		5		10		15		20		25	
	HIGH	YEAR	LOW	YEAR	HIGH	LOW	HIGH	LOW	HIGH	LOW	HIGH	LOW	HIGH	LOW	HIGH	LOW
STOCKS	37.6%	1995	-26.3%	1974	31.2%	-9.2%	24.1%	-2.4%	19.2%	1.2%	17.9%	4.3%	17.7%	6.5%	14.9%	7.9%
BONDS	45.5%	1982	-8.1%	1969	21.9%	-3.5%	22.5%	-2.0%	16.4%	0.9%	13.6%	0.7%	10.8%	0.9%	9.8%	1.2%
CASH	15.1%	1981	2.4%	1961	12.7%	2.7%	11.5%	2.7%	9.5%	2.2%	8.6%	1.8%	7.9%	1.4%	7.5%	1.2%

Source: The Vanguard Group

tween stocks and bonds, and virtually no relationship between stocks and money market securities.

Developing a portfolio is generally based on the idea of holding a variety of investments rather than concentrating on a single investment. This is the opposite of putting all one's eggs in one basket. Investors use this approach in order to reduce the risks of loss and even out the returns of the different investments. The latter point is illustrated with the following hypothetical example of a portfolio.

Assume the investor buys:	Total Investment
1,500 shares of Toys 'R Us. at $37 per share	$ 55,500
and 100 convertible bonds of ABC Co. at $1000 per bond	100,000
Total	$155,500

A year later, the portfolio is valued as follows:

1,500 shares of Toys R Us at $17 per share	$ 25,500
and 100 convertible bonds of ABC Co. at $1060 per bond	106,000
Total	$131,500

The investor has spread the risks of loss by owning two different types of securities as well as averaging the returns of the two types of investments. Certainly, the investor would have done much better had he or she invested totally in ABC Company's bonds, but hindsight always produces the highest returns. The fact that we are not clairvoyant points to the benefits of diversifying across a broad segment of investment types. In other words, diversification seeks a balance between the risk-return trade-off (discussed in Chapter 9, Managing a Bond Portfolio).

Diversification is achieved by selecting a portfolio of investments of different types of securities in different industries. For example, investing in the stocks and bonds of General Motors, Ford, and Chrysler hardly achieves any diversification. By carefully selecting the stocks and bonds of different companies in different industries and/or investing in stock and bond mutual funds, some of the risks of loss on any one security (or type of fund) will be evened out.

What is the right allocation of stocks and bonds? The answer depends on the amount of risk that the investor is willing to absorb. Generally, stocks are riskier investments than bonds. By increasing the time horizon for stock investments, investors can even out the volatility in the stock market. Maturities on bonds can be matched to the time horizons of the investor's needs. Short-term bonds with maturities of one to five years are available, as well as intermediate bonds with maturities between five and 10 years, and long-term bonds with maturities of greater than 10 years (generally 30-year maturities, although 100-year maturity bonds exist). If an investor cannot sleep at night when the amount of his/her investments decline, the investor does not tolerate risk very well and should not have a large percentage invested in stocks. Thus, investors who can tolerate the risk of loss and who have long time horizons would have a larger percentage allocated to stocks.

Besides risk, the investor's objectives determine the allocation of the assets. Investors who need to live off the interest of their investments will be inclined to allocate more of their portfolio assets to bond investments, which generate regular fixed interest payments. Investors with a long time horizon, who do not need to live on the income from their capital, can allocate a greater percentage toward stocks in order to generate growth for the portfolio.

Asset allocation does not follow a rigid formula. Rather, it is a good idea to think about the concept as a guideline for investing money. The percentage allocated to the different types of assets can always be changed depending on circumstances. As individual circumstances change, the investor's objectives change. If the emphasis shifts, for example, to greater income generation and preservation of capital from capital growth, the percentage of the investments in the portfolio can be changed accordingly.

Figure 2-2 illustrates some of the determinants for asset allocation models and Figure 2-3 breaks the models down into greater detail.

The most important aspect of investing is to have an asset allocation plan that reflects the broad mix of stocks and bonds to strive for. Once these have been determined, the individual investments can be pur-

Figure 2-2   Different Asset Allocation Models
Years to Retirement or until the Money is Needed

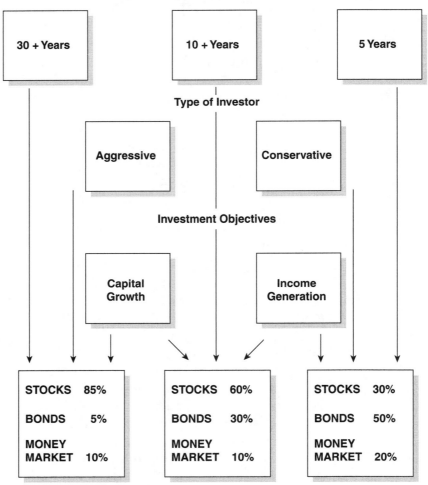

Figure 2-3 Asset allocation models

An **ultra conservative portfolio** is one in which the investment goals are to preserve capital and provide some growth. The weighting is geared toward high-quality bonds and a small portion toward stocks.

Conservative Portfolio

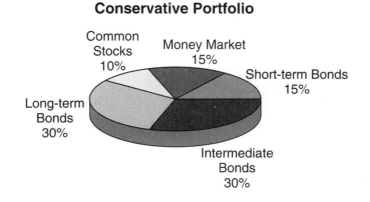

A **balanced portfolio** includes a greater percentage to common stocks, providing capital growth, and keeps a large percentage of assets in bonds, providing income.

Balanced Portfolio

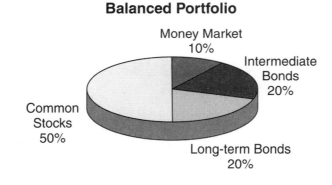

A **very aggressive portfolio** is weighted to common stocks, providing capital growth.

Aggressive Portfolio

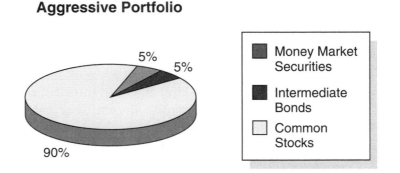

Table 2-4 Benefits of Asset Allocation and Diversification

1. By investing in different classes of investments, the risk of loss is spread among the different investments, rather than being concentrated in the one class.
2. A diversified portfolio of investments reduces the total risk. According to Clements, p. C1, a portfolio assembled over the past 70 years consisting of 23 percent common stock and 77 percent bonds would have the same risk as a portfolio of 100 percent bonds.
3. Diversification can increase overall returns. In the portfolio mentioned previously, the overall returns on a diversified portfolio of 23 percent common stock and 77 percent bonds returned were two percent higher per year than a 100 percent bond portfolio (Clements, p. C1).

chased. Funds for emergency purposes should be liquid. In other words, they should be easily convertible into cash without the loss of principal. These are money market securities. Depending on personal circumstances, the rule of thumb is to have the equivalent of three to six months living expenses in money market securities for an emergency fund.

Asset allocation plans are not etched in stone and investors should re-evaluate their plans on a yearly basis or as personal needs and circumstances change. See Table 2-4 for the benefits of asset allocation and diversification.

Raising Capital

Corporations and governments sometimes need additional external sources of capital to finance their expenditures. Long-term and intermediate-term funds are raised in the *capital markets* through the issuance of bonds, common stocks, and preferred stocks. Short-term capital with maturities of one year or less are raised in the *money markets*. The key difference between capital and money markets is the length of time of maturity of the bond issues. In Chapter 1, we saw that the issuance of debt (bonds) is the predominant form of raising cash for corporations. Figure 2-4 illustrates the mix of capital raised from the selling of securities by corporations during the period 1981 to1996 (Scott, et al, p.42).

The capital and money markets are important because they function to allocate the supply of savings in the economy to those who need to use those savings. In other words, the financial markets are vehicles that allocate the supply and demand of savings in the economy.

Raising capital through the issuance of new bonds is generally not a frequent occurrence for most corporations. This is because very large amounts are raised in each new offering. Governments issue new bonds more frequently, and the processes for raising funds vary among the different types of governments. The specific processes are discussed in later chapters.

Figure 2-4   Mix of Capital Raised by Corporations 1981–1996

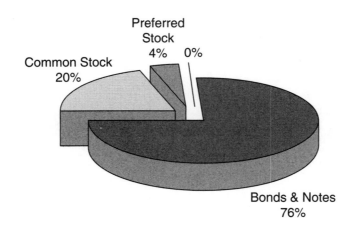

Preferred
Stock
4%   0%

Common Stock
20%

Bonds & Notes
76%

Figure 2-5   Process for Raising Capital

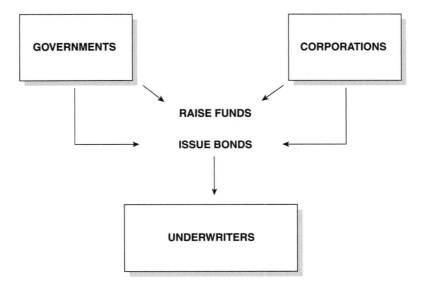

GOVERNMENTS

CORPORATIONS

RAISE FUNDS

ISSUE BONDS

UNDERWRITERS

Figure 2-5 illustrates the process of raising funds in the markets and defines the differences between the primary and secondary markets. Most new bond offerings are sold through underwriters/investment bankers in a *public offering*, who then distribute these securities to the public. A small percentage of new corporate issues are issued directly through *private placement*s to a limited number of institutional investors. The sale of these new securities, for the first time, occurs in the *primary market*. Investors who decide to sell their bonds before maturity, would then sell them in the secondary market to other investors through broker/dealers.

Corporate and some government underwritings are similar in that the investment banker acts as an intermediary between the investing public and issuers. However, many differences appear between corporate and government underwritings. Municipalities are required to obtain

Table 2-5 Typical Information in a SEC Registration

- General information on the issuer
- Purposes of the issue
- Price of the issue to the public
- Price of the issue offered to any special group
- Printers' fees
- Underwriting fees
- Net proceeds to the company
- Remuneration of any officers receiving over $25,000 annually
- Disclosures of any unusual contracts
- Detailed capitalization statement
- Detailed balance sheet
- Detailed earnings statement for three preceding years
- Names and addresses of officers, directors, and underwriters
- Names and addresses of stockholders owning more than 10 percent of any class of stock
- Pending litigation
- Copy of underwriting agreement
- Copy of legal opinions
- Copy of articles of incorporation or association
- Copies of indentures affecting new issues

Source: Radcliffe, Robert C.: *Investment Concepts, Analysis, Strategy.* 5th Ed. 1997, p.123

competitive bids, whereas corporate bond offerings are negotiated. The other major difference in the underwriting process is that most corporate bond offerings fall within the requirements of the Securities Act of 1933. Those corporations must file registration statements with the SEC, which include all the relevant information pertaining to the company and the offering. See Table 2-5 for the typical information listed in a registration statement. Should the company misrepresent or omit any significant information, the purchasers of the issue can sue either the company and/or underwriter.

A 20-day waiting period exists from the time that a registration statement is filed to the time that the new securities may be sold to the public. During this time period, the SEC examines the registration statement to determine if any serious misrepresentations or omissions are present. If none appear, the SEC approves the registration statement. However, this approval does not necessarily imply that the SEC has a favorable opinion of the issue. It merely signifies that there were no significant omissions of information required for the approval.

Potential purchasers of the new issue must be given a *prospectus* (which includes essentially the same information as the registration statement).

Corporate issuers who issue securities through private placements may not have to register with the SEC if they meet certain requirements (less than 25 investors, relatively small-sized issues less than $1.5 million, issues controlled by other federal agencies, among others). The disadvantage of issues that are not registered with the SEC is their lack of marketability, as buyers of the issues are limited in their ability to subsequently sell the bonds before maturity.

The offering price for the new bond issue is usually set the night before or the morning of the effective date to take into account any last minute changes in prevailing market conditions.

New issues of U.S. Treasury securities are sold directly to the investing public through auctions, thus bypassing the use of underwriters.

Reading the Financial Pages

The state of the economy affects the bond market. Both the coupon interest rate and the investor's required rate of return (both are related to the economy) determine the value of a bond. If interest rates and risk are influenced by the state of the economy, it becomes important to understand the relationship between the bond market and the economy.

The following factors directly affect the bond market:

- Interest rates.
- Inflation.
- State of the economy.

Interest Rates

An inverse relationship occurs between market rates of interest and bond prices. When market rates of interest in an economy rise, downward pressure is put on the prices of existing bonds. Similarly, when market rates of interest fall, prices of existing bonds with higher coupon rates rise.

Inflation

An increase in inflation also puts downward pressure on bond prices because a bond pays a fixed amount of interest at the stated coupon rate. With rising inflation, the purchasing power of this interest erodes and the price of the bond decreases. Under these circumstances, issuers of new bonds must, therefore, increase their coupon rates to make it conducive for investors to buy them. Similarly, if inflation is expected to fall, prices of existing bonds rise because bondholders will receive greater *real rates of return*.

Real Rate of Return = Bond Yield (Coupon Rate) − Rate of Inflation

State of the Economy

Generally, an expanding economy may have a negative effect on the bond markets because expansion may be perceived to be inflationary. A sluggish economy is usually good news for the bond markets because interest rates and inflation tend to be low.

Government Reports and Statistics to Watch

Investors pay close attention to interest rates and should try to determine the direction of interest rates before purchasing bonds. Buying bonds when interest rates are rising can cause paper losses or actual capital losses if they are sold before maturity. Similarly, investing in bonds when interest rates are falling can create capital gains if the bonds are sold before maturity.

Federal Reserve Bank and Federal Reserve Open Market Committee

The key to interest rates in the economy lies in the hands of the Federal Reserve Bank. The Federal Reserve Bank has three major tools available to affect the supply of money and interest rates:

- Open market operations
- Reserve requirements
- Discount rate

Open Market Operations The Federal Reserve buys and sells U.S. securities (mainly Treasury bills and repurchase agreements) in the open market to expand and contract the nation's money supply. When the Federal Reserve wants to expand the money supply, it buys securities for its own portfolio from the market. As a result, the nation's money supply increases. The opposite action of this is the contraction of the money supply, as shown in Figure 2-6, where the Federal Reserve sells securities from its portfolio in the open market, which reduces the amount of money in circulation. These actions by the Federal Reserve impact interest rates. A tightening of the money supply causes market rates to rise, and an expansion of the money supply causes interest rates to fall.

The *Federal Reserve Open Market Committee* (FOMC), composed of the Federal Reserve Bank of New York, the board of governors, and the presidents of the other Federal Reserve Banks, conduct these open market operations on a rotating basis. This committee meets every two weeks and the minutes of their meetings are released to the public six weeks after each meeting. However, the Federal open market transactions are reported in the newspapers the day after they occur. Bond traders are acutely aware of the Fed's actions with regard to buying, selling, or refraining from open market transactions.

Reserve Requirements The Federal Reserve can impact interest rates through the reserve requirement. The Federal Reserve Bank requires banks to maintain reserves with the Fed. The percentage of banks' deposits held as reserves is determined by the Fed and is called the *reserve requirement*. The Fed increases the money supply by reducing the reserve requirement: banks then need to keep less in reserve

Figure 2-6   The Effect of Open Market Operations on Interest Rates

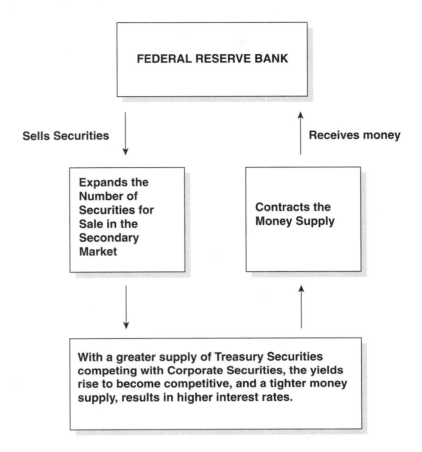

and therefore can increase their lending. The reverse is true when the Fed increases the reserve requirements, increasing interest rates.

The Federal Reserve Bank can also impact changes in interest rates through the *Federal funds rate*. The Fed does not pay interest on the reserves of the banks. Banks with excess reserves lend to banks that need to add to their reserves. These funds are called *Federal funds* and are mostly provided on a short-term (one-day) unsecured basis, although situations have occurred when these funds are provided on a longer-term basis. The rate that banks pay for these funds is called the *Federal funds rate*, which is reported in the financial newspapers. The Fed can alter the money supply by changing the Federal funds rate. These changes to both the Federal funds rate and reserve requirements are widely reported in the newspapers.

Discount Rate   The discount rate is the Fed's third tool. The discount rate is the rate of interest that the Fed charges banks that borrow from the Fed. When the discount rate is too high, banks are discouraged from borrowing reserves from the Fed. When the discount rate is low or lowered, banks are encouraged to borrow. Thus, by changing the discount rate, the Fed can expand or contract the money supply. Changes in the discount rate are also reported in the newspapers.

Monitoring the changes in the open market transactions, reserve requirements, and discount rates can give investors a better feeling for the direction of future interest rates. This is why the investment community carefully monitors the utterances of the Federal Reserve Chairman, Alan Greenspan, as to the Fed's future actions regarding any perceived future changes in interest rate policy that might occur. The Federal Reserve is ever vigilant for signs that inflation might rear its ugly head. Excessive growth in the economy can also cause inflation. When signs of inflation are evident, the Fed raises short-term interest rates, which then impact long-term interest rates.

Reports on Inflation

Inflation is defined as the rate at which the prices for goods and services rise in an economy. Inflation often prevails in a growing economy where the demand for goods and services outstrips production, leading to rising prices. In other words, too much money chases too few goods and services. At the time of this writing, inflation seems to be nonexistent on the short-term horizon. Some economists expect the rate to go below two percent, while others argue for a future increase due to rising wages in a tight job market, and increases in the existing low levels of commodity prices other than oil. The price of oil has risen from a low of $12 per barrel to $34 in August 2000.

The *Consumer Price Index* (CPI) is one measure of inflation, which is calculated monthly by the Bureau of Labor Statistics. The Bureau monitors the changes in prices of items (such as food, clothing, housing, transportation, medical care, and entertainment) in the CPI. It gauges the level of inflation and is more meaningful when it is compared relative to the CPI of previous periods.

Some economists believe that the CPI fuels inflation similar to a cat chasings its tail. Social Security payments and many cost of living increases in employment contracts are tied to increases in the CPI. The CPI may, in fact, exacerbate the level of inflation.

When the level of inflation is high (relative to previous periods), the Federal government will pursue restrictive economic policies to try to reduce the level of inflation.

The *Producer Price Index* (PPI) is announced monthly and monitors the costs of raw materials used to produce products. The PPI is a better predictor of inflation than the CPI because when prices of raw materials increase, a time lag occurs before consumers experience these price increases.

Another key indicator is the Commodity Research Bureau's *commodity price index,* which measures prices of raw materials. When this index rises significantly over a six-month period, it is a warning that inflation is on the horizon.

When other indicators such as the *Leading Inflation Index*, an index that anticipates cyclical turns in consumer price inflation, developed by Columbia University's Center for Business Cycle Research, moves up with commodity prices, it is a clear signal that inflation is ahead.

When an economy is in recovery, the *manufacturing capacity utilization rate* becomes a key indicator to watch. This indicator measures how much of the economy's factory potential is being used. Economists worry about inflation when the nation's factory capacity rises above 82.5 percent. For example, when the recovery is robust and the economy is growing rapidly while interest rates remain low, unemployment declines, which gives rise to increasing wage pressures and increasing prices of goods.

Inflation has a detrimental effect on both the bond and stock markets, as well as on the economy. When the level of inflation increases, real GDP falls (in 1980 in the U.S.) and similarly when inflation decreases, real GDP increases (in 1983 in the U.S.). This inverse relationship might not always hold out as evidenced by the economy in 1992. Despite lower levels of inflation, real GDP showed insignificant growth, which translated into the economy taking a long time to move out of the recession.

For bondholders, the rate of inflation determines their real rates of return. Bond prices react to expectations of future inflation and can be quite volatile. However, bondholders should not react to the daily ups and downs in bond prices by actively trading their bonds. Rather, they should base their opinions on the future, longer-term expectations of inflation to determine whether they should buy or sell their bonds. For example, the core CPI (rate of inflation that excludes food and energy prices) is around two percent while the current yield on a five-year Treasury note is close to six percent. This means a real rate of return of four percent using the core CPI or 3.3 percent using the total CPI.

Reports on the State of the Economy

Gross Domestic Product (GDP) is a measure in dollar value of the economy's total production of goods and services. Comparing the current GDP with previous periods indicates the economy's rate of growth (or lack of it). An increasing GDP indicates that the economy is expanding. GDP grew around 3.5 percent in 1994, slowed to around two percent in 1995, and accelerated to between three and four percent through the 1999. The expectation for GDP is to slow somewhat in the near future. Slower economic growth is expected to slow corporate profits, impacting inventories. With slower sales, companies experience a buildup in inventories, causing them to slow down their production to adjust for this build-up. The state of the economy is far more complex than the mere correlation of two variables. To better assess the state of the economy, many measures such as the inflation rate, unemployment rate, national income, international trade, and manufacturing capacity, should be considered.

Inflation distorts the accuracy of this growth, causing a measure of the real growth of an economy's output, referred to as "real" GDP. Real GDP is adjusted for price level changes and measures each period's goods and services using prices which prevailed in a selected base year. A comparison of real GDP figures with those of prior periods provides a more accurate measurement of the real rate of growth. Therefore, GDP is a measure of the economic health of a country. Inflation currently has been currently low and has not significantly detracted from GDP.

A more narrowly focused measure of a nation's output is *industrial production*, which measures the manufacturing output. Generally, the manufacturing sector leads the economy's short-term swings. Factory production has been down due to weakness in Asia and Latin America, but this should rebound as these economies grow into the early decade of 2000.

The *unemployment rate* is the percentage of the nation's labor force that is without work and is another indicator of the economy's strength (or lack thereof). Currently (2000), the United States has a tight labor market with an unemployment rate that has dropped to 4.1 percent in November 1999, which is the lowest in 29 years. A growing economy and a low unemployment rate is traditionally the combination that fuels inflation. A concern arises when rates for labor rise faster than productivity gains. This is why the bond and stock markets pay so much attention to the utterances of the Federal Reserve Chairman's speech to Congress about interest rates. When even a trace of inflation appears on the horizon, the Federal Reserve could raise short-term interest rates.

The other side of the coin is a high unemployment rate. Governments become concerned when the unemployment rate rises above a certain level (about seven percent) and they will stimulate the economy (through fiscal and monetary policies) to reduce the unemployment rate. These actions may also stimulate inflation.

In the early 1980s, the U.S. experienced both high rates of unemployment and inflation. The government dealt with the inflation first by pursuing restrictive economic policies. This sent the economy into a recession and the unemployment rate increased further. In 1992, the U.S. experienced low inflation but high unemployment. The government's approach was to stimulate the economy by lowering interest rates (through the Federal Reserve Bank).

Housing starts are released monthly and show the strength in housing production. An increase in housing starts, relative to previous months, indicates optimism about the economy as more people are buying homes. Thus, strength in housing starts reveals consumer confidence in the economy.

Economists have designed an index of leading indicators to forecast economic activity. This index of leading indicators includes data series ranging from stock prices, new building permits, and an average work week to changes in business and consumer debt. By analyzing this monthly index, economists hope to forecast economic turns, in order to give advance warning of a turn in the stock market, which can impact the bond markets. However, in reality, when the leading indicators forecast an economic turn, the stock market has already reacted to the change.

This discussion points to the overall relationship between the bond markets, interest rates, inflation, and the state of the economy. Economic expansion can spook the bond markets, which react to fears of inflation. An expanding economy with a low unemployment rate and rising oil prices raises fears of inflation, which will cause the Federal Reserve to raise interest rates to temper any anticipated inflation. This puts downward pressure on the bond markets. Similarly, a declining economy can be associated with a rising bond market because of lower interest rates, which would spur the economy. In general, the bond markets react negatively to good news on the economy and positively to bad news on the state of the economy. Table 2-6 summarizes the relationships between economic variables and the bond market.

Registration of Bonds

Bonds are issued in one of three forms: registered, bearer, or book entry form. The *registered* form is similar to owning stock certificates. Bonds are registered in the owner's name and the interest payments are mailed to the owner. When the bond is sold, the transfer agent registers the bond in the name of the new owner. To redeem the bond at maturity, the bondholder sends the bond certificate to the trustee. Investors who hold registered bonds need to keep a list of the addresses of the trustees of the different bond issues.

In *bearer* (or coupon) form, possession signifies ownership. The bond does not have a registered owner and the issuing company does not know where to mail the interest payments. Therefore, the coupons for

Table 2-6   Relationships of Economic Variables to the Bond Market

Economy	Bond Market
Consecutive quarter real GDP growth	Negative effect on the bond market. Declining GDP is a positive for the bond market.
Increasing unemployment	This may indicate a downturn in business sales, which is a positive sign for the bond market.
Decreasing unemployment	An indication that business is moving towards full employment, which is a negative for the bond market.
Inflation	High level of inflation is detrimental to the bond market as it tends to erode the purchasing power of fixed income payments.
Interest rates	Strong correlation between interest rates and the bond market; declining interest rates are a positive for the bond market; high or increasing interest rates depress existing bond prices.
Money Supply	Increasing money supply is good for the economy and the bond market, provided that it is not inflationary. Tight money supply tends to curb both the economy and the bond market.
Dollar	A strong dollar is good for the bond market as it encourages foreign investment. A weak dollar has a negative impact on the bond market because it discourages foreign investors.

the interest payments are attached to the bearer bonds. At the due date of the interest payment, the bearer clips the coupon and sends it to the issuer's paying agent who will send a check to the bondholder for the interest. The coupon can also be sent to the bondholder's bank, which collects the interest for the bondholder.

Selling bearer bonds is easy because they do not need to be registered. However, they do present problems in terms of safekeeping. Bearer bonds are like money and need to be kept in a safe place since possession signifies ownership. Bonds in bearer form tend to have been issued before the 1980s and new issues in this form are rarely found.

Bonds may also be issued in *book-entry* form, which is the most common form of issue. Instead of a bond certificate, the bondholder receives a confirmation with a computer number, which signifies ownership. Bondholders designate their bank or savings and loan accounts into which interest payments are deposited directly. Selling such a bond requires a simple transfer in the book records of the depository.

Who Should Keep the Investor's Bond Certificates?

Investors often debate whether to take possession of their bond certificates (in bearer or registered form) or whether they should leave them with their brokerage firms.

The advantages of leaving them in the custody of the brokerage firm are as follows:

- They are protected against physical loss if that brokerage firm is covered by the *Securities Insurance Protection Corporation* (SIPC).
- In the event that their bonds are called, the brokerage firm is more likely to become aware of the call and redeem the bonds immediately.

The disadvantages of keeping them in the custody of the brokerage firm are as follows:

- Should an investor decide to sell his/her bonds through another broker, the bonds need to be transferred to the new broker's firm. An investor has three days after the date of sale to deliver the securities before the brokerage firm would assess a late charge.
- Some brokerage firms are slow in remitting the interest payments. For example, one brokerage firm would receive the interest payments at the beginning of the month and only remit the proceeds to their clients at the end of the month. This brokerage firm had the use of clients' money for 30 days.
- When bonds with a sinking fund provision are left in the brokerage firm's name, the brokerage firm will choose which customer's bonds will be redeemed early. This is particularly relevant for the small investor. With a sinking fund provision, an investor is better off

holding his/her own bonds, which can be called directly, but it is not left to the brokerage firm to chose which client's bonds to redeem. Corporations use sinking funds to redeem a certain number of bonds each year before maturity. The company notifies bondholders through the mail and in the newspapers of redemptions.

Exercises

1. Determine the real rate of return on a bond when inflation is around 2.4 percent and the bond yield is 5.6 percent.

2. Determine the real rate of return on a bond when inflation is five percent and the bond yield is 4.6 percent.

3. What economic factors directly affect the bond markets?

4. List the reasons why an investor would consider investing in bonds over stocks.

End Notes

Clements, Jonathan. "Portfolio for the Conservative and the Bold," *The Wall Street Journal,* November 10, 1998, p C1.

Radcliffe, Robert C. *Investment: Concepts, Analysis, Strategy.* 5th Ed. Massachusetts: Addison Wesley, 1997.

Scott, David F., Jr.: *Basic Financial Management.* 8th Ed. New Jersey: Prentice Hall, 1999.

Chapter 3

Beginnings: What Affects Prices?

Several factors account directly for fluctuations in bond prices. These include the relationships between bond prices, coupon rates, yields, maturities (Malkiel, B., 1962, pp. 197–218), and risk assessment.

- The coupon rate (and bond yield) is relative to market rates of interest. When market rates of interest rise and exceed the coupon rate of a bond or bond yield, the price of the bond declines in order to relate the current yield to the market rate of interest. When interest rates fall, the price of the bond rises.
- The length of time to maturity. The longer the maturity, the more volatile the fluctuations in price.
- For a given change in a bond's yield, the longer the maturity of the bond, the greater the magnitude of change in the bond's price.
- For a given change in a bond's yield, the size of the change in the bond's price increases at a diminishing rate, the longer the maturity of the bond.
- For a given change in a bond's yield, the magnitude of the bond's price is inversely related to the bond's coupon yield.
- For a given change in a bond's yield, the magnitude of the price increase caused by a decrease in yield is greater than the price decrease caused by an increase in yield.
- Changes in risk assessment by the market. The lesser the quality, the lower the price, and the greater the quality, the higher the price.

This chapter discusses these direct relationships on bond prices as well as the indirect influences on bond prices. An analysis of bond quotations is the starting point for a better understanding of these relationships.

Analyzing Bond Quotations

The different types of bonds are quoted in different sections of the financial tables. *Corporate bonds* listed on the New York and American Exchanges can be found in the daily newspapers. Over-the-counter bonds, however, are not listed in the newspapers, but investors can obtain quotes from their brokerage firms. The financial newspapers provide a separate table for *Treasury* securities, which includes Treasury bills, notes, and bonds. *Government agency bonds* are listed in the government agency section and include quotes of FNMA issues, Federal Home Loan Bank issues, and bonds of the other government agencies. Both government agencies and Treasury securities are listed in order of maturity. Figure 3-1 shows examples of the different bond quotations.

Figure 3-1   Analyzing bond quotations

Corporate Bonds

Bonds	Cur Yld	Vol	Close	Net Chg
ATT 7s 05	7.1	20	99	-1/4

↓	↓	↓	↓	↓
After the name of the bond, AT&T, is the coupon yield of 7 percent. The s signifies that the bondholder is paid semi-annually ($35 twice a year). The 05 is the matrity date for the bond. It matures in 2005.	The current yield is 7.1%. (Coupon divided by the closing price 70/99 =7.1)	The volume indicates that 20 bonds were traded on the previous day, Jan. 27, 2000	The closing price of the bond was $990.	Shows the change from the previous day's close: down 1/4 from the previous day's close.

Municipal Bonds

Issue	Coupon	Mat	Price	Chg	Bid Yld
CA Hlth Fin Auth	6.125	12-01-30	94 3/8	...	6.55

↓	↓	↓	↓	↓	↓
The name of the issuer is the California Health Finance Authority	These bonds pay 6.125 percent of par ($1000) which is $61.25 per bond per year.	The maturity date is December 1, 2030.	The price of the bond, $943.75.	Shows the change from the previous day's close: there was no change.	The bid yield is the percentage yield of a bond if held for its full term. If this bond was bought at $943.75 and held to maturity the return would be 6.55 percent.

Figure 3-1   Analyzing bond quotations continued

Treasury Notes and Bonds

Maturity	Days to Mat.	Bid	Asked	Chg.	Ask Yld.
7 7/8	Nov 02/07	102:21	102:23	-1	6.79

| The coupon rate is 7.875. This bond pays interest of $78.75 per year. | This bond matures on November 2, 2007. | The bid price is the highest price buyers of this issue will pay. They are willing to pay $102 21/32 or $1026.56. | The asked price is the lowest price offered by sellers, namely, $102 23/32 or $1027.18 per bond. | The change is quoted in 32nds of a point between the bid price of the previous day. This bond was down by 1/32. | The ask yield is the return investors will get if the bond is held to maturity. The return to maturity for this note is 6.79 percent. |

Treasury Bills

Maturity	Days to Mat.	Bid	Asked	Chg.	Ask Yld.
July 27 '00	183	5.52	5.51	...	5.75

| This Treasury bill matures on July 27, 2000. | There are 183 days from the quote of this issue until maturity. | The bid discount is the price that dealers are willing to pay for this issue, $971.90 per bill. See Worksheet 3.1 for the calculation. | The asked discount is the price that dealers are willing to sell this issue, namely, $971.99 per bill. See Worksheet 3.1. | There is no change from the previous day's closing price. | The asked yield of 5.75 percent is the return an investor would get if they bought the bill at the asked price and held it to maturity. |

Worksheet 3-1

How to Determine the Purchase and Selling Price of Treasury Bills

Treasury bills sell at a discount, which is less than the par or face amount of $1,000 and then redeemed at par at maturity. This difference is attributed to interest. The bid discount in the previous example of 5.52 percent is the discount (price) that dealers are willing to pay for this bill on that day, and the asked discount of 5.51 percent is the discount that dealers are willing to sell this security on that day.

The dealer's selling price can be calculated as follows:

$$= \text{Par value} - \text{Par Value (asked discount)} \left[\frac{\text{days to maturity}}{360} \right]$$

$$= \$100 - 100 (0.0551) \left[\frac{183}{360} \right]$$

$$= \$97.199 \text{ or } \$971.99 \text{ per T-bill}$$

The dealer's purchase price can be calculated as follows:

$$= \text{Par value} - \text{Par value (bid discount)} \left[\frac{\text{days to maturity}}{360} \right]$$

$$= \$100 - 100 (0.552) \left[\frac{183}{360} \right]$$

$$= \$97.19 \text{ or } \$971.90 \text{ per T-bill}$$

Interest Rates and Bond Prices

An inverse relationship exists between bond prices and market rates of interest. When market rates of interest rise, prices of existing bonds fall. When interest rates fall, prices of existing bonds rise. The coupon rate of the bond determines the extent of the reaction to bond prices. This determines whether the bond will trade at a discount or a premium price. The generalizations are as follows:

- **Discount:** Bonds trade at a discount when their coupon rates are lower than market rates of interest.
- **Discount:** When the yield to maturity of the bond (ask yield or bid yield) is greater than the coupon rate, the bond generally trades at a discount.

- **Premium**: Bonds trade at a premium when their coupon rates are higher than market rates of interest.
- **Premium:** Bonds generally trade at a premium when the yield to maturity is lower than the coupon rate of the bond.

The maturities of the bonds and interest rates determine the extent of the volatility in price. This is further explained through the concept of duration (see Chapter 6, "Analysis: Evaluation Bond Characteristics").

Interest Rates and Maturity

Some bonds are more sensitive to changes in interest rates than others due to their different maturities. This is explained in the following example:

Bond A has a coupon rate of eight percent with a maturity of 20 years.

Bond B has a coupon rate of eight percent with a maturity of five years.

Both bonds are sold at $1,000 (par price) at issuance and at maturity, both bonds will pay back the par value, $1,000.

- When market interest rates rise above eight percent, the price of the 20-year bond, Bond A, will fall much more than the price of the five-year bond, Bond B.
- When market interest rates fall below eight percent, the price of Bond A will rise more than the price of Bond B.
- When market rates of interest are at eight percent (same as the coupon yield), the price of both bonds will be $1,000.

Figure 3-2 illustrates these concepts. Not only will the longer maturity bond be more volatile than the shorter maturity bond, but the magnitude of changes in price will be greater for bonds with longer maturities.

Figure 3-2 also shows that for a given change in a bond's yield (market rates of interest), the size of the change in the bond's price increases at a diminishing rate, the longer the maturity of the bond.

Table 3-1 illustrates this more effectively. Table 3-1 shows the different bond prices for Bonds A, B, and C with different maturities when interest rates change.

From Table 3-1, when interest rates change from 10 percent to 12 percent, the difference in the 20-year maturity is $128.60 and 86 percent larger than $68.88 on the five-year maturity. On the other hand, the 30-year maturity is $133.76, which is only four percent larger than $128.60 on the 20-year maturity.

Figure 3-2 Effect of changes in market rates of interest and bond prices of different maturities

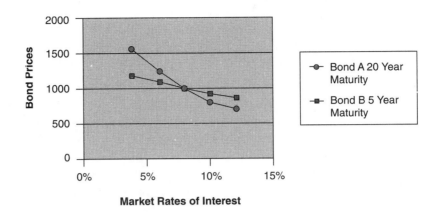

Market Rates of Interest

Table 3-1 Effect of changes in interest rates and bond prices for different maturities of bonds with coupons of eight percent

Market Rates of Interest	4%	6%	8%	10%	12%
Bond C Maturity 30 years	$1691.36	$1275.20	$1000	$811.16	$677.40
Bond A Maturity 20 years	$1543.20	$1229.60	$1000	$830.12	$701.52
Bond B Maturity 5 years	$1178.16	$1083.96	$1000	$924.28	$855.40

	Maturity		
Interest Rates	5 Year	20 Year	30 Year
10%	$924.28	$830.12	$811.16
12%	$855.40	$701.52	$677.40
	$ 68.88	$128.60	$133.76

Interest Rates and Yields

For a given change in a bond's yield, the magnitude of the bond's price is inversely related to the bond's coupon.

The above theorem can be illustrated by comparing the bond prices of different coupon rates of a bond, with the same maturity, 10 years, and the changes in yield to maturity, or market rates of interest (see Table 3-2).

When yields (market rates of interest) increase from seven percent to nine percent, the price of a seven percent coupon bond with a maturity of 10 years declines by $128.74 ($871.26 − $1000), which is a negative 12.87 percent (−128.74/1000). When yields or market rates of interest increase from nine percent to 11 percent for a seven percent bond, the price declines by $107.03 or negative 12.28 percent [($764.23 − $871.26)/$871.26]. This shows that bonds with lower coupon rates are more sensitive to changes in yield to maturity and interest rates.

Table 3-2 Bond prices and yields of bonds with 10-year maturities

Yield to Maturity	Coupon Rates		
	7 Percent	**9 Percent**	**11 Percent**
7 Percent	$1000	$1140.16	$1280.64
9 Percent	$ 871.26	$1000	$1308.71
11 Percent	$ 764.23	$ 882.01	$1000

For a given change in a bond's yield, the magnitude of the price increase caused by a decrease in yield is greater than the price decrease caused by an increase in yield.

By examining Table 3-2, this theorem is easily illustrated. For the seven percent coupon bond, a decrease in yield to maturity (or interest rates) of two percent from nine to seven percent results in an increase in the bond's price of $128.74. For the same coupon bond, an increase in the yield of two percent from nine to 11 percent results in a decrease in the bond's price of $107.03.

Risk Assessment and Bond Prices

Investing in bonds is not without risk. All bond instruments carry risk, but the degree of risk varies with the type of debt and the issuer. Investors should be aware of different types of risks and how the risks affect bond prices.

Treasury notes and bonds are not as risky as corporate bonds primarily because the U.S. Treasury backs their bonds with the full faith and credit of the U.S. government. Corporations cannot issue such watertight guarantees with their corporate bonds. The corporation's ability to maintain its interest payments and repayment of principal over time could deteriorate. This results in a greater risk assessment for that corporation over more creditworthy corporations. Independent ratings services can evaluate the credit risk of municipal and corporate bonds. Ratings are discussed in a later chapter. The direct relationship between risk assessment and bond prices is stated as follows:

Changes in risk assessment by the market: The lesser the quality of the bond, the lower the price. The greater the quality of the bond, the higher the price.

Figure 3-3 illustrates the relationships between the characteristics and the risk assessment of a bond, which affect the investor's required rate of return for that bond, which then determine the price of the bond. The investor's required rate of return includes the risk assessment by the investor and the characteristics of the bond. An investor who perceives one bond to be riskier than another will be more inclined to pay less for the riskier bond. As a result, junk bonds have higher coupon rates than investment grade bonds in order to entice investors to buy them. Thus, the investor's required rate of return for a junk bond will be higher than that for an investment grade bond or Treasury bond. The

Figure 3-3   Factors that affect the price of a bond

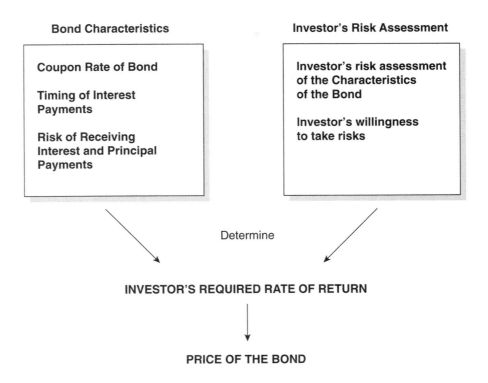

latter has virtually no risk of default on the interest and principal payments.

The investor's required rate of return on a bond is composed of two factors: the risk free rate of return plus an element of risk. The greater the risk component, the greater the required rate of return, and the lower the bond price. Bond valuation is discussed in greater detail in a later chapter.

Call Features

Many corporate bonds have call features, which means that they are subject to *call risk*. This call feature enables the issuer to retire the bonds prior to maturity. When a bond is called, interest no longer accrues, which forces bondholders to retire their bonds. The call feature benefits the issuer rather than the bondholder. This is because issuers tend to call their bonds after a period of high interest rates. For example, if a corporation issued 11 percent coupon bonds when interest rates were high and then rates dropped to seven percent, it would be advantageous for the issuer to refund the old bonds with new bonds at a lower coupon rate. If these bonds were non-callable, investors would continue to receive their 11 percent coupon interest payments. Callable bonds, therefore, sell at lower prices than non-callable bonds of the same maturity and risk level.

Early repayment is always disadvantageous for investors, as issuers rarely refund bonds early if interest rates increase. Calls are especially disadvantageous for investors who bought the bonds with higher coupon yields than the coupon yields of existing bonds.

- Investors should pay particular attention to a bond issue's call and refunding provisions. Three types of call provisions exist:
- *Non-callable bonds* offer investors the most protection, but have many loopholes. Non-callable implies that the bonds will not be called before maturity. However, some cases exist where non-callable bonds have been called as in the case of a fire or act of God; or when a healthy company stops making its interest payments on the bonds, and the trustees call them in and the debt is paid off early. Non-callable for life bonds would be listed in the dealer's quote sheets as NCL.
- *Freely callable bonds* offer investors no protection as issuers can call them anytime.
- *Deferred callable bonds* offer some protection because the bonds cannot be called until after a period of time (usually five, 10, or 15 years after issue). A bond that is non-callable until 2005 would be listed as NC05 on the dealer's quote sheet.

The call provision of the bond specifies the price above the face value that the issuer is willing to pay. This is referred to as the *call premium*, which frequently equals the coupon rate of the bond. It is important to check the call provision of a bond issue before buying. For new issues, investors may want to go one step further and insist on a final copy of the prospectus from the broker. Often the preliminary prospectus is skimpy on early call details (Antilla, 1992).

When buying non-callable or deferred callable bonds, seek written assurances from the broker for their call status.

Besides the call provision, the refunding provision in the bond indenture may be more important. Non-refundable bonds can indeed be called and refunded. However, the refunding must be with "clean money," which is raised either from internal sources of funds or the selling of stocks or assets. Nonrefundable bonds cannot be repaid from the proceeds of selling lower coupon rate debt.

Thus, call and refunding provisions are important to investors particularly if the bonds were purchased at a premium price, and/or market rates of interest are at or near their peak. This is because the call and refunding provisions provide a ceiling price for the bonds. Investors would not be interested in buying a callable bond after the call protection period has expired at a price that is higher than the call price. The issuer could call the bond at the call price at any time. Thus, the call price acts as a ceiling price for the bond.

Put Features

A bond issue with a put provision enables bondholders to resell their bonds to the issuer at par value. *Extendible bonds* have a sequence of designated put dates. These could occur annually or at more frequent intervals.

The put feature provides a floor for the price of the bond. Bondholders know that they can resell their bonds to the issuer at par. This put feature gives bondholders protection against rising interest rates and any deterioration in the credit quality of the issue. However, the price for these advantages is higher bond prices. Bonds with put provisions sell at higher prices than comparable bonds without put provisions.

Sinking Fund Features

Many corporate bonds have *sinking fund* provisions in their indentures, which are used to help the retirement of the bond issues. Instead of the entire bond issue being retired at maturity, a sinking fund enables the corporation to make periodic payments to retire parts of the bond issue before maturity.

With one type of sinking fund, the company randomly selects the bonds to be retired, and then calls them for redemption. Once these bonds are called, they no longer earn interest. For bonds with this kind of sinking fund provision, investors may not want to leave their bonds in street name (in the custody of the brokerage firm), unless they are large investors with tremendous clout in their brokerage firms and know that other investors' bonds will be turned in first.

In another type of sinking fund, a corporation makes payments to a trustee who invests this money and then the entire amount accumulated goes toward retiring the bonds at maturity.

Issuers may also repurchase their bonds in the bond market and retire them. This occurs more frequently when the bonds are trading at a discount. Investors who sell their bonds may not know that it is the issuer who is buying them back.

The significance of a sinking fund feature is twofold:

* It provides some security to bondholders because the issuer sets aside payments into a sinking fund to repay the bondholders. Depending on the circumstances, this could lessen the price volatility of the issue.
* With a random sinking fund plan, bondholders, whose bonds are called, will have their principal repaid before maturity. In this case,

the sinking fund feature acts as a ceiling for the price of the bond issue.

Term Versus Serial Bonds

A *term bond* has a single maturity date. Most corporate bonds are term bonds. On the term date, the bond principal is paid back to the bondholders. In 1993, Walt Disney Company issued 100-year bonds with a call provision after 30-years. All Disney bonds that are not called after 2023 mature in the year 2093. It is common to find call provisions in term bonds.

A *serial bond* issue has portions of the bond issue maturing at different dates. For example, a serial bond issue with a period of 10 years could have one-tenth of the issue mature in each of the 10 years. This example has sequential maturity dates. Generally, serial bonds do not have call provisions.

Convertible Feature*

Convertible bonds have a conversion feature, whereby the bonds can be exchanged for a specified number of common shares of the issuing corporation at the option of the convertible bondholder. In a few cases, convertible bonds have been exchanged for preferred stock or other bond issues.

Convertible securities have their own terminology, which can be confusing. Suppose a corporation wanting to raise funds decides that it does not want to issue more common stock because the market price of the stock is low. To raise enough cash, it would have to issue many more shares of common stock, which would dilute the earnings for existing shareholders. A straight debt issue would also be too costly because the company would have to match the coupon rate of comparable existing corporate debt issues with similar risks and maturities.

Instead, the company decides on a convertible bond. Because of the conversion, feature investors will accept a lower coupon rate on the issue. The company needs to consider the current market price of its common stock to determine the number of shares that each bondholder will receive on conversion. For instance, if the company's stock is currently trading at $18 per share, the company may decide on a conversion price of $25 to make the bonds more appealing to investors. The *conversion ratio*, which is the number of common shares received for each bond, is 40 (shares per bond 1000/25). This is the face value of the bond divided by the conversion price.

*Portions of this section have been previously published by Esme Faerber in *All About Bonds and Bond Mutual Funds,* McGraw-Hill, 2000.

Convertible bonds can be valued either in relation to the conversion value of the stock or as straight debt. In reality, both of these factors are taken into account in the valuation of the convertible security.

The Value of a Convertible Bond as Stock

The value of the convertible security as stock depends on the market price of the common stock. The value is the number of shares into which the bond is convertible multiplied by the market price of the stock. In the hypothetical example above, the convertible may be exchanged into 40 shares, which is multiplied by $18, the current market price of the stock to give a value of $720.

The relationship between the value of the convertible bond as stock and the price of the common stock is illustrated in Table 3-3. From Table 3-3, we see that as the market price of the stock (column 2) rises, the value of the convertible increases. The value of the convertible is obtained by multiplying the conversion ratio by the market price of the stock. When the price of the common stock is below the conversion price of $25, the value of the convertible is less than the face amount of the bond ($1,000).

- When the stock price is above the conversion price of $25, the value of the convertible is greater than the face value of the bond. Thus, the conversion feature allows for the upside potential of capital gains through the appreciation of the stock price.
- Moreover, the price of the convertible will not fall below a floor price, which becomes the straight value of the bond.

For example, assume that in the previous illustration, the market price of the common stock falls to $10 per share. The conversion value is $400, but the market price will not fall below the value of the bond, due to the value of the coupon interest payments on the bond. Similarly, the market price of the convertible will not be less than the conversion value of the security. This is due partly to the activity of arbitrageurs, who will buy and sell the same security in two different markets to take advantage of price differentials. This is discussed in the next section. A graphical explanation of the dual pricing concepts of a convertible bond is shown in Figure 3-4.

Table 3-3 Value of convertible bond as stock

Conversion Ratio*	Market Price of Stock	Value of Convertible as Stock
40	$10	$ 400
40	18	720
40	25	1,000
40	30	1,200
40	35	1,400
40	40	1,600

*The number of shares into which the convertible is exchanged.

Figure 3-4   Pricing of a convertible bond

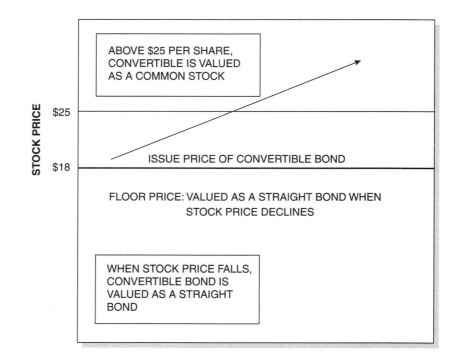

Value of the Convertible Bond as Debt

The value of the convertible as debt depends on the coupon rate, the risk of default on the interest payments, the length of time to maturity, the call provision, and market rates of interest. The investment value of the bond is determined by discounting both the coupon payments that the convertible pays and the face value of the bond at maturity (assuming it is not converted) at the interest rate paid on similar debt. In other words, the value of the convertible bond is the present value of the cash flows of the coupon payments and the face value of the bond at maturity discounted at an interest rate which includes the risk for that security.

As with regular bonds, the value of the convertible bond as debt fluctuates with changes in market rates of interest. When interest rates increase, the price of the convertible bond declines, and conversely, when interest rates decline, the price of the convertible rises. This is because the coupon rate on the convertible is fixed.

The value of the convertible as straight debt is important because it sets a floor price. When the stock price is trading below the conversion price, the straight bond value provides the floor value and the convertible will not fall below this value. This is because the convertible option is of no consequence at lower stock prices. When stock prices go up above the conversion price, the minimum price for the convertible bond is the conversion value as stock. This is where the bond is equity in disguise.

Value of the Convertible Bond as a Hybrid Security

At low stock prices, the floor price of the convertible is no lower than its value as a straight bond, and at sufficiently high stock prices, the price of the convertible is the same as the conversion value into stock. In between these extremes in stock prices, the convertible security generally trades at a premium price over its value as equity and over its value as debt.

These relationships are examined in Table 3-4 using the example of a six percent, 20-year convertible bond which has a conversion ratio of 40 shares. The market rate of interest used is eight percent.

At low stock prices ($5 and $10 per share), the market price of the convertible bond is the same as its value as straight debt and the premium over the stock price is large. At $25 per share, the conversion price, the market price for the convertible is $1,100, which exceeds both the value of the debt by $296.36 and the value as stock by $100. At a significantly high stock price of $40, the market price of the convertible is the same as the value as stock and the premium over the value as debt is very high ($796.36).

The example illustrates that as the stock price rises, the premium paid over its value as straight debt increases. This is due to the importance of the conversion feature on the convertible and the fact that the straight debt becomes less important as the stock price increases.

It is also probable that the bond could be called, which would force conversion when the stock price is greater than the conversion price. For example, assume that the convertible bond was bought at $1,420

Table 3-4 Premiums on convertible bonds

Share Price	Conversion Ratio	Value as Stock	Value as Debt	Market Price of Convertible Bond*	Premium over stock price	Premium over bond price
$ 5	40	$ 200	$803.64	$ 803.64	$603.64	$ 0
10	40	400	803.64	803.64	403.64	0
18	40	720	803.64	850.00	130.00	46.36
25	40	1,000	803.64	1,100.00	100.00	296.36
35	40	1,400	803.64	1,420.00	20.00	616.36
40	40	1,600	803.64	1,600.00	0	796.36

*In reality, it is difficult to calculate the market price of the convertible security due to its hybrid nature and the many factors affecting the market price. Therefore, the market prices between the extremes in stock prices in this example are hypothetical and could fluctuate.

and the company calls in the bonds when the stock price is trading at $35. Convertible bondholders will not turn in their bonds for $1,000 per bond. Instead, they will convert their bonds into equity receiving $1,400 per bond (40 shares $\times$ $35), which results in a loss of $20 per bond for the bondholder. Thus, as the stock price rises and puts downward pressure on the premium over the stock price, the market price for the convertible converges with the stock value of the convertible.

Most convertible securities trade at a premium over either the stock value or the value as a straight bond. Investors should analyze the fundamentals of the company before buying. For example, at Battle Mountain, a mining company, six percent convertible bonds were trading at a 141 percent premium over its equity value, whereas at another mining company, Couer d'Alene, seven percent convertible bonds were trading at a 31 percent premium over the equity value. In this case, the higher premium over the equity value offers greater appreciation potential than the convertible bond with the lower premium over its equity value.

Arbitrage

The activities of arbitrageurs affect the prices of convertible securities. A definition of arbitrage helps to clarify the exploitation of the pricing of convertibles in two different markets. Arbitrage occurs when a similar security is bought and sold in different markets in order to exploit any price differentials. In a strict definition, it requires no risk and it produces an expected level of profit.

For instance, if the market value of the debt is $900 (in the same example used in the previous section), when the stock price moves to $24, arbitrageurs would exploit this price differential for their own profit. The conversion value is $960 (40 shares $\times$ $24 per share), and they sell short the stock. To sell short is to borrow a security and sell it on the market. Short sellers simultaneously buy the convertible bond for $900 and sell short 40 shares of the stock for $960. The conversion option on the convertible bond is exercised, and the shares that were borrowed are tendered. The resulting profit is $60 per bond before taking into account the commissions for the buying and selling of the securities. Arbitrageurs bid up the price of the bonds until a price differential no longer exists. In reality, the price of convertible bonds is rarely the same as the conversion value into stock. Mostly, the price of the convertible exceeds that of the conversion value due to the bond's value. In addition to the upside appreciation from the conversion value, the value of the bond as debt provides a floor price for the convertible bond. Refer to Worksheet 3-2 for another arbitrage example.

Worksheet 3-2

Convertible Bond Arbitrage

Convertible Bond Price: $1,000
Conversion Price: $35
Conversion Ratio: 28.57 shares
Stock Price: $37
What would an investor do to take advantage of the situation?

Answer: 1. Buy the convertible bond at $1,000 per bond. 2. Convert the bond into common stock worth $1057.09 (28.57 × 37 = $1057.09). 3. Sell the stock which equals a profit of $57.09 per bond purchased. 4. The greater the number of bonds purchased, the greater the total profit. Alternatively, an investor could sell the stock short and buy the convertible bonds as outlined in the text above.

Strategies

Understanding the different factors that have direct and indirect influences on bond prices can assist investors with their bond buying strategies. Worksheet 3-3 lists some helpful guidelines.

Exercises

1. Name the factors that account directly for fluctuations in bond prices.

2. Determine the actual purchase and selling price for a Treasury bill quoted at the bid of 5.63 and the ask of 5.62 with 90 days to maturity.

Worksheet 3-3

Strategies to Manage Bond Price Volatility

1. Determine time horizons for objectives. Match bond maturities with the time horizons for the objectives.
2. Anticipate the direction of interest rates in the economy.
   If investors anticipate a decline in interest rates, increase the maturities of bond purchases. Remember, the longer the maturity, the more volatile the price when interest rates change.
   If investors anticipate an increase in interest rates, decrease the maturities of bond purchases, and hold the bonds to maturity.
3. If investors are looking to increasing their returns, they could increase their holdings of lower quality bonds. Examine the yield spread between the high quality and low quality bonds to see if the additional returns are worth the additional risk.
4. Do not buy bonds with a call provision at a premium price before examining the details. The call price acts as a ceiling price, which means that buying a bond above the call price could result in a capital loss.
5. When faced with a choice of bonds to purchase, choose the bonds with higher coupon rates that will be less sensitive to changes

3. Explain why an investor should not buy a callable bond at a premium price that is higher than the call price.

   _____
   _____
   _____
   _____
   _____

4. Explain the floor and ceiling prices for convertible bonds.

End Notes

Antilla, Susan: "Nonrefundable Bonds can Indeed be Refunded," *The New York Times,* November 21, 1992.

Faerber, Esme: *All About Bonds and Bond Mutual Funds.* McGraw-Hill, New York, 2000.

Malkiel, Burton C: "Expectations, Bond Prices, and the Term Structure of Interest Rates," *Quarterly Journal of Economics,* May 1962, pp. 197-218.

Chapter 4

Categories: Types of Bonds

Reasons for Buying Bonds

A couple questions should be considered before purchasing bonds:

- Which types of bonds should investors buy?
- What are the reasons for buying bonds?

In deciding which types of bonds to buy, investors should remember their reasons for investing in them. Generally, bonds tend to be safer than stocks and they provide regular payments of income. However, bonds will not treble overnight like some of the Internet and bio-technology stocks. Stocks have averaged roughly 20 percent annual returns in 1999 versus roughly six percent annual returns for Treasury bonds. On the other hand, bonds provide protection for a portfolio in case of a decline in the stock market. Thus, investors buy bonds to provide insurance against large losses in the value of their assets.

Which bonds should an investor buy? Municipals offer tax advantages for tax payers in high marginal tax brackets, whereas Treasury bonds are the safest in terms of credit and default risk. Corporate bonds provide higher yields, but they also vary in terms of credit quality. Corporate junk bonds provide the highest yields, but also involve much greater risk. Table 4-1 outlines some of the reasons for buying the different types of bonds.

Short-Term Fixed Income Securities

Short-term fixed income securities are liquid, safe investments, and are used by investors for their emergency and short-term funds. Examples of these types of investments are *certificates of deposit* (CD), money market mutual funds, Treasury bills, commercial paper, bankers' acceptances, and repurchase agreements. These investments are also used as temporary, short-term cash substitutes. In other words, idle cash can be invested in these to earn a return. The characteristics of these short-

Table 4-1 Characteristics of the Different Types of Bonds

Treasury Securities	• Safest type of bonds.	• Interest is exempt from state taxes.	• Easiest to buy directly without commissions.
Inflation- Indexed Bonds	• Returns rise with inflation.	• Treasury inflation-indexed bonds are safe.	• If no inflation occurs, returns will be lower than those of other bonds.
Municipal Bonds	• Interest is exempt from Federal income taxes.	• Credit quality varies with the issuer.	
Mortgage-Backed Bonds	• Yield more than Treasuries.	• Income payments may be erratic depending on market rates of interest.	
Corporate Bonds	• Yield more than agency and Treasuries, but have greater risks.		
Corporate Junk Bonds	• High yield, risky bonds.	• Low ratings with regard to the ability to service interest payments and repay principal.	

*Portions of this chapter have been previously published by Esme Faerber in *All About Bonds and Bond Mutual Funds* (McGraw Hill, New York, 2000).

Table 4-2 Short-Term Securities with a Time Horizon of One Year or Less

Investment Objectives	Disadvantages	Types of Investments
Return of Principal.	Low Yields that may not cover inflation.	Savings accounts.
Steady income payments.		Money market accounts/funds.
Access to funds.		Certificates of Deposit.
		Treasury Bills.

term investments are low risk of default with high liquidity and marketability. Table 4-2 outlines the objectives and some of the disadvantages of short-term fixed income securities.

Many other short-term fixed income securities exist, such as commercial paper, bankers' acceptances, and repurchase agreements. These are not widely held by individual investors due to their complexities. Some of the simpler, short-term parking places for funds, namely savings accounts and now checking accounts, will also not be discussed in this book due to their familiarity to most investors.

The easiest parking places for short-term funds are money market mutual funds. Even though money market funds offer a convenient way to invest funds, investors should also understand the nuances of the individual short-term investments, such as Treasury bills and certificates of deposit, for two reasons:

• Money market mutual funds invest their pooled funds in these indi-

vidual short-term fixed income securities. By understanding how these securities work, investors can assess the risks and returns of the different money market mutual funds.
- At times, these individual securities offer greater advantages than using a money market mutual fund.

Money Market Mutual Funds

Money market funds compete directly with bank deposit accounts and over the years, money market funds have grown considerably at the expense of bank accounts. Banks, brokers, and investment companies offer money market mutual funds. Brokerage money market mutual funds may have higher fees, sales commissions (loads), and in the case of short-term bond funds, additional risks. Brokers and financial advisors are motivated to move funds away from the investment companies' money market mutual funds to their own products, where they are compensated through sales commissions (loads). Table 4-3 illustrates the effects of a short-term bond fund with a load versus a no-load money market mutual fund. In addition, operating expenses for these brokerage firms' funds may be higher than those of investment companies (the Vanguard Group, for example).

Investment companies offer the majority of the money market mutual funds. These money market funds provide an alternative parking place for cash and short-term funds, which offer lower risks than investing in stocks and bonds. Investment companies managing money market funds pool investors' money and issue shares to the investors. Then, they invest the money in short-term securities such as Treasury bills, commercial paper, bankers' acceptances, CDs, Euro-dollars, repurchase agreements, and government agency obligations.

Three types of money market funds exist:

- *General purpose funds,* which invest in a wide range of money market securities such as Treasury bills, commercial paper, bankers' acceptances, certificates of deposit, repurchase agreements, and short-term off-shore securities.
- *U.S. government funds,* which invest in short-term Treasury securi-

Table 4-3   Load versus a No-load Fund

Load Fund of 3%		**No- Load Fund**	
Amount Invested	$10, 000	Amount Invested	$10,000
3% Load charge	($300)	No-Load charge	0
Funds Available	$ 9,700	Funds Available	$10,000

This is an illustration of a *front-end load,* which is a charge taken off the initial amount of the funds invested. A *back-end load* **also exists,** which is a charge taken out of the proceeds when shares are sold.

ties and U.S. agency obligations.

- *Tax-exempt money market funds,* which invest in short-term municipal securities. The income from these securities is exempt from federal income taxes.

How Safe Are Money Market Funds?

Money market mutual funds do not carry the *Federal Deposit Insurance Corporation* (FDIC, an independent agency of the U.S. government) insurance carried by bank money market deposit accounts, but they are relatively safe because:

(i) the investments are in securities issued by governments and their agencies, and large corporations; and

(ii) the maturities of these securities are short-term, lowering the risk.

The safest money market funds invest only in U.S. Treasury securities because the full faith and credit of the U.S. government back them. However, all money market funds are relatively safe. Large institutions are unlikely to default on securities issued for a short period of time, and the prices of short-term securities do not fluctuate widely.

Typically, money market funds have a constant share price of $1 per share.

Before investing, read the prospectus, which lists the types of securities that the money market mutual fund invests in. The risk of default has been zero to very low for Treasury bills, certificates of deposit, bankers' acceptances, and commercial paper. Although the risks of default on commercial paper are low, a few companies have defaulted, which affected money market funds holding those issues. However, the investment companies running the funds absorbed the losses instead of the investors.

How to Select a Money Market Fund

Investors can choose from hundreds of money market funds. Before choosing, investors may want to read the prospectus for the following criteria:

- Choose from no-load money market funds.
- Investors should list their objectives to determine which type of money market funds to invest in. If a high quality fund is desired, make sure that the fund chosen invests in top grade securities. If investors are looking for federally tax-exempt income, funds that invest in short-term, tax-exempt municipal bond money market funds should be chosen.
- Examine the return of the fund. The yield or return depends on the

---

Worksheet 4-1

How to Invest in Money Market Funds

To invest in a money market fund, call the fund (most have toll-free telephone numbers) or write to them for a prospectus and application form. The Internet provides a comprehensive list of all the mutual fund families. One of these Web sites is `www.moneymarketmutual-funds.com`. Mutual fund companies are required by the SEC to send the prospectus either by mail or through the Internet to new investors. The prospectus includes information about the fund such as:

- The minimum dollar investment necessary to open an account.
- How the investor can withdraw funds from the account.
- The investment objectives and policies as well as the investment restrictions.
- Who manages the fund, the fees charged by the management company, and an outline of the operating expenses and other charges.
- The fund's financial statements.

Read the prospectus before filling out the application form. The completed form can be sent back with a check to open the account. Investors will receive monthly statements showing the number of shares in their accounts, their deposits, withdrawals, and dividend income. Most funds have a minimum amount (usually $100) for additional investments.

Investors can withdraw money on demand from their money market funds in various ways:

- Through check writing (if check writing is available for that fund).
- Wire transfers from the fund to a bank account.
- Check written by fund and mailed to an account-holder in response to a written withdrawal request.
- Transfer money to other funds within the same investment company's family of funds.
- The investor may request a *systematic withdrawal plan* (SWP) and the fund will send a periodic check to the investor, a third party, or bank.

---

earnings of the fund minus the fees and operating charges. Generally, the safer the fund, the lower the yield. U.S. government securities (T-bills) have lower yields than commercial paper and repurchase agreements, but the U.S. government will not default on its obligations.

- Compare the features that the funds offer, such as whether the fund provides free check writing privileges, the number of funds within that investment family, if limitations on the number and amount of transfers within the family of funds appear, and the minimum dollar amount to open a fund (typically varies from $500 to $2,000).

A comparison of these features guides the investor in their choice of a money market fund. Table 4-4 summarizes the advantages and disadvantages of money market funds.

Caveats

* Choose a money market fund from an investment company that has a wide range of different funds, allowing greater flexibility in the transfers to other types of investment funds.
* Avoid funds that have sales charges, redemption fees, and high management and expense ratios.
* Avoid keeping too much money in money market funds, as over the long-term real rates of return from money market funds are unlikely to exceed the rate of inflation.
* Avoid choosing short-term bond funds over money market mutual funds as a parking place for cash for short periods of time. An investor could experience losses in principal if the share price falls below the purchase price with short-term bond funds.

Treasury Bills

Treasury bills are slightly more difficult to purchase directly than money market funds, but many investors prefer to invest directly in Treasury bills than indirectly through money market funds. Treasury bills are the most popular of the short-term individual investments after money market mutual funds.

Table 4-4 Advantages and Disadvantages of Money Market Funds

Advantages	Disadvantages
• Liquid, safe investments.	• Interest income is taxable at all levels.
• Earn competitive rates of interest.	• May earn more from investing directly in individual money market instruments.
• No tax consequences when adding and withdrawing funds.	

What Are Treasury Bills?

Treasury bills (T-bills) are short-term, safe-haven investments, which are issued by the U.S. Treasury and are backed fully by the U.S. government. The risk of default is extremely low. In fact, if the U.S. government defaulted on any of its obligations, all investments in the U.S. would be suspect. Treasury bills are considered to be the safest of all fixed income investments.

Treasury bills are negotiable, non-interest bearing securities which mature in three months, six months, or one year. They are available in minimum denominations of $10,000 and multiples of $1,000 above that. See Table 4-5 for details on the different Treasury bill issues.

The 13- and 26-week bills are auctioned every week and the 52-week bills are auctioned every four weeks. The announcements for the auctions are made generally two weeks before each auction.

Treasury bills are issued at a discount from their face value. The amount of the discount depends on the prices bid in the Treasury bill auctions. At maturity, the bills are redeemed at full face value. The difference in the amount between the discount value and the face value is treated as interest income. See Worksheet 4-2 for the determination of Treasury bill yields and Worksheet 4-3 on how to buy and sell Treasury bills. Worksheet 4-4 outlines the differences between competitive and non-competitive bids. Table 4-6 lists the advantages and disadvantages of Treasury bills.

Caveats

* When buying T-bills through banks and/or brokers, shop around for the lowest fees/commissions.
* When submitting competitive bids, the possibility always exists that an investor's bid will not be accepted due to unanticipated fluctuations of money market interest rates on the day of the auction.
* Although submitting a non-competitive bid assures the investor of purchase, the uncertainty remains that the investor could receive yields well below current yields due to an unexpected drop in short-term interest rates.

Table 4-5 Treasury bills

Term	Minimum	Multiples	Auction	Auction Time	Issue Date
13 week	$10,000 *	$1,000	Weekly	Monday	Thursday
26 week	$10,000 *	$1,000	Weekly	Monday	Thursday
52 week	$10,000	$1,000	Every four weeks	Thursday	Thursday

* Treasury allowed investors to buy these in denominations of $1,000 August 10,1998 auction.

Worksheet 4-2

How to Determine the Yield on Treasury Bills

Because no stated rate of interest is available, *the yield on Treasury bills* can be determined as follows:

$$\text{Yield} = \frac{(\text{Face value} - \text{Price paid})}{\text{Price paid}} \times \frac{(365)}{\text{Days to maturity}}$$

A six-month Treasury bill purchased for $9,600 and redeemed at face value has an annual yield of 8.33 percent:

$$\text{Yield} = (\$10,000 - 9,600 / 9,600) \times (365/182.5) = 8.33\%$$

However, to make matters more complex, bids submitted to the Federal Reserve Banks are not quoted on an annual basis, as above, but on *a bank discount basis* which is computed as follows:

$$\text{Yield} = (\text{Face value} - \text{Price paid}/100^*) \times (360^{**}/\text{Days to maturity})$$

Using the same example as above, the discount is $4 for the T-bill, selling at $96 per $100 face value with a maturity of six months. The bank discount yield is:

$$= (100 - 96/100) \times (360/180) = 8\%$$

Thus, the bank discount yield is always less than the annual yield.

---

* Yield is quoted for each $100 of face value.

** Note the use of 360 as opposed to 365 days.

Table 4-6 Advantages and Disadvantages of Treasury Bills

Advantages	Disadvantages
Provide a flexible range of maturities.	Need a minimum of $10,000.
Provide maximum safety for the repayment of principal and interest payments.	Yields tend to be less than those offered by CDs and other individual money market securities.
Interest income is exempt from state taxes.	Treasury bills are subject to interest rate risk.
Can buy them directly from the Federal Reserve Banks without incurring any commissions.	Treasury bills do not offer protection against rising inflation.

Worksheet 4-3

How to Buy and Sell Treasury Bills

- New issues of Treasury bills can be bought directly from any of the Federal Reserve Banks in the primary market with no charge of commissions or fees.
- New issues of Treasury bills can be bought indirectly through banks and brokerage firms who charge commissions for their services. Existing T-bills on the secondary markets can be bought and sold through banks and brokerage firms.

Direct Purchase

An investor can buy directly from the Treasury by opening an account and submitting a tender form. See Figures 4-1, 4-2, 4-3 for a list of the offices of the Federal Reserve Banks where forms can be obtained, a copy of a new account request form, and a copy of a tender form for a Treasury bill, respectively.

1. The first step is to fill out the new account request form (Figure 4-2) to establish an account with the Department of the Treasury. Fill in the information requested. The routing number on the form is the identifying number of your financial institution. It is a nine-digit number that can be found on the bottom line of a check before the account number or on a deposit slip before the account number.
2. Submit this form to the Federal Reserve Bank/branch. A confirmation of the establishment of the account and an account number will be received. Purchases of Treasury securities are recorded in this account, which is free up to the amount of $100,000 of securities. Over this amount, the Federal Reserve charges $25 to maintain the account.
3. Fill in the tender form to buy Treasury bills directly from the Federal Reserve Bank. See Figure 4-3 for a copy of a tender form.
4. The Federal Reserve Bank auctions new issues of Treasury bills on a weekly basis. Investors may submit their bids either on a competitive or non-competitive basis.
5. Treasury bills purchased directly through the Federal Reserve system are held in the Treasury direct book-entry system, which is designed primarily for investors who hold their securities to maturity. Should the investor decide to sell T-bills before maturity, he/she would have to fill out a Transfer Request form (PD 5179), which transfers the account to the commercial book-entry system. Then, the T-bills can be sold. The commercial book-entry system records those treasuries bought through financial institutions and government securities dealers. Information on Treasury bills can be obtained from the government's Web site (`www.publicdebt.treas.gov`).

Figure 4-1 List of Federal Reserve Banks and Treasury Servicing Offices

	When you call or visit	When you write:		When you call or visit	When you write:
FRB Atlanta	104 Marietta Street, NW Atlanta, Georgia 404-521-8657 (Recording) 404-521-8653	Securities Service Dept. 104 Marietta Street, NW 30303	**FRB Denver**	1020 16th Street Denver, Colorado 303-572-2475 (Recording) 303-572-2470 or 2473	P.O. Box 5228 Denver, CO 80217-5228
FRB Baltimore	502 South Sharp Street Baltimore, Maryland 410-576-3500 (Recording) 410-576-3300	P.O. Box 1378 Baltimore, MD 21203	**FRB Detroit**	160 West Fort Street Detroit, Michigan 313-963-4936 (Recording) 313-964-6157	P.O. Box 1059 Detroit, MI 48231
FRB Birmingham	1801 Fifth Avenue, North Birmingham, Alabama 205-731-8702 (Recording) 205-731-8708	P.O. Box 830447 Birmingham, AL 35283-0447	**FRB El Paso**	301 East Main El Paso, Texas 915-521-8295 (Recording) 915-521-8272	P.O. Box 100 El Paso, TX 79999
FRB Boston	600 Atlantic Avenue Boston, Massachusetts 617-973-3800 (Recording) 617-973-3810	P.O. Box 2076 Boston, MA 02106	**FRB Houston**	1701 San Jacinto Street Houston, Texas 713-659-4433	P.O. Box 2578 Houston, TX 77252
FRB Buffalo	160 Delaware Avenue Buffalo, New York 716-849-5158 (Recording) 716-849-5000	P.O. Box 961 Buffalo, NY 14240-0961	**FRB Jacksonville**	800 West Water Street Jacksonville, Florida 904-632-1178 (Recording) 904-632-1179	P.O. Box 2499 Jacksonville, FL 32231-2499
FRB Charlotte	530 East Trade Street Charlotte, North Carolina 704-358-2424 (Recording) 704-358-2100	P.O. Box 30248 Charlotte, NC 28230	**FRB Kansas City**	925 Grand Avenue Kansas City, Missouri 816-881-2767 (Recording) 816-881-2883	P.O. Box 419033 Kansas City, MO 64141-6033
FRB Chicago	230 South LaSalle Street Chicago, Illinois 312-786-1110 (Recording) 312-322-5369	P.O. Box 834 Chicago, IL 60690	**FRB Little Rock**	325 West Capitol Avenue Little Rock, Arkansas 501-324-8274 (Recording) 501-324-8272	P.O. Box 1261 Little Rock, AR 72203
FRB Cincinnati	150 East Fourth Street Cincinnati, Ohio 513-721-4794 Ext. 334	P.O. Box 999 Cincinnati, OH 45201	**FRB Los Angeles**	950 South Grand Avenue Los Angeles, California 213-624-7398	P.O. Box 2077 Terminal Annex Los Angeles, CA 90051
FRB Cleveland	1455 East Sixth Street Cleveland, Ohio 216-579-2490 (Recording) 216-579-2000	P.O. Box 6387 Cleveland, OH 44101	**FRB Louisville**	410 South Fifth Street Louisville, Kentucky 502-568-9240 (Recording) 502-568-9238	P.O. Box 32710 Louisville, KY 40232
FRB Dallas	2200 North Pearl Street Dallas, Texas 214-922-6100 214-922-6770 (Recording)	Box 655906 Dallas, TX 75265-5906	**FRB Memphis**	200 North Main Street Memphis, Tennessee 901-523-9380 (Recording) 901-523-7171 Ext. 423	P.O. Box 407 Memphis, TN 38101

Figure 4-1 Continued

	When you call or visit	When you write:		When you call or visit	When you write:
FRB Miami	9100 NW Thirty-Six Street Miami, Florida 305-471-6257 (Recording) 305-471-6497	P.O. Box 520847 Miami, FL 33152	**FRB Salt Lake City**	120 South State Street Salt Lake City, Utah 801-322-7844 (Recording) 801-322-7882	P.O. Box 30780 Salt Lake City, UT 84130-0780
FRB Minneapolis	250 Marquette Avenue Minneapolis, Minnesota 612-340-2051 (Recording) 612-340-2075	250 Marquette Ave. Minneapolis, MN 55480	**FRB San Antonio**	126 East Nueva Street San Antonio, Texas 210-978-1330 (Recording) 210-978-1303 or 1305	P.O. Box 1471 San Antonio, TX 78295
FRB Nashville	301 Eighth Avenue, North Nashville, Tennessee 615-251-7236 (Recording) 615-251-7100	301 Eighth Ave., N. Nashville, TN 37203-4407	**FRB San Francisco**	101 Market Street San Francisco, California 415-974-3491 (Recording) 415-974-2330	P.O. Box 7702 San Francisco, CA 94120
FRB New Orleans	525 St. Charles Avenue New Orleans, Louisiana 504-593-5839 (Recording) 504-593-3200	P.O. Box 52948 New Orleans, LA 70152-2948	**FRB Seattle**	1015 Second Avenue Seattle, Washington 206-343-3615 (Recording) 206-343-3605	P.O. Box 3567 Seattle, WA 98124
FRB New York	33 Liberty Street New York, New York 212-720-5823 (Recording) 212-720-6619	Federal Reserve P.O. Station New York, NY 10045	**FRB St. Louis**	411 Locust Street St. Louis, Missouri 314-444-8703	P.O. Box 14915 St. Louis, MO 63178
FRB Oklahoma City	226 Dean A McGee Avenue Oklahoma City, Oklahoma 405-270-8660 (Recording) 405-270-8652	P.O. Box 25129 Oklahoma City, OK 73125	**Public Debt* Washington, DC**	Capital Area Servicing Center 1300 C Street, S.W. Washington, DC 202-874-4400	Capital Area Servicing Center Bureau of the Public Debt Washington, DC 20239-0001
FRB Omaha	2201 Farnam Street Omaha, Nebraska 402-221-5638 (Recording) 402-221-5636	2201 Farnam Street Omaha, NE 68102		Device for hearing impaired: 202-874-4026	Mail Tenders to: Capital Area Servicing Center Bureau of the Public Debt Department N Washington, DC 20239-1500
FRB Philadelphia	Ten Independence Mall Philadelphia, Pennsylvania 215-574-6580 (Recording) 215-574-6680	P.O. Box 90 Philadelphia, PA 19105			
FRB Pittsburgh	717 Grant Street Pittsburgh, Pennsylvania 412-261-7899 (Recording) 412-261-7802	P.O. Box 867 Pittsburgh, PA 15230-0867			
FRB Portland	915 S.W. Stark Street Portland, Oregon 503-221-5931 (Recording) 503-221-5932	P.O. Box 3436 Portland, OR 97208-3436			
FRB Richmond	701 East Bryd Street Richmond, Virginia 804-697-8355 (Recording) 804-697-8372	P.O. Box 27622 Richmond, VA 23261			

*This servicing office only serves customers residing in the metropolitan Washington, DC area.

Figure 4-2 New account request form to open an account

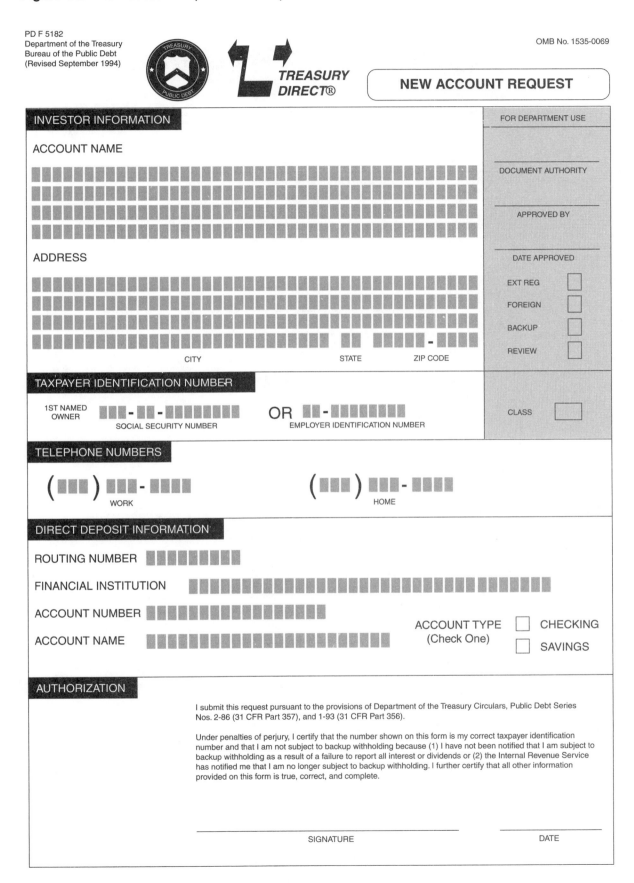

Figure 4-3 Treasury bill, note & bond tender

PD F 5381
Department of the Treasury
Bureau of the Public Debt

TREASURY DIRECT®

OMB No. 1535-0069

TREASURY BILL, NOTE & BOND TENDER

TYPE OR PRINT IN INK ONLY – TENDERS WILL NOT BE ACCEPTED WITH ALTERATIONS OR CORRECTIONS

1. BID INFORMATION *Tender amount must meet or exceed the minimum for the term selected below. (Must Be Completed)*

Par Amount:

$ _____

Bid Type:
(Fill in One)

○ Noncompetitive
○ Competitive at ⌊⌊⌊.⌊⌊⌊⌊ %
(Bill bids must and in 0 or 5.)

| DEPARTMENT USE |
| TENDER NO. |
| RECEIVED BY DATE |

2. TREASURY DIRECT ACCOUNT NUMBER
(If NOT furnished, a new account will be opened.)

⌊⌊⌊⌊⌊-⌊⌊⌊⌊-⌊⌊⌊⌊⌊

3. TAXPAYER ID NUMBER *(Must Be Completed)*

⌊⌊⌊-⌊⌊-⌊⌊⌊⌊ **OR** ⌊⌊-⌊⌊⌊⌊⌊⌊⌊

Social Security Number (First-Named Owner)   Employer ID Number

| ENTERED BY |
| APPROVED BY |

4. TERM SELECTION *(Fill in One)*
(Must Be Completed)

Treasury Bill   Circle the Number of
$10,000 Minimum   Reinvestments

○ 13-Week..........0   1   2   3   4
                       5   6   7   8

○ 26-Week..........0   1   2   3   4

○ 52-Week..........0   1   2

Treasury Note/Bond
$5,000 Minimum

○ 2-Year Note

○ 3-Year Note

- - - - - - - - - - - - - - - - - - - -
$1,000 Minimum

○ 5-Year Note

○ 10-Year Note

○ 30-Year Note

○ Inflation-indexed _____
                        Term

5. ACCOUNT NAME Please Type or Print! *(Must Be Completed)*

6. ADDRESS *(For new account or if changed.)* ○ **New Address?**

City   State   ZIP Code

| ISSUE DATE |
| CUSIP 912794 |
| CUSIP 912827 |
| CUSIP 912810 |
| FOREIGN ☐ |
| BACKUP ☐ |

7. TELEPHONE NUMBERS *(For new account or if changed.)* ○ **New Phone Number?**

Work (____) ____ _____   Home (____) ____ _____

8. DIRECT DEPOSIT INFORMATION *(For new account only.)* Changes? Submit PD F 5178

Routing Number ⌊⌊⌊⌊⌊⌊⌊⌊⌊

Financial Institution Name _____

Account Number ⌊⌊⌊⌊⌊⌊⌊⌊⌊⌊⌊⌊⌊⌊⌊⌊⌊

Name on Account _____

Account Type: *(Fill in One)* ○ Checking   ○ Savings

9. PURCHASE METHOD
(Must Be Completed)

○ *Automatic Withdrawal*
  (Existing Treasury Direct Account Only)

○ Cash: $_____

○ Checks: $_____
               $_____

○ Securities: $_____

Total Payment
Attached: $_____
CHECKS ARE DEPOSITED IMMEDIATELY

| REVIEW ☐ |
| CHECK # |

10. AUTHORIZATION *(Must Be Completed – Original Signature Required)*
Tender Submission: I submit this tender pursuant to the provisions of Department of the Treasury Circulars, Public Debt Series Nos. 2-86 (31 CFR Part 357) and 1-93 (31 CFR Part 356), and the applicable offering announcement. As the first-named owner and under penalties of perjury, I certify that the number shown on this form is my correct taxpayer identification number and that I am not subject to backup withholding because (1) I have not been notified that I am subject to backup withholding as a result of a failure to report all interest or dividends, or (2) the Internal Revenue Service has notified me that I am no longer subject to backup withholding. I further certify that all other information provided on this form is true, correct, and complete.

Automatic Withdrawal: (If using this purchase method.) I authorize a debit to my account at the financial instituton I designated in TREASURY DIRECT to pay for this security. I understand that the purchase price will be charged to my account on or after the settlement date. I also understand that if this transaction cannot be successfully completed, my tender can be rejected and the transaction canceled. If there is a dispute, a copy of this authorization may be provided to my financial institution.

_____   _____
Signature(s)   Date

SEE BACK FOR PRIVACY ACT AND PAPERWORK REDUCTION ACT NOTICE

Worksheet 4-4

Competitive or Non-Competitive Bids?

Competitive Bids

- Submit a bid on a bank discount basis with two decimals. For example, if an investor wanted to buy $100,000 of six-month Treasury bills and pay $96,000, the competitive bid submitted to the Federal Reserve Bank would be 8.00 percent.
- The Federal Reserve accepts those bids that have the lowest discount rates (the highest prices) from all the bids received. The accepted bids have a range of yields, from the lowest to the highest known as the "stop-out yield," which the Federal Reserve will pay. Investors who have their bids accepted at the "stop-out yield" or close to it, will receive greater returns than those received for bids at the lowest accepted yields.
- The yields that investors bid depend on the money market rates that are currently being offered by competing short-term instruments, and the expectations of what current short-term rates for T-bills will be. By studying these rates, an investor has a better chance of submitting a bid that will be accepted. However, with a competitive bid, investors face the risk of not having their bids accepted if their bids are above the *stop-out yields*.

Non-Competitive Bids

- Less expert investors who may not want to work out their bids or for those who want to be assured of their bids being accepted can submit *non-competitive bids*. With non-competitive bids, investors can buy T-bills at the average, accepted competitive bid in the auction. Generally, all non-competitive bids of up to $1 million per investor per auction are accepted, assuring investors of their purchases.
- Tender forms to submit bids may be sent by mail or in person to the Federal Reserve Banks and branches before the close of the auction. Competitive bids must be received by the time designated in the offering circular. Non-competitive bids that are mailed must be postmarked by no later than midnight the day before the auction and received on or before the issue date of the securities.
- Payment must accompany the tender form. Check the type of payment: cash, check, securities, or other. The amount of the payment should be no less than the amount of the tender for a non-competitive bid, and for a competitive bid, no less than the bid amount. If the payment amount is not correct, the tender is rejected and returned.

continued

- On acceptance of the bid, the investor receives a confirmation receipt from the Federal Reserve and a payment, which is the difference between the tender amount submitted and the discounted price of the T-bills. Investors can stipulate on the tender form whether or not they want the Federal Reserve to reinvest the T-bills when they mature. If the reinvestment option is not chosen, the Federal Reserve credits the investor's account for the face value of the Treasury bills at maturity.
- The advantage of buying T-bills directly and holding them to maturity is that the investor avoids paying commissions or fees.

Certificates of Deposit

CDs offer investors with limited resources a convenient form of investing their short-term funds. CDs can be bought through banks and thrift institutions for small amounts for specified periods. For example, an investor might decide to invest $500 in a six-month CD that pays interest of four percent per annum. The $500 is deposited in the bank and in six months time, the bank promises to pay the investor $510 at maturity.

Some money market CDs do not have this time limitation, but they have minimum amounts of $100,000. These money market CDs are negotiable, marketable receipts which can be traded prior to their maturities in a secondary market in New York City. The round lots for these trades are in millions of dollars, although smaller lots than $1 million may also be traded. The prices will not be as good on the smaller size lots. These money market, or jumbo CDs, may be purchased through banks and thrift organizations.

Banks that are members of the FDIC provide insurance of $100,000 per ownership of accounts in a bank. Consequently, many investors have gravitated to CDs as their investment vehicles for their short-term funds.

Table 4-7 lists the advantages and disadvantages of certificates of deposit.

Table 4-7   Advantages and Disadvantages of Certificates of Deposit

Advantages	Disadvantages
Easy to invest in CDs.	Not marketable. Penalties for early withdrawals.
Can invest small amounts.	Rates vary. Investors need to do their homework to find the banks with the most attractive rates.
With FDIC membership, banks offer safety of up to $100,000 per account.	
At maturity can receive proceeds or roll the CD over into a new one.	Returns on CDs may be lower than those offered by Treasury bills and money market mutual funds.
	Interest income is taxed at Federal and state levels of tax.

Treasury Notes and Bonds

The U.S. government issues a wide variety of securities. Treasury notes and bonds are coupon securities and differ from Treasury bills. Coupon securities pay interest every six months, whereas Treasury bills are discount securities for which periodic interest payments are not made.

U.S. Treasury Notes

U.S. Treasury notes are issued with original maturities ranging from two to 10 years. Table 4-8 lists the information on new Treasury notes and bonds.

Treasury notes are not callable and interest payments are made semi-annually (beginning six months from the date of issue).

U.S. Treasury Bonds

Treasury bonds have original maturities of more than 10 years. Currently, 30-year Treasury bonds are offered for sale every three months on the 15th of February, May, August, and November. These 30-year Treasury bonds can be bought with a minimum purchase of $1,000 and then in multiples of $1,000 thereafter.

Many outstanding Treasury bond issues are callable generally within five years of maturity. However, since 1985, the Treasury has not issued any callable bonds.

How to Buy and Sell Treasury Notes and Bonds

Investors may purchase new issues or outstanding Treasury issues trading on the secondary market.

Table 4-8 Treasury Notes and Bonds

Term	Minimum	Multiples	Announcement	Auction Date	Issue Date
2-year Note	$5,000	$1,000	Middle of each Month	One week later	Last day of the month
5-year Note	$1,000	$1,000	Middle of each Month	One week later	2/15, 5/15, 8/15, 11/15
10-year Note	$1,000	$1,000	First Wed. in the quarter	One week later	2/15, 5/15, 8/15, 11/15
30-year Bond	$1,000	$1,000	First Wed. in the quarter	One week later	2/15, 5/15, 8/15, 11/15

New Issues

- New issues of Treasury notes and bonds may be purchased at auctions or through brokerage firms and commercial banks. Buying through banks and brokerage firms involves paying commissions which vary depending on the face value of the securities purchased and the markup charged for the purchase. To avoid paying commissions, investors may purchase new issues auctioned directly by the Federal Reserve Bank.

- Auctions of new issues take place on a regular schedule. Investors can also call the Federal Reserve Bank in their area (refer to Figure 4-1 for the telephone numbers of Federal Reserve Banks in different cities in the U.S.) to be put on the mailing list for new note and bond issues. A 24-hour Reserve Bank information number also lists forthcoming auctions. In addition, the financial newspapers print the schedules of forthcoming auctions.

- When buying directly, an investor should first open an account with the Federal Reserve. By completing a New Account Request form (refer to Figure 4-2), investors establish a Treasury Direct account where the Treasury securities are held in book form. Treasury certificates are no longer issued. After submitting this form to the Federal Reserve Bank/branch in the area, the investor receives confirmation of his/her account with a unique account number pertaining to the information in the account. This account number is used for all of the investor's purchases of Treasury securities (bills, notes, bonds, and indexed-inflation securities), and is maintained free of charge up to $100,000. A $25 fee per year occurs for security amounts over $100,000.

- Investors are now ready to fill out a tender form to buy Treasury notes/bonds on auction from the Federal Reserve Bank. Refer to Figure 4-3 for a copy of the Treasury note and 30-year bond tender form. This is the same general form that is used for Treasury bills and the new inflation-indexed Treasury securities.

- Fill in the personal information on the tender form. The routing number is a nine-digit number, which identifies the investor's financial institution. This number is found on the bottom corner of a check before the account number.

- On the form, investors have a choice of buying Treasuries using a competitive or non-competitive bid. More sophisticated investors use *competitive bids,* where a yield bid to two decimal places (for example, 4.06 percent) is submitted for the issue. Investors can get an idea of the probable range of the yield to submit by watching the pre-auction trading of that issue. Dealers begin trading these securities a few days before the auction on a so-called "when issued basis." The "when issued" yield is often reported in the *Wall Street Journal* and *New York Times* financial section.

- Investors submit their sealed, written bids, and the Treasury accepts bids with the lowest yields until the supply is sold. Thus, within the range of accepted bids, the lowest accepted bidders are penalized with a lesser return than the accepted higher bidders. This is known as the *"winner's curse"* because the bidders with the lowest accepted yields pay a higher price for the issue, and the higher bidders receive a greater rate of return than that received by the lowest bidders on the same issue.

- Investors who bid too aggressively run the risk of losing out in that auction by not having their bids accepted.

- Investors who do not want to run the risk of having their bids rejected, or who may not know what to bid, can submit *non-competitive bids*. With non-competitive bids, investors can buy Treasury notes and bonds at the average, accepted bid in the auction. All non-competitive tenders up to $1,000,000 per bidder are accepted.

- Tender forms to submit bids may be sent by mail or in person to the Federal Reserve Banks/branches before the close of the auction. Competitive bids must be received by the time designated in the offering circular. Non-competitive bids that are mailed must be postmarked by no later than midnight the day before the auction and received on or before the issue date of the securities.

- Payment must accompany the tender form and the amount of the check should be for the face value of the securities. If the auction price is less than the face value, the investor receives a check for the difference. If the auction price of the note/bond is higher than the face value, the investor receives an amount due notice for the difference.

- On acceptance of a bid, the investor receives a confirmation receipt from the Federal Reserve. The Treasury pays interest on notes and bonds every six months.

- About 45 days before the maturity of the notes/bonds, a reinvestment option notification is mailed to all note/bondholders giving them the option of reinvesting in a new issue. If the investor declines the reinvestment option, the redemption payment is made directly into the investor's bank account on the maturity date.

- The U.S. Treasury Department has made Treasury notes and bonds available to investors who would like to purchase them online through the Treasury Direct program. Information, updates on auctions, and news on all Treasury securities can be obtained on the World Wide Web site `www.publicdebt.treas.gov`.

- Should investors decide to sell their Treasury notes/bonds before maturity, an active secondary market composed of dealers is available. Before selling, an investor needs to fill out a Transfer Request form (PD 5179) if the notes/bonds were bought directly from the Federal Reserve. This transfers the account from the Treasury Direct book-entry system to the commercial book-entry system. Then, the investor can sell the Treasury notes/bonds. The commercial book-entry system records Treasuries bought through financial institutions and government security dealers. The investor needs to use a bank/broker to sell Treasuries in the secondary market.

Existing Issues

- Investors buy (and sell) existing issues through banks or brokers. Many issues have a wide range of maturities, trading at discounts or premiums depending on their coupon rates and length of time to maturity. Like corporate bonds, Treasury notes and bonds are quoted in the financial sections of newspapers under the heading "Treasury Issues." Ask a banker/broker for a dealer's quote sheet to see which existing issues are available.
- The secondary market for Treasuries is an over-the-counter market where dealers quote bid and asked prices. The spreads on Treasuries are the smallest (rarely larger than one-eighth of a point) of all the fixed income securities due to the liquidity of many of the issues. It is an active market with huge quantities of Treasuries being traded.

What Are the Risks of Treasury Notes and Bonds?

- Because Treasuries are a direct obligation of the federal government, they have no credit risk and no default risk.
- Treasuries issued after 1985 are free from event risk and call risk.
- Treasuries are subject to interest rate risk and inflation risk.

See Table 4-9 for the advantages and disadvantages of Treasury notes and bonds.

Caveats

Avoid longer maturities unless the investor is confident that both inflation and market rates of interest are headed downwards into the future.

Treasury Inflation-Indexed Securities

Treasury inflation-indexed bonds offer protection against rising inflation, but because inflation is historically low (around two to three percent as of this writing), these bonds have not generated that much enthusiasm.

These inflation-indexed Treasury securities pay a regular coupon rate plus an amount that is indexed for inflation. For example, assume that an investor purchases this bond with a rate of 3 1/2 percent at $1,000. If inflation averages two percent for the year, the price of the bond is adjusted to $1,020 for this inflation. The coupon rate of 3 1/2 percent is paid on the adjusted value of the bond (3 1/2 % × $1,020). The opposite is true if inflation falls. The price of the bond is adjusted downwards and the interest payments are calculated against the lower bond price. See Table 4-10 for more information on these inflation-indexed securities.

Table 4-9 Advantages and Disadvantages of Treasury Securities

Advantages	Disadvantages
No credit or default risk.	Yields are lower than for agency and corporate bonds.
Offers a wide range of maturities.	
	Do not protect against inflation.
Interest is exempt from state taxes.	
	Subject to interest rate risk.
Liquid and marketable due to an active secondary market.	
Buying directly avoids transaction costs.	
Markups on trading are the lowest of all fixed income securities.	
Some issues have minimums of $1,000, making them affordable for small investors.	
Easy to buy directly through the Federal Reserve Bank.	

Table 4-10 Treasury Inflation-Indexed Securities

- The interest rate is set at auction and remains fixed throughout the term of the security.

- The principal amount of the security is adjusted for inflation, but the inflation adjusted principal is paid only at maturity.

- Semi-annual interest payments are based on the inflation-adjusted principal at the time that the interest is paid.

- The auction process uses the single priced or Dutch auction method for these securities.

- The securities are eligible for stripping into principal and interest components in the *Treasury's Separate Trading of Registered Interest and Principal of Securities* (STRIPS) Program.

- At maturity, the securities are redeemed at the greater of their inflation-adjusted principal or par amount at original issue.

Source: www.publicdebt.treas.gov

At the time of this writing, the 10-year Treasury note is yielding 4.875 percent and the 10-year inflation-indexed bond is yielding 4.25 percent. This means that to do better than the regular Treasury note, inflation will have to increase by more than 0.625 percent (4.875% − 4.25%) over the next 10 years.

The downside to these inflation-indexed Treasuries is that holders must pay Federal income taxes on the interest plus the inflation adjustment, even though this inflation adjustment is only paid out when the bond matures. In other words, a negative cash flow on this "phantom" adjustment income exists, which makes these investments more suitable for tax-deferred accounts. Interest is exempt from state and local taxes.

How to Buy Inflation-Indexed Treasury Securities

Investors may purchase new inflation-indexed issues directly from the Federal Reserve Banks/branches or outstanding issues trading on the secondary market through brokers.

New Issues   Investors can buy these securities directly at auctions through the Federal Reserve Bank system as part of the Treasury direct program. Table 4-11 lists the denominations and auction information.

These securities are bought through the Federal Reserve Bank system in the same way as regular Treasury notes and bonds, described in the previous section of this chapter.

Existing Issues   Like regular Treasury notes and bonds, existing inflation-indexed securities are bought and sold through brokers who charge commissions for their services. There is a secondary market for these issues and quotes are available, and can be found in the Treasury note and bond sections of the newspapers. Because of the newness of this type of security, investors do not have many issues to choose from on the secondary markets.

What Are the Risks of Inflation-Indexed Treasury Securities?

- These securities have neither *credit risk* nor *default risk* because they are the direct obligations of the U.S. government. This is why all Treasury securities have lower coupon yields than agency and corporate bonds.
- These securities, like all other fixed income securities, are subject to *interest rate risk*. Yields on these securities are much lower than regular Treasury issues and if inflation remains low, any changes in interest rates will make the prices of these securities more volatile. This is especially true for the longer maturity issues.

Table 4-11   Treasury Inflation-Indexed Securities

Term	Minimum	Multiples	Auction	Issue Date
5-year	$1,000	$1,000	Quarterly	One week later
10-year	$1,000	$1,000	Jan, Apr, July, Oct	One week later
30-year	$1,000	$1,000	Quarterly	One week later

- These securities protect against the ravages of inflation. The opposite is true, however, for the inflation-indexed securities. If inflation remains low, holders of these securities will receive lower returns than regular Treasury notes and bonds of the same maturities.

Table 4-12 lists the advantages and disadvantages of inflation-indexed Treasury securities.

Caveats

Unless inflation rises during the holding period, these securities will yield lower returns than regular Treasury securities.

Government Agency and Pass-Through Securities

Government agency bonds appeal to investors who are interested in high quality bonds with higher yields than Treasury securities. The major federally sponsored agencies, such as the *Federal Home Loan Mortgage Corporation* (FHLMC), *Federal National Mortgage Association* (FNMA), *Federal Home Loan Bank* (FHLB) System, Farm Credit Banks, the *Student Loan Marketing Association* (SLMA), and many others, issue agency bonds. The first three of these agencies (FHLMC, FNMA, and FHLB) provide funds to the mortgage and housing sectors of the economy. The Farm Credit Banks provide funds for the agricultural sector and the SLMA provides funds for loans for higher education. Agencies of the government issue traditional securities in addition to mortgage pass-through securities.

Table 4-12 Advantages and Disadvantages of Inflation-Indexed Treasury Securities

Advantages	Disadvantages
Purchase minimums of $1,000 make them affordable for small investors.	Subject to interest rate risk.
Safe investments with no credit or default risk.	If inflation remains low, returns will be lower than for regular Treasury securities.
Interest payments are exempt from state taxes.	Creates a negative cash flow when holders have to pay federal taxes on the inflation adjustment, which is only received at maturity.
Are liquid and marketable due to an active secondary market.	
Transaction costs can be avoided by buying directly through the Federal Reserve Bank.	
Provide protection against inflation.	

Government Agency Securities

Many different government agencies issue securities, which may vary considerably in their characteristics. However, they do have many common features:

- New issues of agency securities are sold through a syndicate of dealers. These dealers also buy and sell the securities in the secondary markets.
- Large agency issues are marketable and fairly liquid.
- Agency securities are exempt from registration with the SEC.
- Some agency issues have tax advantages where interest income is exempt from state and local taxes.
- Agency securities have either de facto or de jure backing from the federal government, making them safer than corporate bonds.

Agency securities tend to offer yields which are greater than those of Treasuries for comparable maturities, but lower than most AA or AAA rated corporate bonds. The different agency securities, with their wide range of offerings and maturities, appeal to investors who prefer the slightly higher yields than those offered by Treasuries, without sacrificing very much on credit risk.

Mortgage Pass-Through Securities

Mortgage pass-through securities are much more complex than regular fixed income securities. They arise out of mortgage transactions. Various types of mortgage pass-through securities exist, each with their own nuances. Despite their differences, investors in all mortgage pass-through securities are concerned with the following criteria:

- The safety of the issue.
- The liquidity and marketability of the issue.
- The overall rate of return of the issue.
- The expected maturity of the issue.

Three government agencies issue the majority of pass-through securities: the Government National Mortgage Association, the Federal National Mortgage Association, and the Federal Home Loan Mortgage Corporation. However, a marked growth in the number of mortgage pass-through securities issued by private issuers since the mid-1980s has occurred.

How to Buy Agency Securities and Pass-Through Securities

Pass-through securities and agency securities can be purchased at issue through dealers and brokers. Minimum purchase amounts for the different issues vary. Existing issues are bought and sold in the secondary markets. Web sites on the Internet and online brokers have reduced some of the pricing transparency of these issues. *Government National Mortgage Association* (GNMA) bonds, for example, are both liquid and marketable, owing to the large volume of issues traded. When buying these bonds through a broker, investors should be aware of the following:

- Prices quoted in the newspapers or offering sheets are for large buyers (institutions), so small investors are quoted larger spreads (between bid and asked prices).
- Yields quoted are based on prepayment assumptions. If only one yield is quoted, ask the broker for the different prepayment assumptions and the corresponding yields. Use the most conservative yield because even then, it may not be realized.
- The remaining term of the mortgage pool or length of time to maturity is not as important as the weighted-average life because the former assumes no prepayments. In the secondary market, it is assumed that a 30-year GNMA will be repaid on average in 12 years.
- Price is important. If the GNMA is bought at a premium, the investor could suffer a capital loss. When interest rates decline, mortgagors prepay their mortgages in the pool faster than estimated. Hence, an investor may not recover the premium paid over the face value. Buying at a discount offers the opportunity of capital gains, but the coupon yield for the GNMA is lower than those currently offered coupons.

What Are the Risks of Government Agency and Pass-Through Securities?

- Government agency and pass-through mortgage securities provide higher yields than Treasuries because they are subject to greater risk.
- Government agency and pass-through mortgage securities are subject to *interest rate risk*. Generally, when market rates of interest fall, the prices of existing fixed income securities rise. However, pass-through securities have a ceiling on the rise in price. This is because many homeowners are likely to refinance their older, higher interest mortgages for lower interest mortgages. Thus, with falling rates of interest, the prices of pass-through securities do not rise as much as other fixed income securities. The flip side of the coin is that when interest rates rise, homeowners do not refinance their mortgages. This means that holders of pass-through securities receive lower yields than other securities because the pass-through pools have longer lives and holders do not receive their principal to reinvest at higher rates. With rapid swings in interest rates, pass-through securities do not perform as well as other fixed income securities, which then translates into the swings in the share prices of mutual funds. Theoretically, *adjustable rate mortgage* (ARM) securities should perform better when rapid swings in interest rates

occur, but this was not the case in 1994, when ARM securities returned lower yields than money market funds.
- Pass-through mortgage securities are complex because payments are unpredictable and yields are only estimates at best. This makes it more difficult to analyze the risks of pass-through mortgage securities.

Table 4-13 lists the advantages and disadvantages of government agency and mortgage pass-through securities.

Caveats

- To reduce the prepayment risk, investors should avoid buying mortgage pass-through securities from small mortgage pools. By buying into large mortgage pools, investors can spread out the prepayment risks. For this reason, small investors might consider mutual funds where diversification can be achieved through the size of the mutual fund's investments in these securities. By investing in one or a few pools, investors with relatively small amounts cannot achieve the diversification that mutual funds can.

Table 4-13 Advantages and Disadvantages of Government Agency and Pass-Through Securities

Advantages	Disadvantages
Large agency issues are both liquid and marketable.	Subject to interest rate risk.
Pass-through securities offer interest payments on a monthly basis.	For pass-through securities, it is difficult to determine the amount of the monthly cash flows due to prepayments of mortgages in the pools.
Bid and ask spreads tend to be narrow on the large issues.	
Yields tend to be higher than those of Treasuries, but lower than corporate bonds.	Difficult to determine the exact yields for pass-throughs due to uncertainty of the cash flow payments.
Some agency issues are exempt from state and local taxes.	Some issues are fully taxable.
Agency issues with de facto or de jure backing from the federal government are safer than corporate bonds.	
30-year GNMAs are not as volatile as 30-year Treasuries because part of the principal on the GNMA is repaid on a monthly basis.	
Large, sophisticated investors can use the futures markets to hedge their pass-through security portfolios against adverse swings in interest rates.	

- With GNMAs, investors receive a return of principal and interest monthly. Investors should not spend their entire monthly checks, but should rather invest a portion of their proceeds to keep their investment capital intact.
- When mortgage pass-through securities are trading at a premium price, their coupon yields are greater than current coupon rates for new issues. Investors should be cautious of buying at a premium because prepayment volatility is greatest for those issues whose coupons exceed current mortgage rates by three percent (Hayre and Mohebbi 1989, page 283). A faster rate of prepayments may lead to a capital loss.
- Not all agency securities are exempt from state and local taxes, which may mean that a portion of the dividends received from these mutual funds or pass-through securities could be subject to state and local taxes.

Corporate Bonds

Many types of corporate bonds are available such as mortgage bonds, debenture bonds, variable interest bonds, convertible bonds, and zero-coupon bonds. These bonds are either secured or unsecured. Junk bonds are not a special type of bond, but are regular high-risk, low-rated bonds. These corporate bonds have ratings of BBB (by Standard & Poor's) and Baa (by Moody's Investor Services, Inc.), or lesser categories, which consist of a range of poor quality debt close to default. Some of these bonds have no ratings. In order to entice investors, coupon rates of junk bonds are higher than the coupon rates of investment grade bonds.

For *secured bonds*, the issuer pledges an asset as collateral and in the event of a default, the creditor can seize the asset (after proceeding to court). An example of a secured bond is a mortgage bond, which is frequently issued by utility companies. Investors should sleep well at night knowing that their bonds are backed by a power plant, but do investors have the expertise to operate the power plant in the event of a default by the utility company? Although pledging assets increases the safety of the principal of the bonds, in this case, investors should hope that the utility company does not default on its interest and principal payments.

Unsecured bonds or *debenture* bonds are backed only by the issuer's creditworthiness (ability to pay annual interest and principal at maturity). Some companies issue *subordinated debenture* bonds, which are riskier in the event of insolvency, as subordinated debenture holders are last in the line of lenders to be repaid. Seniority becomes important during bankruptcy because secured bonds and senior debt are first in line to be repaid. Riskier issues tend to offer higher coupon rates to entice investors. Generally, investors should be concerned with the issuer's ability to service their debt (or creditworthiness) rather than with the security alone. In the event of bankruptcy, pledged property may not be marketable, and it may involve litigation, which can be time consuming.

What Are the Risks of Corporate Bonds?

The *risk of default* is more of a concern for investors of corporate bonds as a group than for other types of bonds such as U.S. Treasuries and government agency bonds, where the risks of default are much less. U.S. Treasuries are considered to be free of default risk. This is why corporate bonds offer higher yields than Treasuries and government agency bonds. The greater the risk of default, the higher the coupon rate for that issue. For the risk of default on individual corporate bond issues, most investors rely on the ratings of the issues given by the commercial rating companies such as Standard & Poor's, Moody's, and Fitch Investor Services.

Another risk that affects bond prices of existing issues is called an *event risk*. This is the risk that large corporations will issue large amounts of debt to finance the takeovers of other corporations (also known as a leveraged buy-out). This causes the existing bond issues of those takeover corporations to plummet in price because the corporation significantly increases their level of debt, resulting in downgraded ratings. To entice investors to buy these new issues, corporate issuers introduced provisions, which made takeovers more expensive. These are nicknamed *"poison puts,"* which vary from allowing bondholders to resell their bonds to the issuer at par in the event of a takeover or in the event that the bond's ratings are downgraded.

Lower bond coupons often pay for the advantages of a put feature in the bond's indenture. Regardless, a put feature is attractive because it protects against the risk of a rise in interest rates and inflation. When these (interest rates and/or inflation) rise, the price of the bond falls, and holders of the bond can use the put option to resell the bond to the issuer at par value before maturity.

All bonds, except for floating rate bonds, are subject to *interest rate risk*. Citicorp was the first corporation to introduce floating rate bonds in the 1970s. These were unique at the time in that the coupon rate fluctuated with the rate of Treasury bills, and after a two-year period (after issuance), the bondholders could redeem the bonds at par value. Therefore, floating rate bonds do not fluctuate much in price due to changes in interest rates, unlike the prices of regular fixed income bonds. As pointed out in a previous chapter, bond prices fluctuate inversely with market rates of interest. The longer the maturity of the bond, the greater the price fluctuation in relation to changes in interest rates.

Many corporate bonds have call features, meaning that they are subject to *call risk*. This call feature enables the issuer to retire the bonds prior to maturity. When a bond is called, interest no longer accrues, forcing bondholders to retire their bonds. The call feature benefits the issuer rather than the bondholder.

Table 4-14 lists the advantages and disadvantages of corporate bonds.

Table 4-14 Advantages and Disadvantages of Corporate Bonds

Advantages	Disadvantages
Have higher coupon yields than Treasuries.	Subject to inflation and interest rate risk.
Generally, produce higher total returns than Treasuries and Agency bonds.	Exposed to greater credit and event risk than Treasuries and Agency bonds.
	Lower quality bonds may be illiquid.
Income and principal are relatively safe with high-quality corporate debt.	Subject to call risk.
	Spreads on corporate bonds are greater than those of Treasury and Agency bonds.
	Spreads on unlisted junk bonds are large.

Worksheet 4-5

How to Lessen the Impact of Interest Rate Risk

- Spread the maturities of the different bond issues in the portfolio to even out the impact of changing market rates of interest (that is, instead of investing only in bonds with 20-year maturities, ladder the maturities between two, five, 10, 15, and 20 years).
- Diversify the bond portfolio by buying different types of bonds.
- Purchase good quality bonds.
- Lessen the length of the maturities.
- Buy bonds with a put feature, which allows bondholders to resell their bonds to the issuer at face value when interest rates rise.

The downside is that these bonds have lower coupon rates and shorter maturities. However, the optimum strategy, in theory, is to invest in short maturities when market rates of interest are increasing. Then when they peak, buy long term bonds to lock into the high coupon rates. The obvious question is how does the investor know when market rates of interest are going to peak? Locking in at the peak of market interest rates is not as important as at least trying to follow the strategy.

Worksheet 4-6

What to Do about Call Risk

Pay particular attention to a bond issue's call and refunding provisions. Three types of call provisions exist:

- Non-callable bonds offer investors the most protection, but have many loopholes. Non-callable implies that the bonds will not be called before maturity. However, in some cases, non-callable bonds have been called such as in the case of a fire or act of God; or when a healthy company stops making its interest payments on the bonds, and the trustees call them in and the debt is paid off early. Non-callable for life bonds would be listed in the dealer's quote sheets as "NCL."
- Freely callable bonds offer investors no protection as issuers can call them anytime.
- Deferred callable bonds offer some protection because the bonds cannot be called until after a period of time (for example, five, 10 or 15 years after issue). A bond that is non-callable until 2002 is listed as "NC02" in the dealer's quote sheet.

How to Buy Corporate Bonds

Investors may buy corporate bonds through brokerage firms. When a new issue of bonds is bought, the issuing corporation absorbs commissions.

Existing corporate bond issues trade on the over-the-counter market and a number of corporate issues are listed on the *New York Stock Exchange* (NYSE) and American Exchange. The trading of listed bonds does not take place in the same location as common stocks on these exchanges. Actively listed bonds on the NYSE are traded in the Bond Room, where members announce the bid and asked prices. Other members either accept these prices or counter offers are made. Thus, buying and selling is done through these members and not through specialists as in the case of common stocks. Inactively listed bonds are traded through the computer system in the Bond Room. Members respond by entering their orders through the computer terminal.

The advantage of buying listed bonds is that their prices appear in the daily newspapers, which gives investors the opportunity to check up on actual trades. Bonds that trade over-the-counter are unlisted and bond price quotes may vary considerably from dealer to dealer. This is especially true for lower quality, inactively traded bonds where the size of the spread between the bid and asked prices may be quite large. In fact, pressure exists to regulate the unruly trading in the junk bond market by instituting a price quotation system for the most actively traded junk bonds. This system would have to be approved by the SEC before being implemented. Until such time, small investors continue to be disadvantaged by these abusive trading practices. When dealers have to report their prices, many of these inefficiencies will disappear. Thus, when buying unlisted bonds, it is almost imperative that investors shop around for the best quotes from different brokers.

It is always a good idea for investors to ask for both the bid and asked prices of the bonds that they are interested in buying because the size of the spread tells a lot about that bond issue. A large spread (four percent or more) indicates that the bond is more than likely illiquid (cannot resell quickly), inactively traded, and possibly some other bad news such as a potential downgrading in ratings (Thau 1992, 13). A small spread indicates the opposite: active trading with little risk of resale. Higher transaction costs are charged if investors buy or sell a small number of bonds (less than 10 bonds).

For existing bond issues, investors will not see a prospectus, but before investing, they should request the latest company information from their brokers. When buying bonds, investors may pay more than the asked price due to the *accrued interest* on that bond. Bonds earn interest daily, but the corporation only pays out the interest once or twice a year. Therefore, if a bond is purchased between the dates that interest is paid, the buyer then owes the seller the accrued interest for the number of days that the seller owned the bond. The amount of accrued interest is added to the purchase price of the bond. The accrued interest is stated separately on the confirmation statement sent from the brokerage firm when the bonds are bought or sold.

Bonds that are in default and no longer paying interest are said to trade *flat*. These bonds do not trade with accrued interest. An "F" next to the bonds in the financial pages of the newspapers signifies that it is trading flat.

Bondholders can sell their bonds in the secondary market before maturity or call. For listed bonds, investors can get an idea of the price from the newspapers. Bear in mind that newspapers only list one price for bonds (bonds have a bid and asked price).

Several brokerage firms and online trading companies are planning to address some of these difficulties. The Discover Brokerage System of Morgan Stanley provides investors access to the bid and asked spread on any bond. Electronic bond trading may take off in the future, but even with electronic trading, investors should pay attention to finding the lowest costs for their transactions (Zuckerman, *Wall Street Journal*, December 28, 1998, Pages C1, C15).

As mentioned earlier, bonds may be retired before their maturity dates. Many corporate bonds have *sinking fund* provisions in their indentures, which are used to help with the retirement of the bond issues. Instead of the entire bond issue being retired at maturity, a sinking fund enables the corporation to make periodic payments to retire parts of the bond issue before maturity.

Corporations may also repurchase their bonds in the bond market and retire them. This occurs more frequently when the bonds are trading at a discount. Investors who sell their corporate bonds may not know that it is the issuing corporation who is buying them back.

Corporations may decide to repurchase their bonds by announcing their intention to bondholders and offering a certain price to buy them back. In this case, bondholders are not required to resell their bonds to the corporation if they do not want to.

Worksheet 4-7

Assessing the Overall Risks of New Corporate Issues

Before investing in a new issue, examine the company's prospectus to assess the overall risks. From the balance sheet, the level of debt and the number of debt issues, which are senior to this one, can be determined. In the event of bankruptcy, the greater the number of senior issues to this one, the lower the priority of this bond investor's claims.

From the income statement, assess whether or not the level of earnings will provide adequate coverage for the interest payments on all the debt issues outstanding, including the issue to be financed. If a downturn in sales occurs, an investor would want to see how much of an interest cover the company has before the earnings become insufficient to service its debt.

If the company is currently selling off assets to generate funds and the debt to total assets ratio is high, warning flags should go up concerning the issue. This process of analyzing the financial statements is particularly important when considering the purchase of lower quality, new corporate issues. The financial statements of listed companies can be obtained through the Internet on the government Web site **www.edgar-online.com** or **www.freeedgar.com**

Caveats

Before buying corporate bonds, check the following:

- The credit ratings of the issue.
- The seniority of the issue.
- The call and refunding provisions. Investors can avoid losses of principal by not buying higher premium priced bonds with higher coupon rates than market rates, which could be called at lower premium prices. In other words, check whether the premium price exceeds the call price.
- The sinking fund provision.

- Whether "poison put" protection is available against event risk.
- Whether the bonds are part of a small issue (less than $75 million). Avoid buying bonds of small issues.
- Whether the bonds are listed or whether they trade over-the-counter.
- The maturity of the bond. The longer the maturity, the greater the risks. Every now and again, corporations issue bonds with 50-year and 100-year maturities. With this time period, a lot can happen to affect the company's ability to repay the issue. The Disney Corporation issued a 100-year bond, which matures for the next generation's children and grandchildren. For this time span, stocks are a better investment.
- Risk-averse investors should buy good quality corporate bond issues.
- Investing in corporate bonds requires large sums of money to achieve a diversified portfolio to lessen the risks of default.
- Investors in junk bonds should not invest a large portion of their investment funds in this category.

Compare the coupon yield of the corporate issue to those offered on similar maturity Treasuries and government agency bonds first to see if the spread warrants the additional risks to which corporate bonds are exposed. Risk-averse investors should avoid junk bonds and choose high-quality corporate bonds.

Municipal Bonds

Municipal bonds are debt securities issued by state and local governments, their agencies, and enterprises with a public purpose. The most important feature of municipal bonds is that the interest income is exempt from federal income taxes and state and local taxes if investors live in the state issuing the municipal bonds.

Municipal bonds that are issued backed by the full faith and credit of the states and municipalities are called *general obligation bonds*. This is because they are usually secured by the taxing power of the issuer. In other words, the interest paid to bondholders comes from taxes and the issuer's ability to raise more taxes. Theoretically, issuers may have unlimited taxing authority, but in reality, it may not be that easy to enact their "unlimited" taxing powers. This is evidenced by New York City's default on its general obligation notes in 1975. Not all general obligation bonds are equal. Their safety in terms of credit and default risk depends on the economic and financial strengths of the issuers.

Revenue bonds are issued by enterprises such as hospitals, universities, airports, toll roads, and public utilities. The revenues generated by these enterprises or from their projects are used to pay the interest on the debt.

For example, airport revenue bonds may generate revenues based on traffic usage at the airport or from revenues generated by the use of the airport facilities such as leasing out a terminal building. As to the former case of revenue collection, bondholders should determine whether or not a growing demand exists for both passenger and airline traffic usage of the airport, and as to the latter form of revenue collection, whether or not the lease payments are sufficient to service the debt.

Proceeds from highway revenue bonds may be used to build toll roads/bridges or to make improvements to the highway infrastructure. Bondholders have a claim to tolls collected on the roads and bridges, but what about the improvements to the highways? Improving a highway does not generate revenue. Revenue bonds which are not self-supporting have revenues earmarked to secure the debt. Gasoline taxes, license fees, and automobile registration fees are examples of these revenues.

Thus, the security or safety of the revenue bonds depends on how essential the services provided by the enterprise are, the flow of revenues, whether or not these are increasing or decreasing, and whether or not any other claims can be made to the revenues before those of the bondholders. The relative strength of the issuer of the revenue bonds to generate revenues and the ease with which the issuer can cover the interest payments will determine the rating of the revenue bonds.

What Are the Risks of Municipal Bonds?

Although the number of defaults on municipal issues has been small, some highly publicized examples have made investors very conscious of the *risk of default*. See Worksheet 4-8 for some steps to follow that may reduce the risks of default.

Interest rate risk may be greater than the risk of default for quality tax-exempt issues. This is not unique to municipal bonds, but applies to all fixed income securities. The longer the term to maturity, the greater the price volatility due to fluctuations in interest rates.

Although investors receive greater yields from long term (30-year) than shorter term municipals, the increased volatility exists, as well as the fact that yield spreads between maturities tend to be wider for municipals than they are for bonds in the taxable bond market.

The *risk of a municipal bond* being called is a common risk. Most municipal bonds have call or refunding provisions, which enable issuers to call in the bonds when interest rates decrease significantly. Investors should read the call provisions of their bonds before the purchase to see if any unusual features appear. Housing revenue bonds, for example, may not stipulate a call date, meaning that they could be called anytime after issue. Be careful if a premium is paid on these bonds because if they are called, the investor may not recoup his/her premium price.

Municipal securities are not as actively traded as government bonds, which means that the spreads between the bid and asked prices tend to be relatively wide. This is true even for the most actively traded issues. This makes municipal bonds less liquid than Treasury issues and agency bonds. The larger issues of general obligation bonds and the well-known authorities tend to be marketable, but the smaller, thinly traded issues may not be marketable. In fact, some small issues may have no market outside the issuing locality.

Investors run the *risk of paying excessive markups on the pricing of individual municipal bonds.* Under the current pricing practices, investors do not know if they are being charged excessive markups by their brokerage firms when they buy individual municipal bonds because these bonds are traded on the over-the-counter markets where the prices are not publicized. Investors call their brokers and ask for a price quote. The broker may quote any price because the prices are not quoted in the newspapers like they are for stocks. It is difficult to shop around at other brokerage firms unless investors have accounts at these firms. A brokerage firm might not quote their prices for the same bond issues unless the investor has an account. For example, a brokerage firm might buy a particular bond issue at $90 per bond and sell it to investors for $99 per bond. This is a $9 markup or 9.89 percent. This is in lieu of commissions because the brokerage firm owns the bonds and they face the risks of the bonds falling in price. Another brokerage firm might have bought the same issue of bonds at $89 and is offering it to investors at $93 per bond. Lack of pricing information is a big disadvantage, as investors never know if they are paying excessive markups on the individual municipal bonds that they purchase and sell. Thus, investors should buy bonds and hold them to maturity rather than use them as trading vehicles for capital gains. This lack of pricing also affects the sale of the bonds. The *Securities and Exchange Commission* (SEC) is hoping to rectify this problem of the lack of pricing information in the corporate bond and municipal bond markets.

How to Buy and Sell Municipal Bonds

Investors buy municipal bonds at issue or on the secondary market. The financial newspapers, *Barron's, Wall Street Journal*, and *The New York Times* list the forthcoming sales of new municipals for the week. *The Bond Buyer*, a trade publication for municipal bonds, also gives information on the forthcoming sales, as well as the results of the previous week's sales of municipal bonds.

In some cases, state and local governments market their issues by placing them privately in the market, usually directly to institutional buyers. Mostly, they are placed through investment bankers who offer them for sale to the investment community (the public). The investment banker forms a syndicate of brokerage firms to sell the new issue. Investors place orders through their brokerage firms for new issues of interest. If their brokerage firms are part of the syndicate, there are no sales commissions on the purchase. The other advantage of buying at issue is that the bonds are priced at a uniform price (the syndicate offering price) until all the orders for the syndicate have been filled. Only then can the bonds trade at market prices.

Buying municipals on the secondary market is slightly more difficult because the financial newspapers only print the prices of a small list of some of the popular revenue bonds. Prices of government obligation

Worksheet 4-8

How to Reduce the Risks of Default

Following these steps may reduce the risk of default:

1. Ratings. Investors should consider the ratings of the bond offering. Moody's and Standard & Poor's rate these offerings based on a substantial amount of financial information. Because municipal bonds do not have to be registered with the SEC, very little information is available about the issuer's financial status for investors. States and municipalities may not publish their annual financial statements. Therefore, limit purchases to AAA or AA ratings to minimize the risk of default.

2. Insurance. Check whether the issue is insured. Bond insurance can increase the ratings of an issue. When a bond is insured, it is given an AAA rating even if the bond had a lower rating before insurance. A bond issue that has a rating of AAA or AA without insurance is a stronger offering than an insured bond with AAA ratings. Insurance corporations, such as *Municipal Bond Insurance Association* (MBIA) and *Financial Guaranty Insurance Co.* (FGIC) sell insurance, whereby they guarantee the interest payments and the return of principal. The quality of the insurance company also affects the ratings of the issue.

3. Credit Enhancements. Instead of insurance, some issuers have letters of credit from banks and insurance companies. These do not guarantee interest payments by the banks/insurance companies. Instead, these offer the issuer a line of credit. If the issuer does not have enough cash to cover the interest payments, the bank or insurance company lends the issuer the money. This is a lower degree of protection than insurance. Investors should check the ratings of the bank or insurance company providing the line of credit.

4. Official Statement. Obtain a copy of the official statement or offering circular, which is like the prospectus for corporate securities. In it, review the following:
   • The legal opinion. If any doubt as to the tax exemption arises, avoid the issue.
   • How the issue will be repaid. This ought to be fairly clear.
   • The qualifications, such as "no assurance can be given." If phrases are used that cause nervousness, find another issue to invest in.

5. Diversification. Purchase bonds of different issuers, which spreads the risks associated with any one particular issuer.

A word of caution: Ratings are not cast in stone and they can change over time. Thus, do not base a decision on ratings alone.

bonds are not quoted in the newspapers. To learn what bonds are available in the secondary market, an investor may want to obtain a copy of the "Blue List," which is published daily by Standard & Poor's. It lists the bonds that dealers currently own in their portfolios and wish to sell. The listings of each bond include information such as:

- The number of bonds for sale in each issue.
- The name of the issuer.
- The coupon rate and maturity date.
- The price (this does not include the bid and asked spread).
- The name of the dealer selling the bonds.

The "Blue List" is the best source of information, but it is also very costly for most individual investors to subscribe. Consequently, investors should ask their brokers for a copy. Investors should not be surprised to find that by the time they see the "Blue List," some of the bond issues may already be sold. Because the bid and asked spreads are not quoted, some deviation may also appear from the price quoted in the "Blue List."

Many initiatives are underway to provide municipal bond pricing to individual investors. An affiliate, J.J. Kenny, of Standard & Poor's operates a toll-free telephone number (1-800-BOND INFO) where investors can obtain prices of up to 25 bonds which have not traded.

Internet sites also are available where daily information on municipal bonds can be obtained. One such Web site is `www.bondmarkets.com`. This site also has many muncipal bond links. Another Web site is `www.investinginbonds.com`, which lists the municipal bond prices, yields, and credit ratings of the bonds traded.

Many municipal bond dealers throughout the country support the municipal bond secondary market. Brokers serve as intermediaries between dealers and institutional and individual investors in municipal bond issues. Many brokerage firms maintain markets in their local and regional issues.

Pricing of municipal bond issues can vary significantly from dealer to dealer, so when buying (or selling), an investor should get several quotes from different brokerage firms. The bottom line is to shop around because paying high commissions and wide spreads, lowers overall returns.

Another factor, which increases the markup, is whether or not an investor buys in round or odd lots. Buying or selling orders of less than $10,000 to $25,000 are considered to be odd lots. Spreads between the bid and asked prices quoted by dealers for these odd lots tend to be wider because dealers find it harder to sell small numbers of municipal bonds. These higher costs erode investors' returns, so they may want to buy and hold these issues to maturity. Before buying, investors should evaluate the overall risks and returns.

Municipal bonds on the secondary market can trade at a discount or a premium depending on a number of factors such as quality, coupon yield, issuer, and length of time to maturity.

When buying municipal bonds at a discount or premium, an investor should be aware of the likelihood of incurring capital gains when the bonds are sold or called. For example, if an investor buys 50 municipal bonds with a face value of $50,000 at a discount of $45,000 in 1995, and in 1996 buys another 50 municipal bonds with a face value of $50,000 at a premium of $55,000 with both issues maturing in 2000, $5,000 per bond is subject to capital gains in 2000. Puzzled? Well, most people are.

According to the Internal Revenue Tax Code (section 171), no allowable deduction for the amortization of the premium exists for tax-exempt bonds. In other words, the $5,000 gain cannot be offset by the $5,000 loss because the loss is not recognized (which means that the loss cannot be deducted). The premium is amortized down over the life of the bond to maturity or until call. As a result, municipal bondholders are doubly penalized; they could buy high coupon bonds at a premium, only to find that they could be called at a lower price than the premium purchase price paid.

- The loss is not deductible against other capital gains.
- The bonds may be called sooner than anticipated, not giving the bondholder the chance to recoup the costs of having paid a premium price for a high coupon security.

This non-deductibility of the amortization is unique to tax-exempt bonds. Investors should be aware that they may be liable for taxes due to gains from buying bonds at a discount and through the process of amortization of a premium. To illustrate the latter process, consider the example where an investor bought a tax-exempt bond at a premium of $1,100 and in five years, sold the bond for $1,100. As a result of having to amortize or write down the premium over time, the adjusted basis of the tax-exempt bond is less than $1,100. Hence, a taxable gain exists between the adjusted basis and the selling price.

Table 4-15   The Advantages and Disadvantages of Municipal Bonds

Advantages	Disadvantages
Benefits high-income investors because interest is exempt from federal income taxes.	Municipal bonds may be less liquid and marketable than government bonds.
	Default risk due to a small number of defaults in the past is of concern.
Provides regular interest payments for income dependent investors.	Many municipals have call provisions.
	Reinvestment risk when issues are called.
	Subject to interest rate risk.
	Dealer spreads may be wide and vary considerably among dealers.

Municipalities often issue *serial bonds*, which are groups of bonds with different maturities within an issue. Bear in mind that with a serial issue, investors can choose the maturity they desire when the issue is originally sold in the market.

Caveats

- Taxpayers in lower marginal tax brackets should compare the yields of taxable bonds with those of municipal bonds first before investing. See Worksheet 4-9.
- Municipal bonds are not entirely risk-free. Buy municipals with the highest quality ratings and stay away from small, unrated issues and speculative revenue bonds.
- When buying a new issue, check the offering circular for the legal opinion and the ratings for the issue.
- Be aware of the tax nuances—the possibility of incurring capital gains on the redemption of municipals bought at a discount and premium price.
- Interest on *industrial development bonds* (IDBs) issued after August 7, 1986, is treated as a preference item, which may trigger the alternative minimum tax for high-income investors.
- Interest on private activity bonds for nonessential purposes is not tax-exempt from federal income taxes.
- Investors should not buy municipal bonds for their IRAs, Keogh, or tax-deferred pension accounts, as they are already tax-deferred.

Convertible Bonds

Convertibles are hybrid securities that come in two primary forms: convertible bonds and convertible preferred stock. These are bonds and preferred stock that can be exchanged for a specified number of common shares of the issuing corporation, at the option of the convertible holder. In a few cases, convertible bonds have been exchanged for preferred stock or other bond issues. However, some other rare types of hybrid convertibles exist, including *payment in kind* (PIKs), hybrid convertibles, LYONs, commodity-backed bonds, and stock-indexed bonds. Each of these different types of securities has conversion options or relationships to other types of securities or assets. PIKs , for example, pay their holders more of the same units of securities that they hold. Refer to the section in Chapter 3, "Beginning: What Affects Prices?" for the valuation of convertible securities.

What Are the Risks of Convertibles?

As with any debt security, investors are concerned about the *risks of default*. This is especially true for convertible bonds, which tend to be sub-

Worksheet 4-9

How to Determine the Taxable Equivalent Yield of a Municipal Bond

In order to compare municipal bonds with taxable bonds, the tax-exempt yield of a municipal must be converted into the equivalent of a taxable bond. See Table 4-16 for some examples of what taxable bonds would have to yield in order to equal the yields of municipal bonds.

Table 4-16 Comparison of Taxable Bond Yields to Those of Municipals at Different Tax Brackets

A Municipal Bond with a Yield of:

	5%	5.5%	6%	6.5%

is equivalent to a Taxable Bond Yield of:

Federal Income Tax Bracket				
15%	5.8%	6.47%	7.06%	7.65%
28%	6.94%	7.64%	8.33%	9.03%
31%	7.24%	7.97%	8.70%	9.42%
36%	7.81%	8.59%	9.38%	10.16%
39.6%	8.28%	9.11%	9.93%	10.76%

The equivalent yield of a taxable bond at the investor's tax bracket is the yield that an investor would have to earn on a taxable bond to equal the yield on a municipal bond. For example, an investor in the 15 percent tax bracket purchasing a taxable bond with a yield of 7.65 percent would earn the equivalent from a 6 1/2 percent tax-exempt municipal bond. In other words, the investor in the 15 percent tax bracket would purchase a municipal bond yielding 6 1/2 percent only if taxable bonds of similar maturities were yielding less than 7.65 percent. If this investor could earn more than 7.65 percent on taxable bonds, municipal bonds would not be considered. However, for investors in higher tax brackets, the taxable equivalent yield would be much greater. In the 36 percent tax bracket, the taxable equivalent yield on a 6 1/2 percent municipal bond is 10.16 percent. Thus, as tax brackets (rates) increase, the taxable equivalent yields increase, and municipal bonds become more attractive. For a taxpayer in the highest marginal tax bracket of 39.6 percent, a five percent muni-coupon is the equivalent of an 8.28 percent taxable bond coupon.

Brokerage firms publish tables like the one in Table 4-16 of taxable equivalent yields, but it is a simple calculation to convert municipal bond yields to taxable yield equivalents.

continued

The formula is:

Taxable Equivalent Yield $= \dfrac{Tax\ Free\ Yield}{1 - Tax\ Rate}$

A six percent coupon municipal bond bought by an investor in the 28 percent marginal tax bracket has a before tax return of 8.33 percent:

$$\text{Taxable Equivalent Yield} = \frac{6\%}{1 - .28}$$
$$= 8.33\%$$

ordinated to the issuing firm's other debt securities. Convertible bonds are, therefore, not as safe as the company's senior debt, and in the event of bankruptcy, convertible bondholders stand behind the other bondholders in the collection line. Hence, they may only receive a fraction of their invested principal at best.

Interest rate risk exists. Being a fixed income security with coupon rates that tend to be lower than conventional debt issues, an increase in market rates of interest will cause a greater decline in the price of convertible issues than non-convertible bonds.

Generally, high interest rates tend to depress stock market prices, and the convertible bond is doubly cursed if the issuing company's stock is depressed. Stock prices and stock markets can be both uncertain and volatile, which may not help in the appreciation of the convertible. Thus, the risk exists that if the stock price never rises above the conversion value, no conversion occurs, and the convertible bondholder receives a lower return than on a regular bond. This is due to the lower coupon yields of convertible bonds.

In most cases, convertible bonds have call provisions, creating the constant *risk of call*. Generally, bonds are called by corporations when interest rates decline so that the corporations can issue new bonds at lower coupon rates and save money.

How to Buy and Sell Convertible Bonds

Convertible bonds are bought and sold in the same way as corporate bonds. New issues are bought through an underwriter or participating syndicate broker, in which case the investor is not charged a fee or markup.

Convertible securities trading on the secondary market are purchased (sold) through full service brokerage firms, discount brokers, brokerage services offered by banks, and online brokers. Most of the convertible bonds are listed on the over-the-counter markets whereas the convertible bonds of the larger, better known companies are listed on the New York Bond Exchange. The same applies to convertible preferred stocks-listings on the NYSE, American Stock Exchange, and the over-the-counter markets.

Brokerage fees for purchasing convertible bonds are similar to those charged for buying regular bonds. Markups charged per bond vary depending on several factors, such as the number of convertible bonds purchased, the total value of the purchase, and the type of broker (full service or discount). It is important to shop around to find the lowest markups and dealer spreads before buying. Investors have the same difficulties obtaining prices on convertible bonds as they do on other types of bonds such as corporate, agency, and municipal bonds.

See Table 4-17 for the advantages and disadvantages of convertible securities.

Caveats

*   Investors should not buy convertible securities unless they are willing to buy that company's common stock. If the convertible security is never converted to common stock, the interest received on the convertible is less than if the investor had invested in a regular bond.
*   Be wary of buying convertibles that are trading at high premiums over the market values of the common stock and/or the callable price of the convertibles.
*   Check the provisions of the convertibles before buying, such as whether or not a sinking fund exists that will enable the issuing company to redeem a specific number of convertibles each year, the call price, and so on.

Zero-Coupon Bonds

Zero-coupon bonds are debt securities that are issued at deep discounts from their face values. They pay no periodic interest, but are redeemed at face value ($1,000) at maturity. For example, a 10-year, zero-coupon bond (with a face value of $1,000) yielding eight percent would cost

Table 4-17 Advantages and Disadvantages of Convertible Securities

Advantages	Disadvantages
Convertibles can be used to hedge positions in the bond and stock markets.	In the event of liquidation, convertible holders are paid after regular bondholders.
Offer gains through the appreciation of the common stock and the downside protection of the valuation as a straight bond.	When market rates of interest decline, the risk that the convertible bonds may be called increases.
Generally, interest income on bonds exceeds the dividends on the common stock.	On conversion, the risk of dilution of the common stock exists.
Offer some protection against inflation.	Yields are lower than those of regular bonds.

about $463 at issuance. In other words, the investor of this zero-coupon bond buys it for $463, receives no interim interest payments, and at the end of the tenth year, receives $1,000, the face value of the bond. As zero-coupon bonds do not pay interest, they do not have current yields like regular bonds.

The price of a zero-coupon bond is the present value of the face value of the bond at the maturity date, discounted at a particular rate of return. Looked at in another way, the investor's funds grow from $463 to $1,000 in 10 years. The initial price is compounded at a particular rate of interest to equal $1,000 in 10 years.

Zero-coupon bonds do not pay interest, but a negative aspect to this exists which should be appreciated before purchasing this type of bond. The Internal Revenue Service regards the accrued interest on these bonds as actual interest income, even though these payments are not received by the zero-coupon bondholders until maturity. Thus, negative cash flows occur during the life of the bond from paying taxes on accrued (phantom) interest, which makes zero-coupon bonds better suited for investment accounts that are not subject to taxes. These are pension funds, *individual retirement accounts* (IRAs), Keoghs, and SEP accounts. In these plans, accrued interest is taxed only when the funds are withdrawn. Municipal zero-coupon bonds alleviate the tax problems of zero-coupon bonds.

Besides conventional zero-coupon bonds issued by corporations and government entities, many different types of zero-coupon bonds are available. Derivative zero-coupon bonds were introduced by several brokerage houses during the early 1980s, primarily for use in retirement accounts. These are called derivative securities because they are derived from another underlying security. Stripped zero-coupon bonds, municipal zero-coupon bonds, and mortgage backed zero-coupon bonds also exist.

The Relationships Influencing the Price of Zero-Coupon

Bonds   The quality of the bond, the length of time to maturity, the call provision, market rates of interest, and the yield all affect the price of the zero-coupon bond. The *quality* of the zero-coupon bond is important since the return depends on:

- The issuer's ability to redeem them at maturity.
- The investor's ability to sell them before maturity at a higher price than their purchase price.

A zero-coupon bondholder has more to lose in the event of a default, than a conventional bondholder because with the latter, the bondholder would have received some interest payments that could have been reinvested.

The quality of a zero-coupon bond is an assessment of the issuer's ability to pay off the bondholder at maturity. A good, quality zero-coupon bond has less risk of default than a speculative, low quality zero-coupon bond. Investors are willing to pay more for a good quality bond. Thus, a positive relationship between *quality and price* exists.

Ratings assigned by the ratings agencies such as Moody's, and Standard & Poor's are yardsticks to the credit quality, but investors should always be aware that these ratings are subject to changes.

The quality of a zero-coupon bond is also related to the *yield*. A low quality zero-coupon bond offers a higher yield than a good quality zero-coupon bond to entice investors. The flip side of the coin is that investors pay less for a low quality zero-coupon bond than a high quality zero-coupon bond. Therefore, price is inversely related to yield.

However, the yield is also related to the *length of time to maturity*. The longer the maturity, the lower the price, and the higher the yield. This is because the zero-coupon bondholder only gets the interest payment at maturity (or an accrued amount built into the sale price before maturity).

Besides the length of time to maturity and the quality of the issue, zero-coupon prices are sensitive to the *fluctuations in interest rates*. The purchase price of a zero-coupon bond determines the yield over the life of the security because interest is only paid at maturity, and interest accrues at that fixed yield. If market rates of interest rise above the fixed yield of the zero-coupon bond, investors would want to sell their zero-coupon bonds and reinvest at higher rates. This has the effect of depressing the price of the zero-coupon bond more than a conventional type bond, which pays interest annually or semi-annually. The concept of duration explains why zero-coupon bonds are more volatile in price than regular fixed interest payment bonds. Zero-coupon bonds have higher durations than conventional bonds of similar maturities and yields, because holders do not receive any interest payments until the zero-coupon bonds mature. Similarly, when interest rates fall, zero-coupon bonds appreciate more than existing conventional bonds due to the fixed yield on the zero-coupon bond.

Market factors also have a bearing on price. An actively traded zero-coupon bond is priced differently than an inactively traded zero-coupon bond with the same maturity and yield.

What Are the Risks of Zero-Coupon Bonds?

The *risk of default* depends on the financial position of the issuer and is of great importance to the zero-coupon bondholder. This is because the interest and principal is made in a single payment at maturity. If the issuer is not able to make this single payment, the holder receives a "large" zero. Consequently, the quality of the zero-coupon bond is an assessment of the likelihood of the issuer's ability to pay off the bondholder at maturity. The risk of default can be lessened by choosing high quality zero-coupon bond issues and/or government stripped bonds.

Zero-coupon bonds are also subject to *interest rate risk*. When market rates of interest rise (or fall), zero-coupon bonds, like regular bonds, fall (or rise) in price. However, zero-coupon prices tend to be much more volatile than those of regular bonds. This is because the entire amount that the investor receives is a single payment at maturity, whereas for regular fixed interest bearing bonds, the price is the discounted cash flows of the interest payments and the principal at maturity. Generally, with fixed interest paying bonds, the lower the coupon rate of the bond, the greater the price volatility due to changes in market rates of interest. This explains the price volatility of zero-coupon bonds, which have no coupon payments. Some zero-coupon bonds are more volatile in price than other similar yielding zeros as a result of different trading activity, quality differences, call features, and length of time to maturity.

Zero-coupon bonds have call provisions and many are called when interest rates decline.

Zero-coupon bonds have no *reinvestment risk* because the yield is determined by the purchase price and then locked in over the life of the bond. With a regular coupon bond, the holder is faced with the uncertainty of having to reinvest the interest payments at fluctuating market rates of interest. Moreover, the disadvantage is that zero-coupon bondholders are locked in to their existing lower yields when interest rates rise.

If zero-coupon bonds are sold before maturity, investors always face the risk of a loss in principal due to the extreme volatility of zero-coupon bonds. They are the most volatile of all bonds. In addition, markups in the pricing of zero-coupon bonds are high and also vary from dealer to dealer. This makes zero-coupon bonds expensive to buy and sell, as opposed to buying and holding through maturity.

How to Buy and Sell Zero-Coupon Bonds

Zero-coupon bonds are purchased in the primary market at issue (in other words, a new issue to the market). Investors who buy these new issues from the brokerage firms underwriting the issue avoid paying commissions or fees.

Existing zero-coupon bonds trading in the secondary markets are bought through securities brokers, dealers, and banks, as well as through online brokers. Brokers charge fees, which can be relatively high for zero-coupon securities. Bear in mind that investors are investing smaller amounts of money (due to the deep discounts) than they would for the same number of regular bonds. These markups vary considerably from broker to broker, and an investor should not be deceived if a broker announces that his/her firm does not charge a fee or commission. Very often the markups, which include the commissions on zero-coupon bonds, are quite high. The transaction fees for a small number of zero-coupon bonds can also be considerable.

Some brokerage firms may make a market in certain zero-coupon issues. Brokerage firms and the conditions on the market determine the prices that these are bought and sold. Consequently, the investor does not pay a commission, but the size of the markup determines whether the investor is getting a break.

It is important to shop around at different brokerage firms for the best prices when buying and selling zero-coupon securities. Many brokerage firms have inventories of different zero-coupon issues, and they may be more competitively priced. If the issue is quoted in the newspapers, an investor has a baseline price. Most zero-coupon issues are traded over-the-counter, but some issues are quoted on the New York Bond Exchange.

Be aware that when buying zero-coupon issues from sponsoring brokerage houses at issue, these brokerage houses are not required or obligated to make a market in these issues. The high transaction costs on zero-coupon issues make them less liquid than other fixed income securities and consequently, they are more suited to a buy and hold strategy. By holding zeros to maturity, investors improve their returns.

Rather than buy individual zero-coupon issues, investors may choose to put their money into mutual funds that specialize in zero-coupon bonds. As with all mutual funds, fees are deducted from the earnings (and/or the net assets) of the funds and they can be quite high.

See Table 4-18 for the advantages and disadvantages of zero-coupon bonds.

Caveats

*   When investing in zero-coupon bonds, outside of tax-deferred accounts such as IRAS, Keoghs, and pension accounts, investors should be aware of the tax consequences. They can be quite complicated, and it might necessitate the hiring of an accountant or tax professional to compute investors' tax liabilities. The Internal Revenue Service publishes two free guides that are quite helpful in determining the tax liability on zero-coupon bonds. These are IRS Publication 550 on "Investment Income and Expense," and IRS Publication 1212, "List of Original Issue Discount Obligations."

Table 4-18   Advantages and Disadvantages of Zero-Coupon Bonds

Advantages	Disadvantages
Greater appreciation than other bonds when interest rates decline.	Negative cash flow from paying taxes on accrued interest that is only received at maturity.
Investments require less capital than for regular bonds.	Extremely volatile when interest rates change.
No reinvestment rate risk.	Many issues have call provisions.
Provide fixed yields when held to maturity.	Can lose more than from a conventional bond if the issuer defaults.
Many issues from which to choose.	Markups high on zero-coupon issues.
Different types of zero-coupon bonds from which to choose.	May not be as marketable as ordinary bonds.
Well-suited for tax deferred accounts.	

- When computing the tax consequences of a zero-coupon bond, investors should know the yield and when the security was issued. The latter point is important because the computation for the phantom interest is different for zero-coupon bonds issued before December 31, 1984, than for those issued after that date.
- If the investor's tax situation is relatively uncomplicated, and the investor is unable to determine the tax liability as a result of investing in zero-coupon bonds, a tax accountant would have to be hired. In such a situation, the investor is better off investing in other more straight-forward, fixed income securities.

Exercises

1. When should investors invest in money market securities?

2. List the reasons for investing in Treasury securities (notes and bonds).

3. What are the advantages of inflation-indexed Treasury securities?

4. Why consider agency and corporate bonds over Treasuries?

5. What are the major reasons why investors should consider buying convertible bonds?

6. What are the risks of zero-coupon securities?

End Notes

Faerber, Esme: *All About Bonds and Mutual Funds*. McGraw-Hill, New York, 2000.

Hayre, Lakbir S., and Cyrus Mohebbi: "Mortgage Pass-Through Securities," in Frank J. Fabozzi (ed.), *Advances and Innovations in the Bond and Mortgage Markets,* McGraw-Hill, New York, 1989.

Thau, Annette: *The Bond Book,* McGraw-Hill, New York, 1992.

Zuckerman, Gregory: "Online Push Barely Budges Bond Trading," *The Wall Street Journal,* December 28, 1998, pp. C1, C15.

Chapter 5

Trading: Buying and Selling Bonds

Tools and Tips for Entering the Markets

The different types of bonds were discussed in the previous chapter, which leads the investor to ask the question: which types of bonds should one buy?

Bonds vary not only by issuer, but also in their characteristics. Most bonds provide known streams of cash flow payments in the form of interest and the return of the bondholder's principal at the maturity date of the bond. Issuers are assessed as to the relative certainty that they can make these interest payments and principal repayments. Generally, those issuers with greater assurances of ability to make these payments have lower coupon yields and tend to have lower price volatility. Issuers who are assessed with greater variability in their ability to fulfill their payment obligations to the bondholders are considered to be more risky. As a result, the prices of their bonds tend to fluctuate more, and in order to entice investors to buy their bonds, they will pay higher coupon yields than the "safer" issuers.

Besides these vanilla type bonds, hybrid types of bonds with different features are available. Convertible securities pay fixed interest payments, but they have the added feature of being convertible into the common shares of the company by the bondholder. Thus, a convertible bond can be classified as straight debt, but on conversion, the bondholder becomes a stockholder. When the company's stock price rises, the convertible bonds appreciate in price, offering the capital appreciation associated more with the characteristics of equity than debt.

Zero-coupon bond securities are also a hybrid form of debt in that the zero-coupon bondholders do not receive actual payments of interest over the life of the bond. Instead, investors buy these bonds at deep discounts and the accrued interest payments are paid only to holders at maturity.

Investors need to weigh these different safety and risk factors with the investment's ability to generate income and/or capital growth. Investors should consider a number of steps and processes before deciding which bonds to buy.

Risk

Investors have different reasons or *objectives* for investing, which are just as important for bond investors as they are for stock investors. This is because the objectives determine not only the levels of risk tolerance, but also the types of bonds in which to invest. The most prominent objectives for investors are:

- Capital preservation.
- Income generation.
- Income and growth.
- Growth.

Figure 5-1 illustrates a continuum of these objectives as well as the corresponding levels of risk. The level of risk increases as the objectives change from capital preservation to growth on the other extreme.

Figure 5-2 shows the levels of risk of the different fixed income securities. The investments at the base of the triangle have the lowest risk. With each ascending level of investments to the apex of the triangle, the risk increases. The riskiest of the bond types are zero-coupon bonds, which as a group are often referred to as providing a "roller coaster ride." However, the risk levels for these categories are relative

Figure 5-1   Objectives and Level of Risk

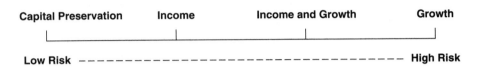

Figure 5-2   Fixed Income Securities and Levels of Risk

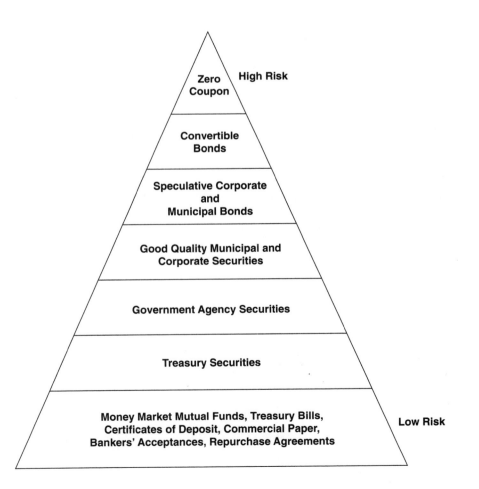

and are not cast in stone. For example, a corporate junk bond descending along the path to bankruptcy is riskier than a good quality zero-coupon bond. Higher yields are used to entice investors to invest in riskier securities.

The main objective of *capital preservation* is the full return of the invested capital, with income generation not being as important. The securities that fit this description are money market securities. If the investor has a longer time horizon, Treasury securities also fit this description. This is because the latter group has no credit or default risk. With money market securities, investors have very little risk of default of the principal invested, so they are assured of the return of their capital while earning whatever rates these securities pay. For investors with longer time horizons, Treasury securities also are assured of a return of capital at maturity. These investors can improve on the rates of return over those of money market securities.

The focus of the *income generation* objective is more on earning income than preserving the original amount of principal invested. Although the latter is important, this objective gives investors a wider choice in seeking bond investments with higher rates of return. In other words, investors with this objective are not deterred from investing in bonds that are more volatile in price in order to receive the higher coupon yields over Treasury securities. With this objective, an investor's risk tolerance allows for the choice of government agency bonds and good quality corporate and municipal bonds over Treasuries for greater returns. See Figure 5-3 for a yield comparison of the different bond securities. The yield differential between the different types of bonds makes it easier to decide whether the increased returns from the higher yielding bonds warrant the increased risks. For example, a four-point differential exists between high quality corporate bonds and junk bonds in Figure 5-3. An investor with this objective might be tempted by the possibility of earning four more percentage points, but the risk of default may deter the investor from taking this much risk. Instead, the investor could improve returns by pursuing slightly lesser rated corporate bonds, such as A rated corporate bonds, rather than top quality corporate bonds.

The *income and growth objective* includes investments that return both income and capital growth. Capital growth may be achieved by buying bonds at lower prices and selling them at higher prices. This means buying bonds that have greater upside potential, which is another way of saying, buy more risky, volatile bonds. Bonds with the potential for greater price appreciation than Treasuries for example, also have the potential for greater price depreciation when conditions go awry. Another point to consider when using bonds as trading vehicles is that they have larger transaction costs than stocks and do not have the same pricing transparency as stocks. Bonds in this category include junk corporates, municipals, and convertible securities.

With a *growth objective,* the focus is on capital growth and not income. Zero-coupon bonds fit this category, but have one great disadvantage. Interest payments are not paid until maturity, but are taxed at the

Figure 5-3 Yield Comparison of Ten-Year Bonds

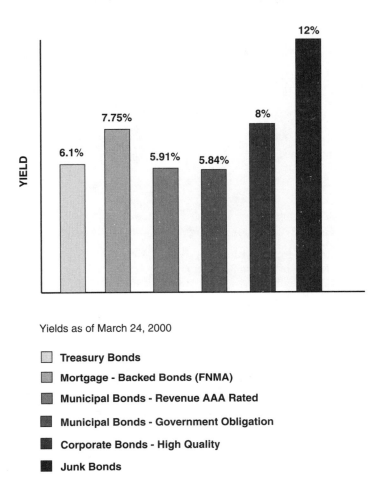

Yields as of March 24, 2000

☐ **Treasury Bonds**

▨ **Mortgage - Backed Bonds (FNMA)**

▨ **Municipal Bonds - Revenue AAA Rated**

▨ **Municipal Bonds - Government Obligation**

■ **Corporate Bonds - High Quality**

■ **Junk Bonds**

federal level as if they were paid on a yearly basis. This creates negative cash flows for this type of bond. For this reason, zero-coupon bonds are better suited as investments in tax-deferred accounts. However, when market rates of interest decline, zero-coupon bonds appreciate more than conventional fixed income securities.

The investor's reasons for investing define the levels of acceptable risk, leading to the next step: determining the types of bonds to purchase.

Which Bonds Should One Buy?

An asset allocation plan assists in determining how much of the portfolio to invest in the different categories of bonds. Figure 5-4 is a suggested allocation plan for a sixty-five year old investor. A diversified portfolio of bond investments can provide a level of safety during turbulent markets. See Table 5-1 for an example of the types of securities in this asset allocation plan.

Figure 5-4   Asset Allocation Model for a Sixty-five year old

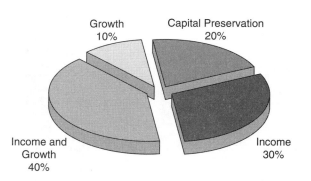

Table 5-1   Types of Securities in the Asset Allocation Plan of Figure 5-4

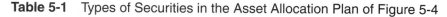

Capital Preservation	**20%**
Money market mutual funds	
Treasury bills	
Income Generation	**30%**
Treasury Notes and Bonds	
Government Agency Bonds	
AAA rated Corporate Bonds	
Municipal Bonds	
Income and Growth	**40%**
AA rated Convertible Bonds	
A rated Corporate Bonds	
Blue chip stocks	
Growth	**10%**
Top quality technology stocks	
AAA rated Zero-coupon bonds	

Rather than concentrating solely on Treasury securities, which are currently yielding around 6.1 percent, government agency and mortgage-pass-through bonds may be considered, which are yielding around 7.75 percent. These are also relatively safe investments with their implied backing by the government. Corporate and municipal bonds may be exposed to greater levels of credit and default risk, so they require careful analysis of the financial positions of their issuers. Worksheet 5-1 is a useful yardstick in determining the yield differentials of the different types of bonds, which assist in the overall decision of which bonds to buy.

High tax bracket investors may find municipal bonds to be beneficial investments. A 5.91 percent yielding municipal bond to an investor in the 39.6 percent tax bracket has a tax equivalent yield of 9.78 percent (5.91%/1 − .396). This yield is higher than those of Treasuries, government agency, and good quality corporate bonds in Figure 5-3.

Worksheet 5-1

Yield Comparison of Ten-Year Bonds

Step 1: Determine Investment Objectives and Acceptable Levels of Risk

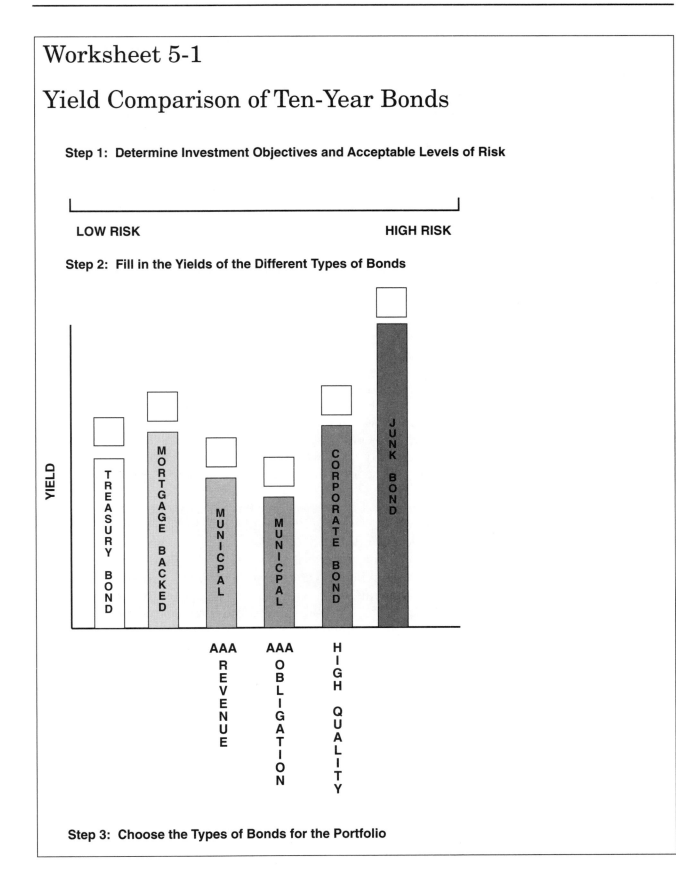

LOW RISK   **HIGH RISK**

Step 2: Fill in the Yields of the Different Types of Bonds

Step 3: Choose the Types of Bonds for the Portfolio

The Route of an Order

Figure 5-5 illustrates the route of a buy order for bonds. Assume that Mr. A would like to buy some good quality corporate bonds with a nine-year maturity. Mr. A can either call his broker to find out what bonds the broker has available in inventory or look online at the broker's inventory, if this option is available. Then, the broker quotes the prices of the different bonds available. A description of the bonds available might be:

AT&T 6% 09 bid 89 ask 91

This means that the AT&T bond has a coupon of six percent, matures in 2009, and is bid at $890 and an asked price of $910. In other words, Mr. A can buy this bond from the broker at $910, and turn around and sell it back to the broker at $890. This spread of $20 per bond tells something about the bond. It is based on several factors such as the quality of the issuer, the length of time to maturity, supply and demand for the bonds, coupon rate and market rates of interest, call features, and the coupon rates of other comparable bonds of similar quality. A large spread (four percent or more) may indicate that it is not a widely traded bond or that creditworthiness may be low. Although other factors play a role, a bond issue with a large spread should be avoided. Spreads are generally the lowest for Treasury securities, and may be quite high for junk bonds and poor quality, thinly traded municipal bonds.

If Mr. A wanted to buy this specific bond that was not held in the inventory of his brokerage firm, he would ask his broker to get him a quote. The broker would send this request to the trading floor of the firm, which would get a quote from a market maker or dealer in this bond. In this case, the bid and asked spread may be wider to include the price that the brokerage firm would have to pay to buy this bond. This process is described in Figure 5-6, where the firm buys a specific bond that they do not hold in inventory.

Figure 5-5   Route of an Order to Buy Bonds

Figure 5-6 Route of an order to buy a specific bond not held in the inventory of the brokerage firm

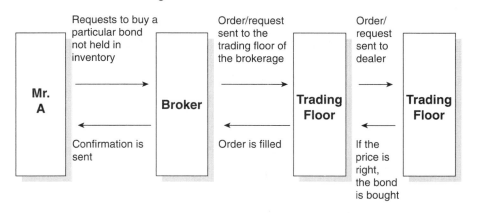

When the investor is interested in buying a specific bond, the investor should obtain different bid and asked quotes from different brokerage firms in order to seek out the best price. This is because prices do differ depending on what the brokerage firm pays to obtain the bond, and what their markups and markdowns are on the securities. For example, another brokerage firm might quote the above mentioned bond at

89 bid, 90 1/2 asked.

For all transactions, a broker fills out a buy or sell order, shown in Figure 5-7, either on their computer screens or if the brokerage is not fully computerized, a paper copy of the buy/sell ticket. This is sent electronically or physically to the brokerage firm's trading floor. Investors who buy or sell their bonds online fill out a similar buy or sell order on their computer monitors and submit their orders to the brokerage firm's trading floor to be enacted.

Using Bond Tables

Quotes of corporate bonds listed on the New York and American Exchanges are found in the daily financial newspapers. Similarly, daily quotes of Treasury securities are listed in the financial newspapers. However, the majority of traded bonds are unlisted and trade on the over-the-counter markets through dealers where investors do not have ready access to prices. The development of the Internet may make the pricing of unlisted bonds more transparent in the future as online brokers continue to offer more services to make online bond trading more accessible for investors.

Figure 5-7   Example of a Buy and Sell Order Ticket

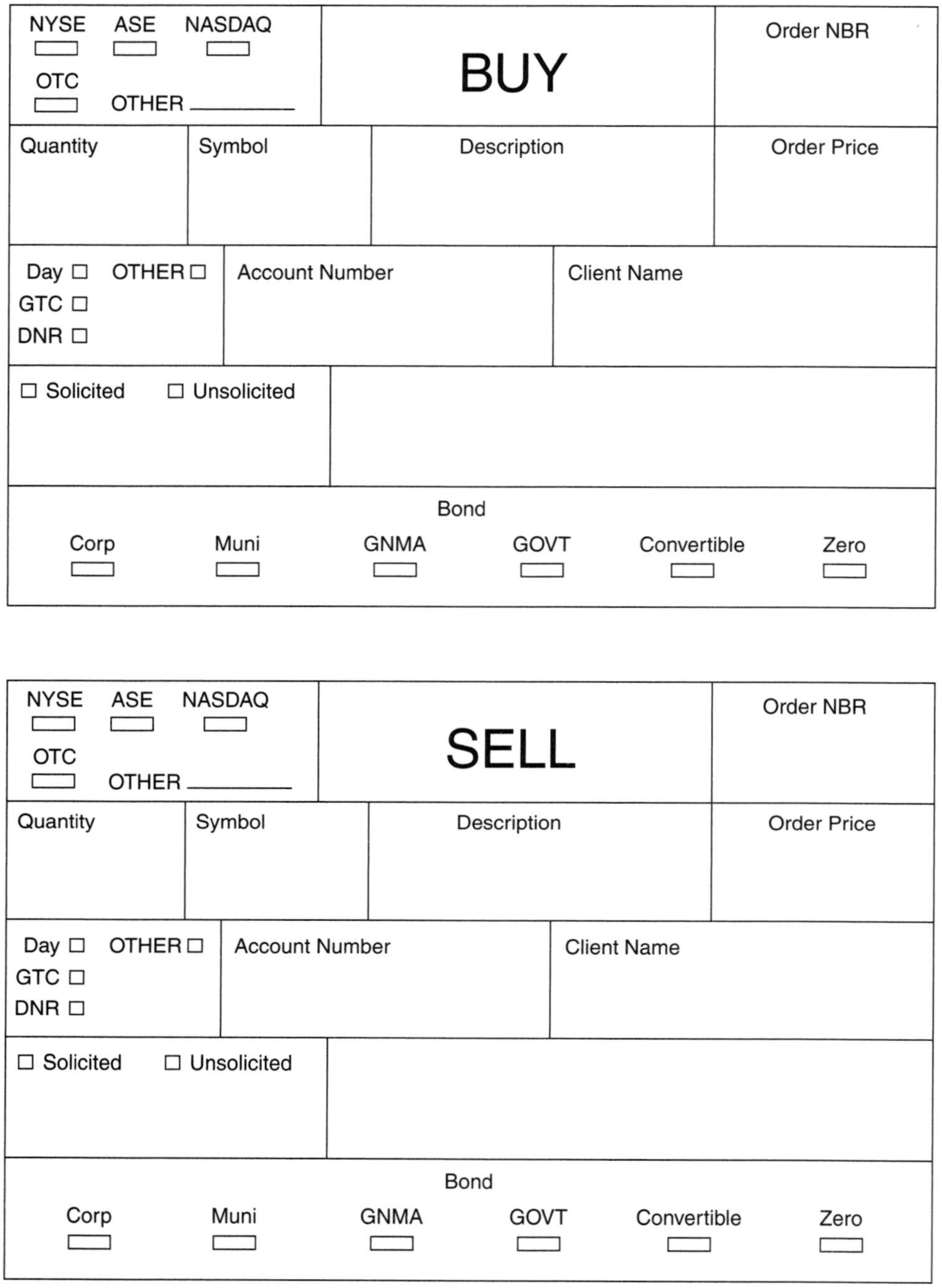

NYSE ☐ ASE ☐ NASDAQ ☐ OTC ☐ OTHER _____	**BUY**	Order NBR
Quantity	Symbol	Description	Order Price
Day ☐ OTHER ☐ GTC ☐ DNR ☐	Account Number	Client Name
☐ Solicited ☐ Unsolicited	
Bond		

| | Corp ☐ | Muni ☐ | GNMA ☐ | GOVT ☐ | Convertible ☐ | Zero ☐ |

NYSE ☐ ASE ☐ NASDAQ ☐ OTC ☐ OTHER _____	**SELL**	Order NBR
Quantity	Symbol	Description	Order Price
Day ☐ OTHER ☐ GTC ☐ DNR ☐	Account Number	Client Name
☐ Solicited ☐ Unsolicited	
Bond		

| | Corp ☐ | Muni ☐ | GNMA ☐ | GOVT ☐ | Convertible ☐ | Zero ☐ |

When investing in bonds, which are not listed on the exchanges, the investor should obtain the following information from the brokerage firm before investing:

- The price spread (bid and asked price).
- The coupon yield.
- The frequency of interest payments (whether annual or semi-annual).
- The date of maturity.
- The yield to maturity.
- The call or refunding provisions.
- The yield to call.

This information on the bond of interest should be considered to determine the value of the bond. Much of this information can be obtained from the quotes for bonds that are listed in the daily newspapers. Refer to the section on how to read the different types of bond quotations in Chapter Three, "Beginnings: What Affects Prices?".

Interpreting the Data

Bonds may be purchased at par value ($1000 per bond), at a discount (below $1000), or at a premium price (above $1000 per bond).

Par Value   If the investor purchases a bond at par value and holds the bond to maturity, the investor earns the coupon rate of the bond. For example, if the investor pays $1000 for a 10-year bond with a coupon rate of seven percent and holds the bond until maturity, the investor earns seven percent on the bond. The return on the investment is the same as the coupon rate. A relationship exists between market rates of interest and bond prices. Thus, if newly issued 10-year bonds of similar quality come to market at par with the same coupon rate of seven percent, then existing bonds with seven percent coupons would also trade at par or close to it. However, if market rates of interest rise, new bonds with the same maturity and quality will be issued with higher coupon rates. This depresses the prices of existing bonds with lower coupon rates.

Premium Price   Bonds that trade at a premium have prices above $1,000 per bond. Bonds trade at premium prices for many reasons, with the most important being that coupon rates of these premium priced bonds are higher than the coupon rates of newly issued bonds. Looked at another way, investors are willing to pay more for a bond with a higher coupon rate. Because investors pay premium prices, the overall yield to maturity (discussed in Chapter 6, "Analysis: Evaluating Bond Characteristics") or the return on their investment is lower than the coupon rate. The quality of the bond also affects the price of the bond. Many junk bonds with higher coupon rates than newly issued bonds are not trading at premium prices. This is because they may be facing higher credit or default risks or some other negative information is depressing their prices.

Discount Price   Bonds that trade at discounts have prices below $1,000. When market rates of interest rise, newly issued bonds have higher coupons than existing bonds that were issued when market rates of interest were lower. Thus, coupon rates of bonds trading at a discount are generally lower than similar quality, newly issued bonds.

A direct relationship between interest rates and bond prices determines whether bonds trade at premiums, discounts, or par prices. Worksheet 5-2 addresses the issue of what the investor should look for when buying bonds.

Worksheet 5-2

Guidelines for Buying Bonds

1. Check the yield to maturity on the bond. The price of a bond is important and the question of whether to purchase a bond at a premium or discount may be answered by looking at the yield to maturity. The yield to maturity is the annual effective rate of return earned on a bond held to maturity. Compare different bonds with the same maturities and similar risks, and choose the bonds with the highest yield to maturity. When the yield to maturity is greater than the coupon rate, the bond trades at a discounted price. Similarly, when the yield to maturity is less than the coupon rate, the bond trades at a premium price.

2. Be cautious when buying a premium priced bond. The investor should check out the call or refunding provisions first before buying a premium priced bond. When the market premium price of the bond is greater than the call price, the investor stands to lose principal if the bond is called at the lower price. Avoid bonds that trade at higher prices than their call prices.

3. Be aware of the reason(s) a bond is being traded at a discount. Although the yield to maturity is greater than the coupon rates for bonds trading at a discount, which generally occurs when market rates of interest rise, other reasons may contribute to why the bonds are trading at discounted prices. These may be due to the risks of credit and default, or other bad news regarding the issuer, which depresses the price. Compare the bonds with other bonds of similar quality and maturity to determine if the discount is due to these other risks.

Exercises

1. List the likely types of bonds that would be considered by an investor with a low tolerance for risk and with the objective of generating income for the next 10 years.

2. List the likely types of bonds that would be considered by an investor with medium risk tolerance and with the objectives of generating both income and growth for the next 10 years.

3. What factors should be considered when deciding between the purchase of a bond trading at a discount and one trading at a premium price?

Chapter 6

Analysis: Evaluating Bond Characteristics

This chapter focuses on an evaluation of the different bond characteristics that enable investors to make better choices in the bonds that they purchase and hold.

Bond Ratings

Bond ratings assist investors in appraising the credit and default risks of bonds. Creditworthiness is the issuer's ability to make scheduled interest payments and repay the principal when the bonds mature. Credit risk varies with bond issuers. For instance, U.S. Treasury issues carry virtually no risk of default, whereas U.S. agency debt has slightly increased risks of default. Municipal bonds issued by different state and local governments depend on the financial health of the particular issuer and their ability to raise revenue. For corporate issuers, credit risks are linked to the status or financial condition of their balance sheets, income statements, and their earnings capacities.

Independent ratings services can evaluate the credit risks of municipal and corporate bonds. See Table 6-1 for a list of credit ratings ranging from the best credit quality for the issuers with the strongest financial status to the lowest ratings for issuers in default.

Moody's and *Standard & Poor's* (S&P) are two of the best-known, independent ratings agencies, and their ratings are similar, though not identical. Other established ratings agencies include Fitch Investor Service, and *Duff and Phelps* (D&P). The higher the ratings, the greater the probable safety of the interest and principal payments. Ratings of AAA, AA, A, and BBB from S&P are considered to be investment grade quality. Bonds with ratings below BBB are considered to be junk bonds and are speculative. These junk bonds have lower ratings, meaning that the issuers have a greater likelihood of default on their interest and principal repayments. Before buying a bond issue, investors should ask their brokers for the ratings on that issue. Most online brokers provide this information with their price quotes.

Investors should stick to issues with ratings of BBB and above to insure against sleepless nights. These ratings, however, provide only a relative guide for investors because the financial status of the issuer could deteriorate over time and result in the issue being downgraded to a lower rating. A downgrading usually causes a decline in the market price of the bond. The opposite occurs when a bond issue is upgraded. The same issuer with many different bond issues outstanding could have different ratings for each issue. For example, in May 1999, Moody's downgraded Conti Financial Corporation's senior, unsecured debt from B1 to Caa1.

Investors should not be duly alarmed if their bonds are downgraded from AAA to A because this still indicates good quality. However, if the issue is downgraded below BBB, an investor should review whether to continue owning that bond.

Credit risks are minimized by buying bonds with investment grade ratings of A and above by S&P, which have a reduced likelihood of de-

Table 6-1 Bond Ratings

Moody's	Standard & Poor's	Interpretation of Ratings
Aaa	AAA	Highest quality obligations.
Aa	AA	High quality obligations.
A	A	Bonds that have a strong capacity to repay principal and interest, but may be impaired in the future.
Baa	BBB	Medium grade quality.
Ba	BB B	Interest and principal is neither highly protected nor poorly secured. Lower ratings in this category have some speculative characteristics.
B Caa Ca C	CCC CC C DDD DD D	Speculative bonds with great uncertainty. In default.

fault, and through diversification. In other words, instead of investing all your money in the bonds of one issuer, buy bonds of different issuers, particularly with corporate and municipal bonds.

Rate of Return

Calculating a rate of return is important for a number of reasons.

- It is a measure of the growth or decline of the investor's wealth.
- It is a yardstick against which investors can evaluate the performance of their bond investments against their objectives.

Investors invest in bonds to earn interest income, and/or capital appreciation (when the face value of the bond at maturity or the sale price is greater than the purchase price). The simple definition of total return includes both income and capital gains/losses.

The total rate of return is calculated as follows:

Rate of return = (Ending Value − Beginning Value) + Income / Gross Purchase Price

Spreads and commissions should be included in the calculations. For example, if the gross purchase price of a bond bought at the beginning of the year is $850, and the bond is sold for $950 at the end of the year with a commission of $25, and interest of $50 was received, the rate of return is:

$$\text{Rate of return} = [(925 - 850) + 50]/850$$
$$= 14.71\%$$

This is not the most accurate rate of return as it ignores the time value of money. A more comprehensive measure of the rate of return of a bond is the *yield to maturity*, which takes into account the time value of money. The *time value of money* is a concept that recognizes that a dollar today is worth more in the future because of its earnings potential. A dollar invested at five percent for one year would equal $1.05 at the end of the year. Similarly, a dollar received at the end of one year would be worth less than a dollar at the beginning of the year.

This average rate of return of 14.71 percent discussed previously does not take into account the earnings capacity of the interest received. In other words, the $50 of interest received is reinvested, increasing the rate of return above 14.71 percent. See Worksheet 6-1 for the calculation of rates of return for bonds held for different time periods.

Yield

A relationship between bond prices and yield exists. A bond's cash flows and the required rate of return or yield used to discount the cash flows determines bond prices. Four basic types of yields exist, which are explained in this section.

Coupon Yield

The coupon yield is the stated yield of the bond issue. This is the specified amount of interest that the issuer of the bond promises to pay the bondholder each year. This annual amount of interest is stated as a percentage of the par value of the bond or as a dollar amount. For instance, a bond with a par value of $1,000 that pays $70 of annual interest has a seven percent coupon yield.

The coupon yield is fixed through the life of the bond issue unless it is a variable interest coupon that fluctuates through the life of the bond.

Current Yield

The current yield is the relationship between the price of the bond and its yield. The current yield is determined as follows:

$$\textbf{Current Yield} = \frac{\text{Coupon Interest Amount}}{\text{Purchase Price of the Bond}}$$

Worksheet 6-1

Calculation of Rates of Return for Different Time Periods

Determine the rate of return for a bond bought at $99 and sold two years later at $101 with a coupon of seven percent payable semi-annually.

Answer

Cash Flows

Rate of Return = [(1010 - 990) + 140] / 990
= 16.16%

Annualized Rate of Return = 16.16% / 2 years
= 8.08%

Reason: The rate of return of 16.16 percent is for the two year period and for an annualized return; this is divided by two.

Determine the rate of return for a bond bought at $98 and sold after six months at $99 with a receipt of one interest payment of $40.

Answer

Rate of Return = [(990 − 980) + 40] / 980
= 5.1%

Annualized Rate of Return = 5.1% × 2
= 10.2%

Reason: The rate of return for 6 months is 5.1 percent, which is multiplied by two for an annualized return.

If a bond is purchased at par, $1000, and the coupon is five percent (interest is $50 per year), then the current yield is five percent (same as the coupon yield). However, on the secondary market, most bonds trade above or below par. For a bond purchased at $1,100 with a five percent coupon, the current yield is 4.54% (50/1100).

A relationship exists among bond prices, current yields, and coupon rates. Bonds trading at a discount to their par values have current yields that are higher than their coupon rates. Similarly, bonds trading at a premium to their par values have current yields that are lower than their coupon rates. This relationship is summarized below:

Bond Price

Discount	Current Yield	>	Coupon Yield
Par	Current Yield	=	Coupon Yield
Premium	Current Yield	<	Coupon Yield

For investors who are concerned with high current income, the current yield is a useful measure.

Yield to Maturity

The yield to maturity is a calculation relating the maturity value of the bond and the interest payments with the time value of money to the present price of the bond. In other words, the yield to maturity is the discount rate calculated by mathematically equaling the cash flows of the interest and principal payments with the price of the bond. This is also referred to as the internal rate of return of the bond.

The yield to maturity can be solved easily with the use of a computer or a financial calculator with built-in financial tables. For example, a bond that was purchased for $770.36 and pays a coupon of five percent ($50 annually) with a maturity of 10 years, has a yield to maturity of 8.5 percent.

The process on the financial calculator would be:

1. The purchase price of $770.36 is entered into the *present value* (PV) button.
2. The coupon payment of $50 is entered into the *payment* (PMT) button.
3. The maturity value ($1,000 par value) is entered into the *future value* (FV) button.
4. The time to maturity is entered into the number of payment periods per year multiplied by the number of years (*n*) button.
5. Press the interest/yield to maturity (*I*) button and the calculator solves the yield to maturity.

Without the use of a financial calculator, the following formula gives the approximate *yield to maturity* (YTM):

$$YTM = (\text{Coupon Payment} + 1,000 - \text{Purchase Price / Years to Maturity}) / (1,000 + \text{Purchase Price / 2})$$

$$= [(50 + (1,000 - 770.36 / 10)] / (1,000 + 770.36 / 2)$$

$$= 8.24\%$$

Using the approximation formula, the yield of 8.24 percent understates the true YTM calculated with a financial calculator.

The YTM can also be calculated with pencil, paper, and financial tables (present value of a single sum and the present value of an annuity of one tables) by solving the following equation for "r" (which is the YTM):

Purchase Price of Bond = Σ PV Coupon / $(1 + r)^n$ + PV 1,000 / $(1 + r)^n$

    where Σ = summation

    n = number of years to maturity

    PV is the present value

For the above:

    $770.36 = \Sigma$ PV 50 / $(1 + r)^{10}$ + PV 1,000 / $(1 + r)^{10}$

Solving this equation is a tedious task as it involves a trial and error approach to determine the value of r. Choose a value for r and plug it into the calculation. If this value does not equate the right side of the equation to the left side, choose another value until the right value is found.

The YTM incorporates the compounding effects of the interest payments, but it also hinges on two assumptions:

1. The investor holds the bond to maturity.
2. The investor reinvests the interest payments received at the same YTM rate.

If the bond is not held to maturity, the internal rate of return of the bond is calculated by substituting the sale price of the bond for the maturity value.

The YTM rate assumes that the investor reinvests the interest received at the same YTM. If this does not occur, the investor's actual rate of return differs from the quoted YTM rate. For example, if the interest received is spent and not reinvested, the coupon interest does not earn interest; the investor earns much less than the stated YTM. Similarly, if the stated YTM is eight percent and the investor reinvests the interest at lesser (or greater) rates, the eight percent will not be achieved.

In reality, it is difficult to match the YTM rate for the interest received because interest rates are constantly changing. The interest received is usually reinvested at different rates from the stated YTM rate.

The YTM is useful in comparing and evaluating different bonds of varying quality with different coupons and prices. For example, by comparing the YTM of an AAA rated bond with a BBB rated bond, the investor easily can see how much the increment in yield would be in choosing the lower rated bond. The investor can also see the yield differential between bonds with different maturities.

The YTM does not indicate the price volatility of different coupon bonds with different maturities. When comparing different bonds with different maturities, investors will want to know which of the bond's price will decrease more, when interest rates rise. This is answered by calculating the bond's duration.

The relationship between the coupon yield, current yield, YTM, and bond price is summarized here:

Bond Price

Discount	Coupon Yield	<	Current Yield	<	Yield to Maturity
Par	Coupon Yield	=	Current Yield	=	Yield to Maturity
Premium	Coupon Yield	>	Current Yield	>	Yield to Maturity

Yield to Call

When the bond has a call feature, investors calculate the *yield to call* by substituting the call price for the maturity price in the equations discussed previously in the YTM section. For bonds with call provisions, investors should determine both the yield to call and the YTM because if the bond is called, the yield to call is the annual return the investor receives on the bond.

Duration

Duration is defined as the average time that it takes for a bondholder to receive the total interest and principal. It is the point in time in the life of the bond where the bond's return remains the same or unchanged despite the movement of market rates of interest. For example, the duration on a $1,000 face value bond with a coupon of six percent, maturing in three years with a market price of $973.44, and current market rates of interest of seven percent, is calculated using the following formula (Mayo, 1991):

$$\text{Duration} = \frac{(1 + y)}{y} - \frac{(1 + y) + n(c - y)}{c[(1 + y)^n - 1] + y}$$

where c = coupon rate
y = yield to maturity
n = number of years to maturity

Substituting the figures in the example:

$$\text{Duration} = \frac{(1 + .07)}{.07} - \frac{(1 + .07) + 3\,(.06 - .07)}{.06\,[(1 + .07)^3 - 1] + .07)}$$
$$= 2.83 \text{ years}$$

Another method of determining the duration of a bond is to use the time value of money concept. Using the same example above, for a bond with a coupon of six percent, maturing in three years with a market price of $973.44, and current market rates of interest of seven percent, duration is determined as follows:

Time Period of Payment		Payment Amount (Coupon & Principal)		Present Value (Interest Factor)		Present Value of Time Weighted Payments
1	×	$ 60	×	.9346	=	$ 56.08
2	×	60	×	.8734	=	$ 104.80
3	×	1060	×	.8163	=	$2595.83
						$2756.71

Duration = <u>Summation of Present Value of Time Weighted Payments</u>
Market Price of the Bond

= <u>$2,756.71</u>
$ 973.44

= 2.83 years/periods

Duration is a time weighted average of the summation of the present values of the coupon and interest payments multiplied by the time periods of the payments, which is then divided by the market price of the bond. The present value is the opposite of the future or compound value in the time value of money concept. A dollar today is worth more in the future because of its earnings potential. Similarly, a dollar in the future can be discounted to today's value and is worth less now than in the future.

A duration of 2.83 means that the bondholder will collect the average of the coupon and the principal payments of this particular bond in 2.83 years.

The impact of interest rate risk can be lessened using the concept of duration. Bonds with different maturities and different coupons have different durations. Bonds with higher durations experience greater price volatility as market rates of interest change and bonds with smaller durations have lower price volatility. Different bonds with the same durations have similar price fluctuations to changes in market rates of interest.

This is explained in Table 6-2, which shows the prices of six percent coupon bonds with different maturities when market rates of interest change.

When market rates of interest decline below the coupon rate (of six percent) to five percent, the price of the bond increases above par value.

Table 6-2   Impact of Market Fluctuations in Interest Rates on a Par Value Bond with a Coupon Rate of Six Percent with Different Maturities

Maturity	Market Rate of Interest 5%	Market Rate of Interest 7%
2 year	$1018.56	$ 981.88
5 year	$1042.27	$ 959.01
10 year	$1077.21	$ 929.72
20 year	$1124.63	$ 894.04

Correspondingly, as the maturities increase from two years to 20 years, so do the prices of the bond. The opposite is true when market rates of interest rise to seven percent above the coupon rate of six percent as shown in Table 6-2. Bond prices fall below par and decline further as maturities extend into the future.

The following are the generalizations for bonds with which duration can be better explained:

- The longer the maturity of a bond, the greater the price volatility.
- An inverse relationship exists between bond prices and market rates of interest. When market rates of interest rise, bond prices fall, and when market rates of interest fall, bond prices increase.

As pointed out in the discussion, a bondholder with a coupon of six percent and a maturity of 30 years faces greater price volatility than a similar coupon bond with a shorter maturity. A lower coupon bond (for example, four percent) with the same maturity experiences even greater price volatility with changes in market rates of interest. This is because the bondholder with the lower coupon bond receives lower cash flows ($40 per year through maturity versus $60 per year), which when reinvested, produces lower future values. The longer the maturity of the bond, the longer the bondholder has to wait to receive the face or par value of the bond. Hence, the present value of the par value of the bond is discounted to a lesser amount than the present value of the par value of a bond maturing earlier.

Duration accounts for this reinvestment rate risk, the coupon rate, and the term to maturity of a bond as follows in Table 6-3:

Duration explains why a zero-coupon bond has the same duration as its term to maturity. With a zero-coupon bond, no coupon payments are made and only the principal is received at maturity. Thus, except for zero-coupon bonds, the duration for all other bonds are less than their terms to maturities.

Duration is a tool that can be used to manage interest rate risk and the maturity of the bonds with the timing of the investor's needs for the funds. By matching the duration of bonds with the timing of the funds, investors can lessen their risks of loss on their bonds.

Table 6-3   Duration and Bond Characteristics

- The lower the coupon, the higher the duration.

- The higher the coupon, the lower the duration.

- The longer the term to maturity, the higher the duration.

- The shorter the term to maturity, the lower the duration.

- The smaller the duration, the smaller the price volatility of the bond.

- The greater the duration, the greater the price volatility of the bond.

Convexity

The previous discussion on duration shows the usefulness of the concept when market rates of interest change in small increments. However, when changes in interest rates are large, estimates made using the concept of duration are not accurate because the relationships are not linear. The concept of convexity can help reduce errors when the changes in interest rates are large.

Convexity is a measure of the curve of the line showing the relationship between bond prices and the different yields to maturity. When bond yields decline, bond prices rise at an increasing rate. Similarly, bond prices fall at a decreasing rate when yields rise. In other words, bond prices do not move up and down at the same rate. Bond prices rise faster than they decline, which means that the price yield curve has a positive convexity curve. This is a property of all non-callable bonds. This means that investors can make more money when interest rates decline than they will lose when interest rates increase. The amount of money that can be made or lost resulting from changes in bond yields depends on duration and convexity (characteristics of the bond).

Table 6-4 shows the price yield relationships for three bonds, and Figure 6-1 illustrates the convexity of these bonds with the different coupon yields and maturities.

Bond A, in Figure 6-1, with the highest coupon and the shortest maturity (13 percent coupon maturing in three years) has an almost flat curve with very little convexity, whereas Bond B with an eight percent coupon and 10-year maturity has a more convex line. Bond C with a zero-coupon and 30-year maturity has the greatest convexity of the bonds shown. These curves show that the greatest change in YTM has the greatest impact on the prices of bonds with the greater convexities. In general, the relationships regarding convexity are:

- The greater the YTM, the lower the convexity.
- The lower the coupon, the higher the convexity.

Figure 6-2 illustrates the relationships between duration and convexity when changes in yield occur. The convexity of Bond A is shown along with the duration lines at two different points on the bond curve. These lines indicate the slope or duration at the points where they touch the bond curve. As the yield declines on the graph, the slope of the line becomes steeper. Similarly, as the yield increases, the slope of the line gets flatter.

In general, the relationships between yield and duration are as follows:

- When YTM decreases, the duration of the bond increases.
- When the YTM increases, the duration (slope) of the bond falls.

Table 6-4 Relationship between Yields to Maturity and Bond Prices

Bond A 13%, 3 year bond		Bond B 8%, 10 year bond		Bond C Zero-coupon, 30 year bond	
Yield to Maturity	Bond Price	Yield to Maturity	Bond Price	Yield to Maturity	Bond Price
1%	$1352.93	1%	$1663.00	1%	$742.90
2%	$1316.92	2%	$1538.64	2%	$552.00
3%	$1282.56	3%	$1426.64	3%	$412.00
4%	$1249.75	4%	$1324.88	4%	$308.00
5%	$1217.82	5%	$1231.64	5%	$231.40
6%	$1187.09	6%	$1147.21	6%	$174.10
7%	$1157.46	7%	$1070.19	7%	$131.40
8%	$1128.82	8%	$1000.00	8%	$ 99.40
9%	$1101.27	9%	$ 935.82	9%	$ 75.40
10%	$1074.60	10%	$ 877.07	10%	$ 57.30
11%	$1048.88	11%	$ 824.14	11%	$ 43.70
12%	$1024.03	12%	$ 774.02	12%	$ 33.40
13%	$1000.00	13%	$ 731.56	13%	$ 25.60

Figure 6-1 Bond convexity

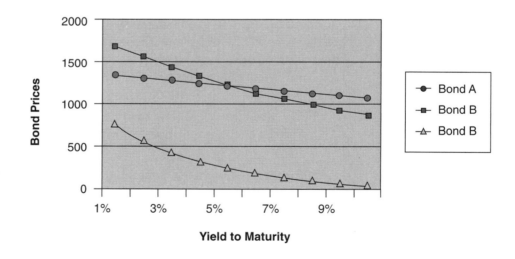

Duration is fairly accurate in determining the price of a bond when the change in yield is small. However, with large changes in yield, duration estimates the price of the bond at less than the actual price as shown by arrow B in Figure 6-2. Duration uses a linear measure rather than the actual curvilinear relationship used for convexity.

Figure 6-2 Relationship between duration and convexity

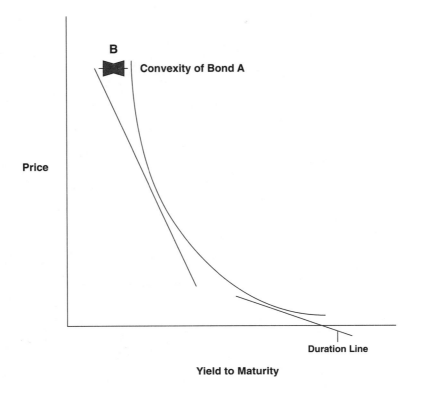

What Is the Value of Convexity for Investors?

Investors can use the concept of convexity to determine which bonds to buy. For example, when investors are faced with a choice between two bonds, both with the same duration and yield, the convexity of the bonds can assist in the decision-making process. Figure 6-3 illustrates the different convexities of two bonds, Bond 1 and Bond 2, which are trading at the same price, yield, and duration. It does not matter what happens to interest rates because Bond 1 will always trade at higher prices than Bond 2. This is because Bond 1 has a higher convexity than Bond 2.

The question is how much more would investors be willing to pay for Bond 1 over Bond 2 at different yields? The answer lies in the expected changes in interest rates. If interest rates are expected to change very little into the future, then the advantages of the changes in bond prices of Bond 1 over those of Bond 2 will not be that significant. In other words, investors might not be willing to pay premium prices for Bond 1 over Bond 2. However, if interest rates are expected to be quite volatile, investors may be more willing to pay premium prices for Bond 1 over those of Bond 2.

Figure 6-3   Convexity and duration

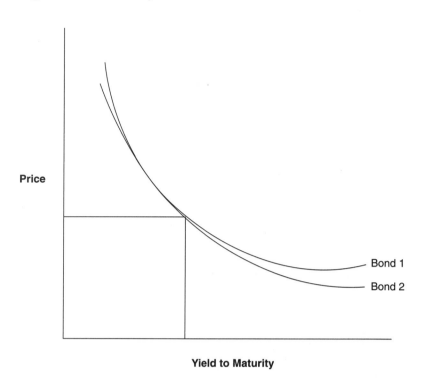

Taxes and Returns

Taxes diminish an investor's rate of return. Interest income is taxed at ordinary rates at the federal level. Currently, capital gains are taxed at lower marginal tax rates if the securities are held for the required length of time to qualify. If the securities are held for less than the prescribed time, the capital gains on bonds are taxed at the higher, ordinary tax rates.

As taxes (federal, state, and possibly local) are levied on income and capital gains, the *after tax return* of different bonds should be compared. The after tax return is calculated as follows:

After Tax Return = (1 − tax rate)(Rate before taxes)

For example, an investor in the 39.6 percent marginal tax bracket who invests in a corporate bond yielding 6.8 percent has an after tax return of 4.107 percent:

After Tax Return = (1 − .396)(.068)
= 4.107%

This can be compared to the rate of return of a municipal bond, which is tax-free at the federal level. In many cases, taxes affect the choice of investments, so effective tax planning may reduce the level of taxes paid.

Inflation, taxes, and commissions (spreads) diminish the rates of return. Investors should consider these factors to ensure that their investments yield positive returns after these have been deducted. This is particularly important during periods when inflation rates are high or interest rates are low.

Liquidity

Liquidity is defined as the ability to convert an investment into cash without losing a significant amount of the funds invested. Funds, which are to be used in a short period of time, should be invested in assets that are high in liquidity (savings accounts, CDs, Treasury bills, and money market funds). A Treasury bill can be sold very quickly with a slight concession in selling price, whereas a 20-year to maturity junk bond may not only take time to sell, but may also sell at a significant price concession. This is especially true for bonds that are thinly traded, that is, where relatively few of these bonds are traded and the trades take place only with large spreads between the bid and the ask prices. Thus, thinly traded bonds are not *marketable*, meaning they can't be sold quickly.

Risks

Investing in bonds is not risk-free. All bond instruments carry risk, but the degree of risk varies with the type of bond and the issuer. When investors sell bonds before maturity, they always run the risk of losing part of their principal if market rates of interest go up after purchase. This does not mean that investors should stash their money under mattresses because that too involves risks of loss. Different types of risk exist; therefore, investors should be aware of how they affect their bond investments. Table 6-5 lists the different types of risk that affect bond prices.

Interest Rate Risk

The price of fixed income securities changes inversely to the changes in interest rates. During periods of rising interest rates, investors holding fixed income securities find that the market prices of their bonds fall because new investors in bonds want a competitive yield. Similarly, in periods of declining interest rates, prices of fixed income securities rise. The longer the time to maturity, the greater the potential interest rate risk.

Interest rate risk can be lessened by reducing maturities and also by staggering bond investments with different maturities. Interest rate risk is minimized if investors hold onto their bonds until maturity.

Table 6-5   The Different Types of Risk

Interest Rate Risk refers to the changes in market rates of interest that have a direct effect on bond prices.

Risk of Default depends on the creditworthiness of the issuer of the bond. This is the issuer's ability to make scheduled payments of interest and repay the principal of the bonds at maturity.

Risk of Call Bonds with a call provision have *call risk*.

Purchasing Power or Inflation Risk erodes the value of the bond and value of the cash flow payments for the holder.

Reinvestment Rate Risk affects all bonds with coupon payments.

Currency Risk affect bonds denominated in foreign currencies.

Risk of Default

Credit risk varies with bond issuers. U.S. Treasury issues carry virtually no risk of default. U.S. agency debt has slightly increased risks of default. Bonds issued by state and local governments depend on the financial health of the particular issuer and their ability to raise revenue. For corporate issuers, credit risks are linked to their financial condition (status of their balance sheets, income statements, and their earnings capacities).

Independent ratings services can evaluate the credit risks of municipal and corporate bonds. Refer to Table 6-1 for a list of credit ratings ranging from the best credit quality for the issuers with the strongest financial status to the lowest ratings for issuers in default.

Credit risks can be minimized by buying bonds with investment grade ratings of A and above by S&P, which have a reduced likelihood of default, and by diversifying investments. In other words, instead of investors investing all their money in the bonds of one issuer, they should buy bonds of different issuers.

Call Risk

Many corporate and municipal bond issues are callable by their issuers. This means that the issuers can repurchase their bonds at a specified (call) price before maturity. This is beneficial to the issuer and detrimental to the investor because when interest rates drop significantly below the coupon rate of the bond, the issuer can call the bonds. The issuer then reissues new bonds at a lower coupon rate.

Call risk poses a potential loss of principal when the bonds are purchased at a premium and the call price is less than the premium price. Call risk can be anticipated by estimating the level to which the interest rates must fall before the issuer would find it worthwhile to call the issue. The call provision of a bond makes the duration of the bond uncertain.

To minimize call risks, examine the call provisions of the bond and choose bonds that are unlikely to be called. This is particularly important if an investor is contemplating the purchase of bonds trading above their par values (at a premium).

Purchasing Power Risk

Bond coupon or interest payments are generally fixed amounts; thus, the value of the payments is affected by inflation. When the rate of inflation rises, bond prices tend to fall because the purchasing power of the coupon payments is reduced. Thus, to say the least, bonds are not a good hedge against inflation. Bond prices react favorably to low rates of inflation.

To combat purchasing power risk, invest in bonds whose rates of return will be greater than anticipated inflation rates. If future inflation is anticipated, invest in floating rate bonds whose coupon rate adjusts up and down with market interest rates.

Reinvestment Rate Risk

Interest payments received may be reinvested at a lower interest rate than the coupon rate of the bond, particularly if market rates of interest decline or have declined. Zero-coupon bonds, which make no periodic interest payments, have no reinvestment risk.

Foreign Currency Risk

Foreign bonds are subject to *foreign currency risks*. A rise in the dollar against a foreign currency can decimate any returns and result in a loss in principal when the bond matures.

What to Do about Risk

It is evident that risk cannot be avoided even with the most conservative investments, such as savings accounts and Treasury bills. Even stashing money under the mattress entails risks. However, through diversification, which is investing in different types of bonds rather than investing completely in one bond issue, certain levels of risk can be minimized. By understanding and recognizing the different levels of risk for each type of bond, the total risk can be better managed in the construction of a bond portfolio.

As we have learned, a direct correlation between risk and return exists. The greater the risk of an investment, the greater the return is in order to entice investors. However, in most cases, investing in bonds with the greatest rate of return and therefore, the greatest risk, can lead to financial ruin if the odds do not pan out as expected.

Valuation of Bonds

Bond prices fluctuate up and down due to the relationship between their coupon and market rates of interest, and their creditworthiness and the length of time to maturity. After bonds are issued, they rarely trade at their par values ($1,000) in the secondary markets because interest rates are always changing. Certain bonds sell at premiums and others sell at discounts.

A mathematical formula can determine the price of a bond, but bear in mind that prices may deviate from this valuation depending on circumstances. The market price of a bond depends on the stream of the bond's coupon payments and the principal repayment in the future. Using the time value of money, this stream of future payments is discounted at market rates of interest to its present value in today's dollars. It is the same formula used for calculating the YTM. In this case, the present value is solved for using the input, I, that reflects both market rates of interest and a value of the risk premium assessed for the bond.

For example, a bond that pays a coupon interest of $100 per year and matures in three years, with market rates of interest projected at an average of six percent per year, has a price of $1,107.30 according to the valuation calculation. Thus, the price of the bond is linked to the coupon yield, market rates of interest, discount rate, and the length of time to maturity.

If the price of a U.S. Treasury note with the same coupon rate and maturity as that of a corporate bond is compared, their prices differ. The Treasury note trades at a higher price than that of the corporate bond because a greater risk of default exists with the corporate bond; thus, the price is calculated with a higher discount rate (or YTM). As a result, investors require a greater yield on the corporate bond for assuming greater risks of default. This confirms why an AAA rated corporate bond trades at a higher price than a BBB rated corporate bond if the coupon and maturity are the same. The difference in yield between the AAA and BBB rated bonds is referred to as the excess yield which issuers must pay for the extra grade of credit risk.

Bond prices fluctuate depending on investors' assessment of their risks. The greater the risk, the greater the yield, and the lower the market price.

Exercises

1. What is the importance of bond ratings?

2. Discuss the relevance of the different types of yields.

3. Discuss how the use of the concepts, convexity, and duration, can assist investors in the management of their bond portfolios.

4. Discuss the major risks that affect bonds.

End Notes

Mayo, Herbert B.: *Investments,* 3rd ed., Dryden Press, New York, 1991.

Chapter 7

Risk versus Return: Enhancing Investment Performance

Techniques for Assessing and Balancing Risk and Return

The previous chapter emphasized the necessity for recognizing the different types of risk involved when investing in bonds. The financial markets use interest rates to set prices for bond securities. A risk factor accompanies this rate of interest. For example, two factors primarily determine the rate on a Treasury security: the supply and demand for money in the economy, and the rate of inflation. The rate of return on a Treasury bill is also referred to as the *risk-less rate*, as it has no credit risk or risk of default. For bonds subject to credit and default risks, a risk premium is added to this risk-less rate. In addition, the marketability of the securities should also be considered. These concepts are illustrated in Figure 7-1.

Corporate and municipal bond issues are assessed a risk premium, which include two major types of risk: the business and financial risk.

Business risk involves the variability in the returns of the assets invested. For example, the bonds of an oil-exploration company or a start-up dot.com company are riskier than those of established banks or retail companies. Hence, the earnings of the former two companies are less predictable and likely to be more volatile than the earnings of the latter two companies. The type of business determines the business risk and the level of risk for the company's bonds and common stocks.

Financial risk involves the variability of returns attributable to the type of financing of the assets. A company that has financed the major-

Figure 7-1   Relationship between risk and return

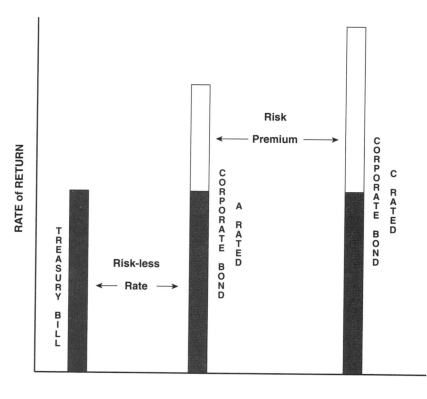

ity of its assets with debt may be perceived as riskier than a similar company in the same industry that has used common stock to finance its assets. Financial risk increases with the level of debt that is used to finance assets. Consequently, the risk of default increases with higher levels of outstanding debt. This is because companies need to earn enough income to service their interest payments and repayment of principal. A default on the payment of interest and/or principal can trigger bankruptcy proceedings by bondholders.

The amount attached to the risk premium can vary among potential investors. Conceivably, investors could attach different risk premiums to the same bond. This is illustrated in Figure 7-2. The same corporate bond could be valued differently by two different investors, prompting one investor to sell and one to buy. The risk premium is built into the in-

Figure 7-2   Risk premium and bond prices

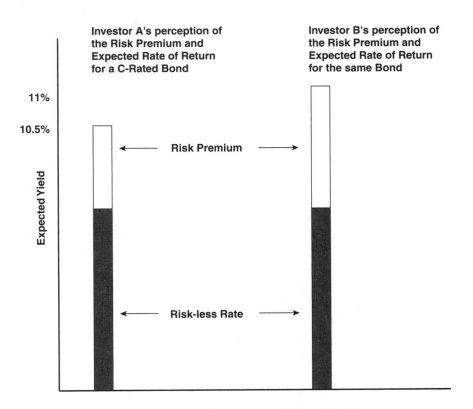

Price of the C-rated bond with a coupon of 10%, maturing in 10 years with an expected rate of return (yield) of 10.5% is $969.90 per bond.

Price of the C-rated bond with a coupon of 10%, maturing in 10 years with an expected rate of return (yield) of 11% is $941.10 per bond.

Investors with these expected rates of return will not pay more than these prices for this particular bond.

vestor's required or expected rate of return for an investment, which also determines the price the investor is willing to pay for that investment. An investor who attaches a higher risk premium requires a greater expected rate of return and will pay a lower price for the same bond than an investor with a lower expected rate of return.

The rate of return on a bond depends on the type of bond, the level of risk, and the time period to maturity. U.S. agency bonds have a slightly increased risk of default for the same maturities over U.S. Treasury bonds. Similarly, a junk bond with an S&P rating of CCC has to pay a considerably higher yield than a bond with an A rating in order to entice investors.

What Rate of Return Should One Expect?

Although no specific answer exists, the following factors need to be considered:

1. The spectrum of rates for different types of fixed income securities.
2. The level of risk that gives the comfort of being able to sleep well at night.
3. The types of bonds and maturities that match the investor's financial needs, objectives, and time horizons.

Market rates of interest have fallen over the past nine years through 1999. Through 1999 to mid-2000, the Federal Reserve Bank hiked interest rates. Bond investors are interested in the actions of the Federal Reserve Board because of the influence interest rates have on bond prices. Bond prices of existing issues fall when interest rates go up and rise when interest rates fall. Table 7-1 lists the yields of the different types of maturities at the time of this writing. Worksheet 7-1 provides the framework for investors to fill in the yields and maturities of the different types of bonds, to assist in the decision making process of determining the expected returns from these bonds and the types of bonds to buy.

Generally, by increasing the level of risk and extending the maturities of bonds, investors can increase their rates of return. However, from an examination of Table 7-1, this is not altogether true for Treasuries. Two-year Treasury notes offer higher yields than longer maturity Treasury bonds. This is due primarily to two factors:

1. The hikes in short-term interest rates by the Federal Reserve.
2. The repurchase of 30-year Treasuries by the government, which has reduced the supply.

Table 7-1 Rates for the Different Types of Bonds

Treasuries

10-year U.S. Treasury Notes	6.06%
5-year U.S. Treasury Notes	6.27%
2-year U.S. Treasury Notes	6.45%

U.S. Agency Issues

10 + years U.S. Agency Bonds	6.92%
1-10 year U.S. Agency Bonds	6.26%

Municipal Issues

22+ year Revenue Bonds (AA)	5.94%
12-22 year Government Obligation Bonds (AA)	5.68%
7-12 year Government Obligation Bonds (AA)	5.04%

Corporate Bonds

10+ year AAA-AA rated	7.87%
10+ year A-BBB	8.36%
1-10 year AAA-AA	7.33%
1-10 year A-BBB	7.65%

Money Market Securities

3-month Treasury Bill	5.852%
3-month Bank Certificate of Deposit	5.98%*
90-day Commercial Paper	6.57%

*Average rates by New York banks for amounts greater than $100,000. Rates as of June 19, 2000.

Basing investments on the greatest yield can also be disastrous. Raising the level of risk by choosing Agency securities and good quality corporate and municipal bonds over Treasuries can increase returns as shown in the following list:

10 + year Agency Bonds	6.92%
10 + year AAA Corporate Bonds	7.87%
12-22 year GO Bonds	5.68% (Before tax yield at the marginal tax bracket of 39.6% is 9.4%)

Municipal bonds become more attractive to investors in high marginal tax brackets as shown in the example above. The before tax return share of a government obligation municipal bond is 9.4 percent, which is far greater than Agency or corporate bonds of the same maturities with similar credit ratings. See Worksheet 7-2 for the formula that converts the after tax yields of municipals to before tax yields.

Going for the highest yields and ignoring risk does not always produce high returns over a period of time. For example, choosing low quality corporate bond issues that go into default translates into a loss of principal and negative returns. Investors must decide whether the additional returns of lower quality bonds warrant the additional credit and default risks. This is known as the risk-return trade-off. Investors should choose the level of risk with which they feel comfortable.

Worksheet 7-1

Comparison of the Rates for the Different Types of Bonds

1. Fill in the different yields.

Treasuries
30-year U.S. Treasury Bonds	_____%
10-year U.S. Treasury Notes	_____%
5-year U.S. Treasury Notes	_____%
2-year U.S. Treasury Notes	_____%

U.S. Agency Issues
10 + years U.S. Agency Bonds	_____%
1-10 year U.S. Agency Bonds	_____%

Municipal Issues
22+ year Revenue Bonds (AA)	_____%
12-22 year Government Obligation Bonds (AA)	_____%
7-12 year Government Obligation Bonds (AA)	_____%

Corporate Bonds
10+ year AAA-AA rated	_____%
10+ year A-BBB	_____%
1-10 year AAA-AA	_____%
1-10 year A-BBB	_____%

Money Market Securities
3-month Treasury Bill	_____%
3-month Bank Certificate of Deposit	_____%
90-day Commercial Paper	_____%

2. Analyze the yield differential between the different types of securities for the different maturities.

3. Determine the "acceptable" level of risk.

4. Fill in the best buys.

On the other hand, by playing it too safe and investing in securities with minimal risks, investors are assured of low, minimal returns. To receive higher returns, investors have to accept greater risks.

As pointed out earlier, when investors extend the maturities on their investments without regard for their financial needs, the result can be a loss in principal due to interest rate risk. The other extreme is just as bad: when investors invest every cent of their savings in short-term bank accounts and money market funds. This approach ensures the safety of principal, but produces low yields. Determine the yield spreads between short- and long-term maturities and also the spreads between the different types of bonds.

Worksheet 7-2

How to Convert Municipal Bond Yields to Before Tax Yields

The before tax yields of municipal bonds should be calculated and compared with the before tax yields of other types of bonds.

$$\text{Before Tax Yield} = \frac{\text{Municipal Bond Yield}}{(1 - \text{Investor's Marginal Tax Rate})}$$

Example:
Find the before tax yield for a Massachusetts Regional School Bond yielding 4.7 percent and maturing in two years for an investor in the 39.6 percent marginal tax bracket:

$$\text{Before Tax Yield} = \frac{4.7\%}{(1 - .396)}$$
$$= 7.781\%$$

Find the before tax yield for the above municipal bond for an investor in the 15 percent marginal tax bracket:

$$\text{Before Tax Yield} = \frac{4.7\%}{(1 - .15)}$$
$$= 5.53\%$$

Compare the before tax yields of municipals with those of Treasuries, agency, and corporate bonds to assist in the purchase decision.

Increasing yields within acceptable risk levels can enhance overall returns for investors. Consider the future values of two investments with $1,000 invested in a bank savings accounts yielding three percent versus $1,000 invested in a money market mutual fund yielding five percent p.a. over a one-year, five-year, and ten-year period.

		End of Yr. 1	End of Yr. 5	End of Yr. 10
Bank Savings Account	3%	$1,030.00	$1,159.30	$1,343.90
Money Market Mutual Fund	5%	$1,050.00	$1,276.30	$1,628.90

By investing in money market mutual funds with an additional yield of two percent over a 10-year period, an investor can increase his/her investment by $285.00 ($1,628.90 – $1,343.90) for each $1,000 of principal invested.

Two important factors affect the rates of return earned on investments: inflation and taxes. If an investment earns four percent per year and inflation is three percent for the same period, the real rate of return is only one percent. If inflation increases to four percent or more, investors holding fixed income securities yielding four percent will not be jumping for joy at the prospect of earning zero or negative returns. This is why market prices of long-term bonds decline so rapidly when inflation increases. Bondholders receive fixed amounts of interest. Market prices of existing bonds on the secondary markets decline in price in order to make their rates of return more competitive (to include the rate of inflation), which will entice investors to buy them.

When inflation is anticipated, choose investments that yield rates of return that are greater than the anticipated rate of inflation. In times of rising inflation, investors tend to avoid long-term fixed income securities and invest in short-term investments (money market accounts and Treasury bills), where rates of return can increase with the rates of inflation.

Various strategies, such as laddering and the barbell approach, can be used in the choice of investments with different maturities. Refer to the discussion of these in Chapter 9, "Managing a Bond Portfolio." The question of whether to choose long-term or short-term maturities depends on the outlook for future interest rates. The yield curve provides some clues to future yields.

The Yield Curve and How to Use It

The *yield curve* depicts the relationship between the yield and the length of time to maturity of bonds with the same level of risk. Figure 7-3 shows the yield curve for U. S. Treasury securities for June 21, 2000. Yields for the three-month, six-month, one-year, two-year, five-year, 10-year, 20-year, and 30-year Treasury securities were plotted. These were as follows:

3-month Treasury bill	5.63%
6-month Treasury bill	5.92%
1-year Treasury bill	6.46%
2-year Treasury Note	6.43%
10-year Treasury Note	6.02%
30 year Treasury Bond	5.89%

By examining the yield curve on any particular day, investors have a snapshot of the different yields of various maturities for different types of securities. Figure 7-3 shows the yield curve for Treasuries, but this can also be done for other bond types such as municipals, corporate bonds, and agency bonds.

Note the shape of the curve in Figure 7-3. It has an upward slope from three-months to one-year, a leveling off for the one to two-year maturities and then a declining curve for longer maturities through 30 years. This is called an inverted curve, which is generally atypical. Typically, yield curves assume four general shapes: rising, flat, falling,

Figure 7-3 Treasury yield curve (as of June 21, 2000)

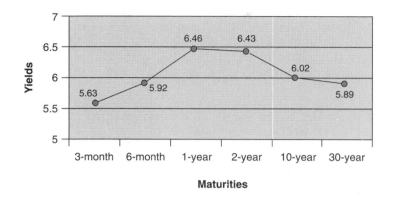

and humped such as Figure 7-3. The most common is the rising yield curve. One would expect an upward sloping curve because the longer the maturity, the greater is the bondholder's exposure to risks. Hence, bond issuers tend to pay more to compensate investors for these risks.

The yield curve has had a downward slope where short-term yields have exceeded long-term yields on only a few occasions historically. In other words, yields decline as maturities increase. This happened in 1979, 1981, and 1982.

An inverted yield curve means that investors are taking greater risks for lesser returns by extending maturities. The reason for the inversion can be explained as follows:

> The Federal Reserve raised short-term interest rates while the prices of 30-year bonds rallied, which depressed their yields. Part of the reason for this rally was the U.S. government's program of buying back 30-year Treasuries, which reduced the supply. The 10-year Treasury was caught in the middle and did not move much.

To get a better feeling for yields, the yield curve should be drawn for several weeks and then compared. Figure 7-4 shows the yield curve using two sets of data: June 21, and June 28, 2000. Yields of short-term (3-month and 6-month) Treasuries for June 28 increased slightly over those of the previous week, whereas yields of one- and two-year Treasury notes remained the same. The 30-year yield for June 28 declined to 5.9 percent due to the increased repurchase of the securities by the Treasury Department. This action increased the price of the securities and depressed the yield.

The shape of the yield curve changes daily with the changes in yield due to fluctuations in market rates of interest. A number of theories explain the shape of the yield curve. Table 7-2 discusses the three most quoted theories: the expectation theory, the liquidity preference theory, and the market segmentation theory.

Figure 7-4   Treasury Yield Curve for June 21 and June 28, 2000

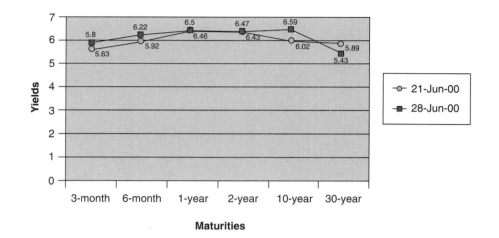

Table 7-2   Theories that Explain the Shape of the Yield Curve

Expectation Theory	According to this theory, expected future interest rates determine the shape of the yield curve. If investors expect future interest rates to rise, they will invest their funds into short-term maturities. Consequently, long-term security rates will increase as prices come down, making them more attractive to investors. On the other hand, if expectations are for lower long-term interest rates in the future, investors will buy long-term maturities to lock-in the higher yields. This pushes prices of these securities up and the yields go down.
Liquidity Preference Theory	This theory adds the element of risk into the expectations of future interest rates. Generally, investors prefer short-term maturities. They would prefer longer-term maturities only if they expect long-term interest rates to rise enough to compensate them for the risks of the expected fluctuations in future interest rates. In other words, investors require an additional amount of return, called a risk premium, in order to expose themselves to the future uncertainties of longer-term interest rates. If they do not expect to receive this additional risk premium, they will continue to invest in short-term maturities and roll them over at maturity into new short-term securities.
Market Segmentation Theory	This theory is based on the preferences of institutional investors for particular types of maturities, which would then determine the yield curve through supply and demand of these securities. For example, life insurance companies invest more in longer maturity bonds generally, whereas banks stick to short- and medium-term maturities. Investors with low market risk prefer short-term maturities, which provide stability of principal. On the other side of the coin are long-term maturity bond investors who prefer income to stability of principal.

How the Yield Curve Can Help Investors

The yield curve can assist investors in choosing the maturities of their fixed income securities. By examining the current yield curve, investors have information on the yields of the different maturities, which can help them in their decision-making about maturities.

The yield curve in Figure 7-3 shows a relatively small spread between the three-month Treasury bill of 5.63 percent and a 30-year Treasury bond of 5.89 percent. With this kind of curve, investors are not receiving much more yield for the risks that they are taking by extending their maturities. In fact, the 10-year Treasury note earned a greater yield than the 30-year Treasury bond. This anomaly can be explained by the fact that the 10-year bond was not as actively traded as the 30-year bond. In other words, it cost more to buy the 30-year bond, which pushed the yield down.

Yield curves can be constructed for other types of bonds besides Treasury securities, which can be used to assess the risks of extending maturities.

Investors should keep the following in mind:

- Most of the time, the yield curve is sloping upward, whereas yields on long-term securities are greater than the yields of short-term securities.
- Changes in the yield curve generally take the form of shifts up and down over time. When short-term yields are rising, long-term yields generally rise. Similarly, when short-term yields are falling, long-term yields also fall.
- During a recession, short-term yields fall faster than long-term yields, and during a period of economic expansion, short-term yields rise faster than long-term yields.

Investment Plans

An investor should have a plan regarding his/her investments. Buying stocks and bonds is relatively easy, but knowing which ones to buy and how they fit into a portfolio is more difficult. The investment plan is based on the investor's objectives, which determine the time horizons, risk-return level, and types of securities to choose for the portfolio. The questionnaire in Figure 7-5 gives the investor some guidance with regard to time horizons, risk tolerance, and types of investments to choose.

What works for one investor most likely will not work for another. An evaluation of the answers to the questions in Figure 7-5 will assist the investor in his/her allocation of investment assets. Having a plan

Figure 7-5 Questionnaire to Determine the Types of Assets in an Investor's
Portfolio

1. Does the investor have an emergency fund consisting of at least three months
salary?

  a. No
  b. Yes, but less than three months
  c. Yes

Investment Planning: If not, funds should be invested in liquid assets (money
market securities) to avoid any loss in principal when the money is needed. The first
step is to establish an emergency fund, after which an investment fund can be established.

2. When will the investment funds (over and above your emergency fund) be
needed?

  a. Within one year
  b. Within five years
  c. Between five and 10 years
  d. Longer than 10 years

Investment Planning: If the money is needed within one year, the investor
needs to invest in liquid investments. Money needed within a five year time frame
should be invested in short-term securities. Investments with a longer than five year
time frame can be invested more aggressively depending on the investor's circumstances and the investor's risk tolerance, such as long-term bonds and stocks.

3. What percentage of the total investment funds is in retirement accounts?

  a. Below 25 percent
  b. Between 25 and 50 precent
  c. Between 51 and 75 percent
  d. Above 75 percent

Investment Planning: The lower the percentage in retirement funds, the more
aggressively the funds can be invested.

4. How stable is income from employment likely to be over the next five years?

  a. Likely to decrease
  b. Likely to stay the same
  c. Likely to keep pace with inflation
  d. Likely to increase above inflation

Investment Planning: If uncertainty arises about future earnings, an investor
may have to withdraw funds from investments, which means that a corresponding
amount should be invested in liquid securities. If investors see a good chance that
employment earnings will increase in the future, investment choices can be more
aggressive.

5. How many dependents does the investor have?

   a. None
   b. One
   c. Two
   d. More than two

   Investment Planning: The greater the dependents, the greater the responsibilities. Generally, this may require being a little more conservative in the investment approach.

6. What percentage of earnings goes towards paying off debts (including a mortgage)?

   a. Less than 10 percent
   b. Between 10 and 25 percent
   c. Between 25 and 50 percent
   d. Over 50 percent

   Investment Planning: The higher the percentage of the earnings that goes towards paying off debts, the greater the likelihood that an investor may need to dip into his investment account, which may prompt for a more conservative approach.

7. With regard to investment assets, where on the scale below is the comfort level?

Willing to invest	Comfortable with	Uncomfortable when
aggressively for the maximum possible growth even if there is the potential for losses due to market fluctuations.	some level of fluctuations in funds in order to achieve reasonable levels of growth	investment funds go down in value due to market fluctuations.

   Investment Planning: Appetite for risk will determine whether investments can be aggressive, somewhere in the middle, or conservative.

8. Does the investor feel comfortable when potential returns are increased by taking on more risk?

   a. Yes
   b. No

   Investment Planning: If yes, the investor can be a little more aggressive in his investments. If no, the investor should invest in those assets that he/she feels comfortable with.

9. What rate of return is expected from investments?

   a. Keep ahead of inflation while seeking stability of principal.

continues

b. Earn returns that are greater than inflation even if some potential for loss in principal exists.

c. Earn high returns regardless of the increased potential for loss in principal.

Investment Planning: Acceptance of risks of loss in principal will determine whether an investor should invest aggressively, conservatively, or somewhere in the middle.

10. What are the objectives for investment assets?

a. Investment Income
b. Long term capital growth

Investment Planning: If income is needed, the investment assets should be allocated more towards bonds. Long-term capital growth can be obtained from diversified investments in common stocks.

Source: Adapted from Fidelity Investments Institutional Service Company Inc.

that includes a broad mix of asset types is the most important part of investing. Examples of these plans are shown in Table 7-4. Individual investments should be chosen only after deciding on an asset allocation plan.

Selection of Individual Investments

The investor's objectives determine the time horizons and acceptable risk levels for the different individual investments. Funds for immediate needs and emergency purposes should be *liquid*, that is, in investments that can be converted easily into cash without a loss in principal. These investments include money market mutual funds, checking accounts, and savings accounts, which are readily convertible into cash. By increasing the time horizon from immediate needs to short-term needs, investors can marginally increase their rates of return by investing in CDs, Treasury bills, and commercial paper. Of these, only Treasury bills are *marketable*, which means that they can be sold on the secondary market before maturity.

These individual investments (savings accounts, CDs, money market mutual funds, Treasury bills, and commercial paper) provide some income that is taxable and liquid, but not marketable (except for

Treasury bills). These types of investments do not offer the possibilities of capital gains. Although investors will not lose any of their principal by investing in this group of investments, they run the risk that the returns from these investments may not keep up with inflation.

Intermediate term objectives stretch several years into the future, such as the purchase of a car, house, appliance, and/or the funding of a child's education, in addition to emergency uses of funds that crop up in the future. These investments need to produce a greater rate of return than leaving the money in a savings account or in short-term money market securities. Short- to intermediate-term bonds offer increased rates of return over money market securities, as well as the possibility of capital gains or losses if the investor needs the money before maturity. Generally, returns are greater from intermediate-term securities, but they are not as liquid as short-term securities. Treasury notes and bonds have no credit risk or risk of default. This means that Treasury notes and bonds require no need to diversify, whereas with corporate, municipal, and agency bonds, it is a good idea for investors to spread the risks of default (and call) by buying the bonds of different issuers.

Financing a child's education in five years requires an investment that is relatively safe. Most people would not gamble with the money earmarked for their children's education. Thus, the credit quality of the issuer is important. Similarly, if the yield spread between Treasuries and other types of intermediate bonds is not significant, it may be advantageous to stick with Treasury securities. This is because they are free of default risk and their interest payments are tax-free at the state and local levels of taxation. However, if the yield differential on other types of bonds (agency bonds, corporate bonds, and municipals) over Treasuries is large, investors should invest in these other bond types. Once again, it becomes important to choose a diversified portfolio rather than invest all the intermediate term funds in the securities of one issuer. Federal taxes and changes in the individual tax rates can steer the choice towards municipal bonds.

Long-term objectives, such as saving for retirement or an infant's college education in 18 years, require investments that offer long-term growth prospects as well as greater returns. The level of risk that can be withstood on these investments will depend on the individual investor's circumstances.

A more conservative long-term portfolio would consist of long-term bonds, "blue chip" stocks, and conservative growth stocks. The emphasis of this strategy is to invest in good quality bonds and stocks of established companies, which pay dividends and offer the prospects of steady growth over a long period of time. Securities offering capital growth are important even in conservative portfolios, which provide some cover against any possible erosion in future purchasing power due to inflation.

A more speculative portfolio where the investor can absorb greater levels of risk and strive for greater growth and returns would include growth stocks, stocks of small emerging companies, convertible bonds, junk bonds, real estate, options, commodities, and futures. By including the last three types of investments, options, commodities, and futures, the author is not advocating that these should play a major role in a portfolio. They are for speculative investors who understand these investments and these types of securities should account for no more than five percent of the total portfolio. Foreign bonds and stocks should also be considered, but investors should do their homework first so that they understand the risks fully. International mutual funds may be more helpful to spread some of the risks, although currency risks always exist when investing in off-shore investments.

Some investors may not feel comfortable buying individual bonds and stocks, so they should stick with mutual funds. Investors willing to make their own investment decisions on individual securities can eliminate the fees and expenses charged by mutual funds. However, they need to make sure that brokerage commissions charged are discounted and competitive. Many full service brokers will discount their commissions if they know that the investors have done their homework and will lose them to discount brokers if the commissions are not matched. Online investing can reduce commissions significantly.

When considering the different types of securities to choose for a portfolio, investors should weigh the characteristics of the type of investment along with the risks to assist them in their overall choice. See Worksheet 7-3 for an overview of a hypothetical portfolio for a balanced portfolio using the asset allocation model in Figure 7-6.

Figure 7-6 Asset Allocation Models

Conservative Portfolio A portfolio where the investment goals are to preserve capital with some growth. The weighting is geared towards high quality bonds and some common stocks for growth.

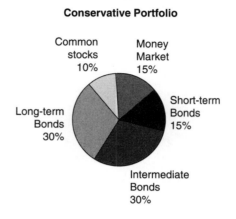

Conservative Portfolio

Balanced Portfolio Includes a greater percentage of common stocks, which provides the capital growth, as well as keeping a large percentage of assets in fixed income securities, which provide income.

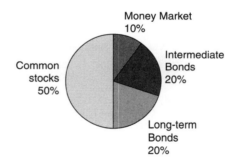

Balanced Portfolio

Aggressive Portfolio Weighted more towards common stocks, which provide capital growth.

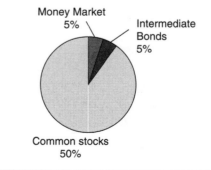

Aggressive Portfolio

Worksheet 7-3

Balanced Portfolio for Investor A

Balanced Portfolio for Investor A	Years to Maturity	Amount
Money Market Mutual Funds	0-1	20,000
Intermediate Term Bonds		
U.S. Treasury Note 6 1/2% 2/02	2	5,000
Raytheon Co. 7.9% 3/1/03	3	10,000
Fannie Mae 7.125% 2/15/05	5	15,000
Tulsa Authority Rev. 6.625% 10/01/07	7	10,000
Long Term Bonds		
Metro Trans. Auth. N.Y. 6.375% 7/01/10	10	20,000
U.S. Treasury Bond 9 7/8% 11/15	15	20,000
Common Stock		
200 shares Intel Corp.		14,000
200 shares Motorola Corp.		6,000
200 shares Ford Motor Corp.		8,600
200 shares Exxon Mobil		15,600
200 shares Johnson & Johnson		20,400
200 shares Cisco Systems		12,800
200 shares AOL		10,600
100 shares International Paper		3,200
200 shares Pepsi Cola		8,800
Total Portfolio		200,000

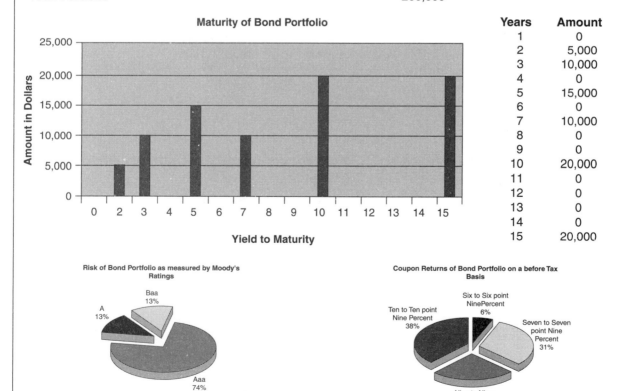

Years	Amount
1	0
2	5,000
3	10,000
4	0
5	15,000
6	0
7	10,000
8	0
9	0
10	20,000
11	0
12	0
13	0
14	0
15	20,000

Maturity of Bond Portfolio

Amount in Dollars / Yield to Maturity

Risk of Bond Portfolio as measured by Moody's Ratings

Baa 13%
A 13%
Aaa 74%

Coupon Returns of Bond Portfolio on a before Tax Basis

Six to Six point Nine Percent 6%
Ten to Ten point Nine Percent 38%
Seven to Seven point Nine Percent 31%
Nine to Nine point Nine Percent 25%

The bond portfolio from the example in Worksheet 7-3 shows the maturity schedule, the risk, and coupon returns.

Time Horizon

The schedule of bond maturities should match the time horizons of the investor's objectives to avoid the potential risk of loss from selling securities before maturity. To determine the schedule of the intermediate-term and long-term bond portfolio, fill in the amounts of the maturities from years one through 15.

The maturity dates are listed after the coupon yields in Worksheet 7-3. For example, the U.S. Treasury notes mature in February 2002 and total $5,000. Raytheon Company bonds mature in March 2003, and the maturity amount is $10,000. The table shows the maturity schedule and maturity amounts in dollars for all of the bonds in the portfolio.

Risk

The relative risk of this bond portfolio is measured by Moody's ratings. These ratings give an idea of the relative credit risk and risk of default for each bond. The schedule for the graph was composed as follows:

Bond	Moody's Ratings	Amount	
U.S. Treasury Notes	Aaa *	$ 5,000	
Fannie Mae	Aaa	15,000	
Metro Transp. Auth	Aaa	20,000	
U.S. Treasury Bonds	Aaa *	20,000	
			$60,000
Tulsa Authority	A	10,000	
			$10,000
Raytheon Company	Baa	10,000	
			$10,000
Total			**$80,000**

U.S. Treasury securities have no credit or default risk and are grouped with the Aaa Category.

Percentage Composition of Risk		
Aaa	$60,000/80,000	75%
A	$10,000/80,000	12.5%
Baa	$10,000/80,000	12.5%

This bond portfolio is composed primarily of high quality bonds with only 12.5 percent in bonds with ratings lower than Aaa. These are the Raytheon Company bonds, which are medium quality with Baa ratings. By switching to lower quality bonds, investors may improve their returns, but this comes with the price of increased credit and default risk. Diversification into different types of bonds such as corporate, municipal, agency, and mortgage-backed bonds may also reduce the risk of loss.

Return

The pie chart shows the distribution of the coupon yields as a percentage of the total bond portfolio. The after tax yields of the two municipal bond issues were converted to before tax yields as follows, using Investor A's marginal tax rate of 39.6 percent:

Tulsa Authority After Tax Coupon 6.625 Percent

Before Tax Yield = 6.625/ (1–39.6%)
= 10.96%

Metro Transit After Tax Coupon 6.375 Percent

Before Tax Yield = 6.375%/ (1–39.6%)
= 10.55%

	Coupon	Amount	Total	% of Total
U.S. Treasury Notes	6.5%	$ 5,000		
Raytheon Company	7.9%	10,000		
Fannie Mae	7.125%	15,000		
Tulsa Authority	10.96%	10,000		
U.S. Treasury Bonds	9.78%	20,000		
Metro Transp. Auth.	10.55%	20,000		
6-6.9% Return	6.5%	$ 5,000	5,000	6.25%
7-7.9% Return	7.9%	10,000		
	7.125%	15,000		
			$25,000	31.25%
9-9.5% Return	9.78%	20,000	$20,000	25%
10-10.9% Return	10.96%	10,000		
	10.55%	20,000		
			$30,000	37.5%
Total		**$80,000**		

Analyzing a portfolio in such a way once or twice a year gives the investor a more precise picture of the maturity schedule, risk, and return of the portfolio.

Exercises

1. Explain the risk premium on a bond.

2. Explain what is meant by the risk-return trade-off.

3. Explain how the yield curve can assist bond investors.

Chapter 8

Diversifying: Bond Mutual Funds

Mutual funds enable investors who do not have the time, knowledge, or expertise of different financial instruments to invest their money in stock, bonds, and money market instruments. So many mutual funds are available to choose from, numbering in the thousands, that investors should be as careful in their selection of mutual funds as they are when they invest in individual securities. Three steps can facilitate the decision-making process of which mutual funds to invest in:

1. Understand mutual funds and how they work.
2. Determine the types of investments that the fund invests in.
3. Evaluate the performance of the fund from the prospectus.

By following these steps, investors can narrow their choices of the different types of funds, placing them in a better position to make a decision as to the overall choice of fund.

Mutual Funds and How They Work

All mutual funds work in similar ways. The investment company that sponsors the mutual fund sells shares to investors and then invests the funds in a portfolio of securities. Pooling the investor's funds enables the fund to diversify their acquisition of different securities such as stocks for stock funds and bonds for bond funds. The *objectives* of the mutual fund determine the type of investments chosen. For example, if a bond fund's objectives are to provide tax-free income, the fund invests in municipal bonds. The fund buys different municipal bond issues to achieve a diversified portfolio, which also reduces the risk of loss due to default.

When interest on these securities is paid, fund shareholders receive a proportionate share. Consequently, an investor who invests $1,000 receives the same rate of return as another investor who invests $100,000 in the same fund.

When the prices of the securities fluctuate, the total value of the fund is affected. These fluctuations in price are due to many different factors, such as the intrinsic risk of the types of securities in the portfolio, as well as economic, market, and political factors. The objectives of the fund are important because they indicate the type and quality of the investments chosen by the fund. From these objectives, investors are better able to assess the risks that the fund is willing to take to improve income (return) and/or capital gains.

Investment companies offer three different types of mutual funds:

•   Open-end mutual funds.
•   Closed-end mutual funds.
•   Unit investment trusts.

Table 8-1 outlines the differences in these investment companies.

Table 8–1   Closed-End Funds and Unit Investment Trusts versus Open-end Funds

Closed-End Funds and Unit Investment Trusts	Open-End Funds
1. Issue a fixed number of shares, which are sold to ordinary shareholders. 2. Shares (after issue) are traded on the stock exchanges. 3. Shares may trade at, above, or below net asset values. 4. Share prices depend not only on the fundamentals, but also on the supply and demand for the shares. 5. Closed-end funds do not mature. Unit investment trusts do. 6. Unit trusts invest in bond securities which are held to maturity.	1. Issue an unlimited number of shares. 2. Shares (including new shares) may be bought (and sold) from (to) the fund. 3. Shares trade at net asset values. 4. Share prices depend on the fundamentals of the assets in the fund. 5. Open-end funds do not mature except for zero-coupon funds.

Open-End Mutual Funds versus Closed-End Funds

Two types of mutual funds are available: open-end and closed-end. With *open-end* funds, the fund's investment company issues an unlimited number of shares. Investors may buy more shares from the mutual fund company or sell them back to the mutual fund company, which means that the number of shares will increase or decrease, respectively. *Closed-end* funds issue a fixed number of shares and when all are sold, they do not issue any more. In other words, they have a fixed capital structure. Investors who want to invest in these existing closed-end funds after all the shares have been sold must buy them from shareholders who are willing to sell them in the market. Shares of closed-end funds are listed on stock exchanges and over-the-counter markets, whereas shares of open-end mutual funds are bought from and sold to the investment company sponsoring the fund. Thus, share prices of closed-end funds are not only a function of their net-asset values, but also the supply and demand for the stock in the market.

Another type of closed-end fund is the unit investment trust. *Unit investment trusts* issue a fixed number of shares, which are originally sold by the sponsor of the trust. The proceeds from the sale are used to buy bonds for the trust, which are held to maturity. Unlike open-end and closed-end bond funds, no active trading of the bonds in the portfolio occurs. Consequently, unit investment trusts have no active management of trusts, which should mean lower management fees, but this is not always the case. Trusts have a maturity date and the proceeds are then returned to the shareholders of the trust.

All unit investment trusts charge a sales commission, whereas with open-end funds, investors have a choice between the purchase of funds that do not charge sales commissions and those that do have sales charges.

Open-end funds are the focus of the discussion for the balance of this chapter. The information may also be applied to closed-end funds except for the differences as noted in Table 8-1.

Open-end Mutual Funds

Investors invest their money in mutual funds by buying shares at the *net asset value* (NAV). The fund's NAV price of the shares is the total assets minus the liabilities of the fund divided by the number of outstanding shares.

It is easy for a fund to determine the market value of its assets at the end of each trading day. For instance, if the fund is a balanced fund, which means that it invests in both common stocks and bonds, the fund uses the closing prices of the stocks and bonds for the day. The prices are multiplied by the number of shares of stocks and bonds that the fund owns. The resulting totals are added up and any liabilities that the fund has (for example, accrued fees) are subtracted. The total is then divided by the number of shares outstanding in the fund to give the NAV price per share. Worksheet 8-1 has a numerical example that shows how the NAV is calculated.

The NAV changes daily due to the market fluctuations of the stock and bond prices. Table 8-2 outlines the importance of NAVs for investors.

The NAVs of the different funds are quoted in the daily newspapers. Table 8-3 shows how mutual funds were listed in the newspapers several years ago to illustrate the importance of differentiating the sales commission charged on some funds. Currently, only the NAVs are reported in the newspapers, making it difficult to differentiate the load funds from the no-load funds by looking at the quotes. Potential investors in the funds would have to call the investment companies or visit their Web sites to determine whether or not they have sales commissions (loads).

In the Vanguard Group, the *Ginnie Mae* (GNMA) fund, which invests in bonds (as opposed to the STAR fund, which invests in stocks and bonds), has a NAV of $10.53 per share. The investment objective col-

Worksheet 8-1

How the Net Asset Value Is Determined

Market Value of Stocks and Bonds	$100,000,000
Minus Total Liabilities	−150,000
Net Worth	$99,850,000
Number of Shares Outstanding	7,500,000
Net Asset Value	$13.31 (99,850,000/7,500,000)

Table 8-2 Importance of Net Asset Values (NAV) for Investors

1. The price that is used to determine the value of the investor's holding in the mutual fund (number of shares held multiplied by the net asset value price per share).
2. The price at which new shares are purchased or redeemed.

Table 8-3 Mutual Fund Quotations*

	Inv. Obj.	NAV	Offer Price	NAV Change
Vanguard Group:				
STAR	S&B	13.39	NL	+ 0.07
GNMA	BND	10.53	NL	+ 0.02
IG Corp	BND	9.20	NL	+ 0.02
Westcore:				
GNMA	BND	16.45	17.23	+ 0.02
ST Govt.	BST	15.87	16.19	. . .

*Source: *Wall Street Journal*
This table has been previously published by Esme Faerber in *All About Bonds and Bond Mutual Funds,* McGraw-Hill, New York, 2000.

umn indicates the types of investments a fund will invest in. A *NL* in the offer price column signifies that the fund is a no-load fund, which means that investors can buy and sell shares at the NAV of $10.53. The NAV change column signifies the change in price from the previous day's closing price. The Vanguard GNMA fund closed $0.02 up from the previous day's closing price.

The two fund examples in the Westcore Group are load funds because they charge a sales commission to buy and sell their shares. This is evidenced by the offer price, which is different from the NAV price. To buy shares in Westcore's Short-Term Government Fund, investors would buy at the offer price of $16.19 per share and sell their shares at the NAV price ($15.87). The difference ($0.32 per share) between the offer price ($16.19) and the NAV price ($15.87) represents the load or commission that investors pay to buy or sell shares in this fund.

Shareholders receive monthly and annual statements showing the interest, dividends, capital gains and losses, and other relevant data that should be retained for tax purposes. In fact, not only is the interest income and capital gains information important for tax purposes, but when investing in different fixed income mutual funds, investors should also keep track of the NAV prices of the shares purchased and sold. This information is used in the computation of gains and losses when shares are redeemed.

The Different Types of Bond Funds

Table 8-4 shows different fixed income security mutual funds by investment objectives. Many different types of bond funds are available and their differences may be significant. The overriding difference between

Table 8-4 Types of Fixed Income Funds

Funds	Objectives
Corporate Bond Funds	Seek high levels of income. Invest in corporate bonds, Treasury bonds, and agency bonds.
High Yield Bond Funds	Seek higher yields by investing in less-than-investment grade bonds (junk bonds).
Municipal Bond Funds Long-Term Maturities	Seek income that is exempt from federal income taxes. Invest in bonds issued by state and local governments with long-term maturities.
Municipal Bond Funds Intermediate-Term Maturities	Seek income that is exempt from federal income taxes. Invest in bonds issued by state and local governments with intermediate-term maturities.
Municipal Bond Funds Short-Term Maturities	Invest in municipal securities with relatively short-term maturities. Also known as tax-exempt money market funds.
U.S. Government Income Funds	Invest in different types of government securities such as Treasury securities, agency securities, and federally backed mortgage-backed securities.
GNMA Funds	Invest in Government National Mortgage Association securities and other mortgage-backed securities.
Index Funds	Invest in the bonds that comprise the index.
Global Income Funds	Invest in the bonds of companies and countries worldwide, including those in the U.S.
Money Market Funds	Invest in money market securities with relatively short maturities.

Worksheet 8-2

How Do Investors Earn Money from Their Mutual Funds?

- When interest and/or dividends earned on the fund's investments are passed through to shareholders.
- When the fund's management sells investment securities at a profit, the capital gains are passed through to shareholders. If these securities are sold at a loss, the gains of the fund offset the capital loss, and the net gain or loss is passed through to the shareholders.
- When the NAV per share increases, the value of the shareholder's investment increases.

the types of bond funds is that they invest in different sectors of the bond markets. For instance, municipal bond funds are very different from zero-coupon bond funds. Similarly, short-term government funds differ from both municipal bond funds and zero-coupon bond funds. The types of securities that funds invest in determine the risks of the fund, namely the reaction to changes in interest rates, credit quality, the risk of default, length of time to maturity, and the yield of the fund.

Money market funds are the only types of bond funds that maintain constant share prices. These are mostly $1 a share and the investment company maintains the $1 per share NAV. Any expenses or short-term losses from the sale of securities are deducted from the revenues generated from the investments in order to keep the share price constant. This is more easily accomplished for funds that invest in money market securities, which are short-term, meaning that not that much volatility in the prices of the investment assets is present.

All the other types of bond funds have share prices that fluctuate depending on the value of the assets (investments) of the funds. Certain types of fixed income securities fluctuate more in price than other securities. For instance, Ginnie Mae securities will be much more volatile to changes in interest rates than similar maturity Treasury notes and bonds. In order to gauge the extent of the volatility in the mutual fund's price, investors should understand how the different bond securities react to changes in interest rates. Generally, funds with longer maturity bonds fluctuate more than shorter-term maturity bond funds. However, investors increase their returns by extending the maturities of their bonds. This point is illustrated by the following example.

Instead of investing in money market mutual funds yielding three to four percent p.a., investors can increase their returns by investing in short-term bond funds with securities maturing within three years. Should market rates of interest decline, the share price of the short-term bond fund will increase. The opposite is also true; when market rates of interest rise, the share price of the short-tem bond fund declines.

To lessen the potential price volatility, investors can invest in shorter-term maturity bond funds, which tend to fluctuate less than longer-term maturity funds. Money market funds, which have constant share prices, have an average maturity of 90 days. This is why money market funds are considered safe investments. Short-term funds have maturities of three years or less, which means that they have less volatility in NAV prices than longer maturity funds due to changes in interest rates. Remember, less risk does not mean no risk. Long-term maturity funds have average maturities in the range of 20 years, which will see the greatest fluctuations in price as interest rates change. Fund managers are quick to take advantage of changing rates of interest by either increasing or decreasing the maturities of their investments. For instance, when interest rates are on their way down, fund managers purchase bond issues with longer maturities, which of course, increase the yield and the fund's total return. See Worksheet 8-3 for a grid to assist investors in their choice of mutual funds.

Worksheet 8-3

Different Types of Mutual Funds

Quality

	High	Medium	Low	
Low Risk	High Quality Short-term Fund	Medium Quality Short-term Fund	Low Quality Short-term Fund	**High Risk** — Short-term
	High Quality Intermediate-term Fund	Medium Quality Intermediate-term Fund	Low Quality Intermediate-term Fund	Intermediate-term
High Risk	High Quality Long-term Fund	Medium Quality Long-term Fund	Low Quality Long-term Fund	Long-term

Maturity

High quality bonds have a low risk of default and at the other extreme are low quality bonds, junk bonds, which have a high risk of default.

Short-Term bond funds have an average maturity of 1-3 years for their bonds.

Intermediate-Term bond funds have an average maturity of 7-10 years for their bonds.

Long-Term bond funds have an average maturity of 15-25 years for their bonds.

The choice of mutual fund(s) depends on the investor's objectives and risk tolerance.

A conservative investor should be aware that investing in a bond fund composed of junk bonds (high yield bond fund) can fluctuate as much as 50 percent in NAV price. During the junk bond sell-off in the 1980s, some fund's prices declined by as much as 50 percent. Similarly, in the past, occasional sell-offs in GNMA bond funds and in the municipal bond market have occurred. Share prices of adjustable rate mortgage funds fell even when interest rates declined. This was because homeowners were refinancing their mortgages. These mortgages were paid back to their holders at 100 percent of their face value, but many funds could have paid premiums for these securities. Those losses then translated into lower NAV prices.

Understanding how individual types of bonds react to changes in interest rates will interpret more or less into how the fund's prices react to these changes. Generally, the higher the risk of the securities, the greater the potential return, and the greater the potential loss on the down-side.

The credit quality of the investments has an influence on price volatility as well as the yield. The lower the ratings of the individual bond issues in the fund, the higher the fluctuations in price, and the greater the yields. Because of the many issues held in a bond fund, credit risk does not affect bond funds in the same way it does when individual investors buy bond issues. For instance, most individual bond issues in a bond fund account for less than two percent of the total value of a typical large bond fund, which means that a default by the issuer would not have a significant impact on the NAV price. This would not be true for an individual investor's bond portfolio unless it is unduly large. The exception is the high-risk bond fund. This type of fund invests in below-investment grade bond issues, namely junk bonds where credit risk and the risk of default are of greater concern. Investors in these funds are compensated with higher yields for bearing these risks, which translate into greater NAV price volatility.

Many bond fund managers have boosted their yields by investing in exotic types of bonds, such as *collateralized mortgage obligations* (CMOs). Some bond funds held as much as 15 percent of their assets in CMOs. CMOs have the potential of boosting returns for funds, but because of the complexities of this type of investment, it is difficult to price them on a daily basis. Inverse floaters, a derivative type of municipal bond, were mainly acquired by municipal bond funds to boost their yields. These are also difficult to price because of their volatility.

By understanding the characteristics of the investments in a fund, shareholders are better able to gauge the extent of the fluctuations in the NAV of the fund. However, if investors do not know what the fund is investing in, it becomes harder to anticipate the changes to NAV prices. If the fund's holdings are not clearly spelled out in the prospectus of the fund, investors are in the dark with regard to the types of securities. The securities that the funds invest in are listed in the prospectus information, but the type and characteristics of the bonds may not be fully disclosed. Hence, an investor might see the number of the bond in a mortgage pool with the coupon rate, but other information might not be disclosed. For example, investors may not know if it is a floating rate bond or a fixed rate bond, the weighted average life of the bond and the tranche it is in, if it is a CMO.

An *index* bond mutual fund seeks to match the returns of a particular index, such as the Lehman Brothers Aggregate Bond Index, by replicating the holdings of the bonds in the index. The main benefit from indexing is that it does not require active management. After the bonds are purchased, actively managing the portfolio is unnecessary. Thus, an index fund experiences lower portfolio trading, which translates into lower transaction costs and lower expense ratios than actively managed bond mutual funds. The aim of an index fund is to match the returns of the index and not beat the market, whereas actively managed mutual funds aim to beat the markets.

How Does Performance Affect the Choice of a Mutual Fund?

The overall performance of a fund depends on the following:

- Yield
- Total return
- Expenses

Only looking at the yields or returns of funds does not provide a complete picture. Funds with high yields may have high expense ratios, which when deducted from the yields, may result in poor total performance. Performance by itself is an elusive property because most funds can boast attaining the number one position in some area of performance at some point in time throughout their existence. Similarly, as with any investment, good past performance may not be indicative of good future performance. Some funds that have performed well in the past have had poor performance thereafter. In fact, some funds that did well in the past are no longer in existence today.

New funds do not have track records; therefore, investors may not have a yardstick to measure the performance during a period of declining prices. This is especially true for funds, which come into existence during bull markets.

Some organizations such as Morningstar, a Chicago firm that tracks mutual funds, rate a mutual fund's performance relative to other funds with the same investment objectives. However, this too can be misleading for investors trying to choose a fund. (Morningstar's Internet address is *www.morningstar.com*.) First, the funds may not be comparable even though they have similar objectives; one fund may have riskier assets than another fund, and hence, a comparison would be inappropriate. And, again, past performance may not be a reliable indicator of future performance.

In choosing a fund, investors are best off looking at what the fund invests in (as best as can be determined), and trying to determine the volatility in terms of up and down markets.

Yield is only one aspect of performance. Yield is defined as the interest/dividends that are paid to shareholders as a percentage of the NAV price. Money market funds quote yields over a seven-day period. This is an average dividend yield over seven days, which can be annualized. Long-term bond funds also quote an annualized average yield, but it is generally over 30 days.

Since 1988, the SEC has ruled that funds with average maturities longer than those of money market mutual funds quote the SEC standardized yield. The *SEC standardized yield* includes the interest or dividends accrued by the fund over 30 days as well as an adjustment to the prices of the bonds for the amount of the amortization of any discount or premium that was paid for the bond assets. The SEC standardized yield makes the comparison of different mutual funds more meaningful.

The SEC standardized yield should be used for comparison purposes and not as a means to predict future yields. This yield is a measure of the fund's dividend distribution over a 30-day period and only one aspect of the fund's *total return*. Table 8-5 shows how the total return of a mutual fund is affected.

Table 8-5 The Total Return of a Mutual Fund

Total return includes the following:

- Dividends and capital gains/losses
- Changes in NAVs
- Dividends (interest) on reinvested dividends

Dollar amount of the total return = income dividends + capital gains + changes in share value

For example, an investor who purchased 100 shares for $10 per share in a bond fund for a total investment of $1000, receives income dividends of $0.40 per share, capital gains of $0.02 per share, and then sells the 100 shares for $11 per share has a total return of:

Income dividends (100 × $0.40)	$ 40
Capital gains (100 × $0.02)	2
Change in NAV (100 × $1)	100
Dollar Total Return	**$142**

The coupon interest earned on the bonds held by the fund is paid out to mutual fund shareholders as dividends. Mutual funds also pass on any gains or losses to shareholders, which can increase or decrease the fund's total return.

Another factor that affects total return is the fluctuation in NAV. When the share price increases by six percent, the total return will effectively increase by an additional six percent. Similarly, when the NAV price of the fund declines, the total return will decrease. This explains why funds can have a negative return. This happened when the European currencies went into turmoil towards the latter part of 1992 and affected short-term, global bond mutual funds. These funds had high yields, but they were diminished by the steep declines in their NAV prices.

The interest on reinvested dividends is included in the total return. When the monthly interest or dividend paid out by the fund is reinvested to buy more shares, the yield earned on these reinvested shares will boost the overall return on the invested capital.

Therefore, when comparing the total returns quoted by the different funds, investors must be sure that they are comparing the same type of total return.

When total returns are quoted by funds, investors should determine whether all of the above three components are included in the computation. In other words, it would be a *cumulative total return* for the period. However, examples of funds that choose not to advertise a total cumulative return exist. Some high yield junk bond funds have chosen not to emphasize total returns at times because they were negative due to the deep declines in junk bond prices. Instead, they touted their high yields. Thus, basing your choice of fund on yield alone can be misleading, as yields may be easier to manipulate. Investors should look at the yield and the total return of the fund to get a more balanced picture.

Expenses are a key factor in differentiating the performance of the different bond funds. By painstakingly looking for funds with the highest yields, investors are only looking at half the picture. A fund with a high yield may also be the one that charges higher expenses, which would put that fund behind some of the lower cost funds, which have smaller yields. Fees reduce the total return earned by the funds.

The mutual fund industry has been criticized for the proliferation of fees and charges. Granted, these are all disclosed in the prospectus of each mutual fund, but besides the conspicuous charges, investors need to know where to look to find the less obvious fees. Funds that charge load fees affect investors directly.

Load Funds versus No-Load Funds

Some mutual funds are *no-load funds* where the investor pays no commission or fee to buy or sell the shares of the fund. Investing $10,000 in a no-load fund means that every cent of the $10,000 goes toward buying shares in the fund. Investors can no longer easily identify no-load funds from price quotes in newspapers. However, this information can be determined easily by calling the toll-free number of the mutual fund family to ask about load funds, looking on the Web site of the fund, or examining the fund's prospectus.

A *load fund* charges a sales commission for buying shares in the fund. These charges can be front-ended and/or back-ended, and can be quite substantial, ranging to as much as 8.5 percent of the purchase price of the shares. The amount of the sales (load) charge per share can be determined by deducting the NAV price from the offer price. Refer to Table 8-3 for an example.

A front-end load is deducted from the investor's funds. For example, an investment of $10,000 in a fund with a load of five percent means that the $500 load charge is deducted from the $10,000. In other words, the investor is left with $9,500 of the $10,000 investment that goes toward buying shares in the fund.

Some funds give quantity discounts on their loads to investors who buy large blocks of shares. For example, the sales load might be five percent for amounts under $100,000, 4.25 percent for investing between $100,000 to $200,000, and 3.5 percent for amounts in excess of

$200,000. With load funds, investors should check whether loads are charged on reinvested dividends and capital gains as well.

Some funds also charge a *back end-load* or *exit fee* when investors sell their shares in the fund. This could be a straight percentage or the percentage charged could decline the longer the shares are held in the fund.

The ultimate effect of load charges is to reduce the total return. The impact of the load charge is felt more greatly if the fund is held for a short period of time. For instance, if a fund has a yield of six percent and has a four percent load to buy into the fund, the total return to the investor for the year is sharply reduced. If a back-end load to exit the fund exists, this could be even more expensive to the investor if the share price has increased, as it is the load percentage of a larger amount. Worksheet 8-4 summarizes the reasons for the choice of a load over a no-load fund.

12 (b)-1 fees are less obvious than loads. These are charged by many funds to recover expenses for marketing and distribution. These fees are assessed annually and can be quite steep when added together with load fees. Many no-load funds tout the absence of sales commissions, but tack on 12 (b)-1 fees, which are like a hidden load. A one percent 12 (b)-1 fee may not sound as if it is much, but this is $100 less per annum in the investor's pocket on a $10,000 mutual fund investment.

In addition to the previously-mentioned charges, funds have *management fees* or *investment advisory fees*, which are paid to managers who administer the fund's portfolio of investments. These can be quite high and also take a toll on the investor's total return.

Worksheet 8-4

The Choice: Load or No-Load?

Investors choose load funds because:

- They cannot decide which funds to invest in and it is convenient to leave the decision to a broker or financial planner.
- Brokers and financial planners sell only load funds from which they earn commissions.
- Brokers and planners do not sell no-load funds.

Investors choose no-load funds because:

- They can determine which types of funds to invest in.
- They are aware of the sales commissions of load funds and choose to put all their money to work.
- No-load bond funds tend to outperform load funds. See Table 8-6.

Table 8-6 Do Load Funds Outperform No-Load Funds?

No evidence supports the opinions expressed by many brokers and financial planners that load funds outperform no-load funds. According to CDA/Weisenberger, no difference appeared between the performance of the average no-load funds and load funds over a five-year period (Clements 1993). In fact, when adjusting for sales commissions, investors would have been better off with no-load funds. This makes sense because a load fund would have to outperform a no-load fund for a number of years just to recoup the initial load deducted from the investment amount. Consequently, it makes it much harder for load bond funds to outperform no-load bond funds when the general range of returns earned by bond funds are not that wide.

The decision is not so easily made because operating expenses in some load funds may be lower than those of some no-load funds. Thus, investors should do their homework because they may be exchanging load funds for higher operating costs in no-load funds.

All fees bear watching as they reduce yields and total returns because fees are deducted from net assets. Critics of the mutual fund industry have brought a sense of awareness of the proliferation of all these charges. A proposal from the General Accounting Office asks funds to disclose the exact dollar amount they charge investors on a quarterly basis. Currently, if investors want to determine the amounts charged by their funds, they have to use the expense ratio provided by the fund and then calculate how much they are being charged. The expense ratio provided by the fund may be used to compare the fees with other funds, but it does not give the amount that shareholders actually pay to the fund.

Funds are required to disclose their fees, which means that investors can find them in the fund's prospectus. The financial newspapers also list the types of charges of the different funds in their periodic mutual fund performance reviews. Investors should not be deceived by funds that claim to be what they are not. Lowering front-end loads or eliminating them altogether does not mean that a fund cannot add them in somewhere else.

Here are some guidelines that investors may want to follow to help with the choice of a fund:

- Obtain and read the prospectus. See Table 8-7.
- Examine the performance records of the funds of interest.
- Compare their total expenses and fees.
- Choose the fund in terms of overall performance. If no difference in the performance of the choice of funds appears, go with the fund with the lowest expenses.

Table 8-7 The Importance of the Prospectus

Read the objectives.	The objectives describe the types of securities that the fund invests in, as well as the risk factors associated with the securities. For instance, if the prospectus states that the fund buys securities that are less than investment grade, the investor should not be surprised to find that most of the bonds are junk bonds. The objectives also state whether the fund is seeking current income, stability of capital, or long-term growth. The investment policies outline the latitude of the fund manager to invest in other types of securities. These may be the trading of future contracts and the writing of options to hedge their bets on the direction of interest rates, and/or the investing in derivative securities to boost the yield of the fund. The greater the latitude in investing in these other types of securities, the greater the risk will be if events backfire.
Analyze the selected per share data and ratios information.	The "Selected Per Share Data and Ratios" table in the prospectus summarizes the fund's performance over the time period shown. Worksheet 8-5 illustrates an example of such a table.
Examine the expenses of the fund.	Although annual expenses are also shown in the "Selected Per Share Data and Ratios" section, mutual funds have a separate table with a breakdown of their expenses in the prospectus. This typically shows the different load charges, redemption fees, shareholder accounting costs, 12 (b)-1 fees, distribution costs, and other expenses. An examination of the prospectus enables investors to make informed choices of which mutual funds to invest in.

Worksheet 8-5

Selected Per Share Data and Ratios

	2000	1999	1998
Net Asset Value (NAV) Beginning of the Year	$10.02	$11.01	$10.73
Investment Activities			
line 1 Income	.40	.35	.55
line 2 Expenses	(.03)	(.04)	(.05)
line 3 Net Investment Income	.37	.31	.50
line 4 Distribution of Dividends	(.37)	(.30)	(.47)
Capital Changes			
line 5 Net Realized and Unrealized Gains (Losses) on Investments	$1.00	(75)	1.50
line 6 Distributions of Realized Gains	(.70)	(.25)	1.25
line 7 Net Increase (Decrease) to NAV	.30	(.99)	.28
NAV Beginning of Year	10.02	11.01	10.73
NAV at End of Year	10.32	10.02	11.01
Ratio of Operating Expenses to Average Net Assets	.45%	.46%	.84%
Portfolio Turnover Rate	121%	135%	150%
Shares Outstanding (000)	10,600	8,451	6,339

Analysis

The "Investment Activities" section shows the amount of investment income earned on the securities held by the fund. Generally, these are passed on to the mutual fund shareholders. For instance, in 2000, all of the net investment income of $0.37 was distributed to the shareholders (line 4), but in 1999, only $0.30 of the $0.31 of net income was paid out to shareholders. In that year, the $0.01, which was not distributed to shareholders, increased the NAV (line 7) in the capital changes section. (The capital loss and distribution of gains was reduced by this $0.01, which was not distributed.)

Capital gains and losses also affect the NAV. Funds distribute their realized capital gains (line 6), but the unrealized capital gains (losses) also increase (decrease) the NAV.

The changes in the NAV from year to year give investors some idea of the volatility in share price. For instance, in the year 1999, the NAV decreased by $1.01, which is a 9.17 percent decrease. How comfortable would an investor feel in the short-term if he/she invested $10,000 only to have it decline to $9,082.65 (a 9.17 percent decline)?

An average total return can be calculated by taking into account three sources of return: dividends distributed, capital gains distributed, and the changes in share price, using the following formula:

$$\textbf{Average Total Return} = \frac{(\text{Dividend} + \text{Capital gain distriutions}) + \dfrac{(\text{Ending NAV} - \text{Beginning NAV})}{\text{year}}}{\dfrac{(\text{Ending NAV} + \text{Beginning NAV})}{2}}$$

$$\textbf{Average Total Return for 2000} = \frac{(.37 + .70) + \dfrac{(10.30 - 10.00)}{1}}{\dfrac{10.30 + 10.00}{2}}$$

$$= 13.50\%$$

Calculating this simple total return of 13.5 percent indicates that an investor in this fund would have received double-digit returns, resulting mainly from realized gains and increases in the NAV share price. The more volatile the NAV of the fund, the greater the likelihood of unstable returns. Thus, when considering whether to invest in a particular fund, investors should not go by the advertised yield alone, but also look at the total return.

The ratio of operating expenses to average net assets is fairly low in this hypothetical fund (close to 1/2 of 1 percent). This is the aggregate of the expenses in the fund, which is expressed as a percentage of the assets in the fund. Investors should be interested in this ratio because they are paying for it in the form of a direct deduction from the earnings of the fund. Look for funds with expense ratios of less than one percent.

The portfolio turnover rate indicates how actively the assets in the fund are turned over. Bond funds tend to have higher turnover rates than the average stock funds and 150 percent is not uncommon for bond funds. A turnover rate of 100 percent indicates that all the investments in a portfolio change once a year.

How to Buy and Sell Bond Mutual Funds

Buying and selling shares in bond mutual funds can be accomplished in several ways, depending on whether the fund is a load or no-load fund.

Investors can buy into no-load mutual funds by dealing directly with the mutual fund. Most, if not all funds, have toll-free telephone numbers. Mutual funds will send a prospectus along with an application form to open an account to first time investors. A prospectus and application form may also be downloaded from the fund's Web site on the Internet. Once an investor has opened an account with the fund, he/she can purchase additional shares by sending a check along with a preprinted account stub detached from the account statement. As mentioned earlier, no sales commissions exist with no-load funds, so brokers do not sell them. Shares in no-load funds are bought and sold at their NAVs.

Load funds are sold through brokers, financial planners, and salespeople who charge commissions every time new shares are bought. Some funds also charge redemption fees, such as back-end or reverse loads, for selling shares. If the percentage loads are the same (for front or back-end), it may be preferable to go for a reverse load rather than a front load because all the money is invested immediately with the back-end load.

Some financial planners, brokers, and salespeople may try to convince investors to buy load funds with claims of better performance than no-load funds. No evidence supports this premise. In fact, according to a study by Morningstar, no-load bond funds consistently outperformed load funds over three, five, and 10-year periods through March 31, 1993 (McGough 1993). However, the claim that no-load bond funds are much more volatile than load funds during expanding and contracting markets may hold some truth.

Banks and discount brokerage firms have also entered the mutual fund arena and are selling mutual funds. This, of course, complicates the choice of mutual funds, but investors who feel confident enough to choose their own funds are better off with no-load funds. The difference saved may be minimal over short periods of time, but this difference can grow substantially over a 10-year period due to the compounding of interest (time value of money).

Information may also be obtained from the individual mutual fund companies' Web sites, along with other Web sites on the Internet. One such Web site is **www.fundsinteractive.com**.

Table 8-8 summarizes the information investors should consider in the selection of one mutual fund over another.

Table 8-8 Criteria to Consider When Choosing a Mutual Fund

- Investors should define their long-term objectives and risk tolerance before investing in the funds for the long-term.
- Select funds with low costs.
- Do not overrate past performance. Top performing funds can lose their edge over time.
- Use past performance data to see the range of performance and the risks of the fund.
- Do not buy too many funds. The amount of funds will vary as to the circumstances of the investor and the amount of money to be invested. Many investors erroneously duplicate their bond funds for diversification. This is unnecessary as each fund has a diversified portfolio of investments.

Tax Consequences of Selling Mutual Fund Shares

Investors should be aware of the tax consequences of actively trading their shares in their bond funds. The NAVs of bond funds fluctuate, resulting in gains and losses when shares are sold at different net asset prices from their purchase prices. Tax reporting on mutual funds can be complicated. Tax consequences occur even when investors buy and hold shares in a mutual fund. Dividends, which are paid to investors on a monthly basis, may be automatically reinvested in that fund to buy more shares. At the end of the year, the mutual fund sends a Form 1099 to each mutual fund shareholder showing the amount of dividends and capital gains received for the year. Dividends and capital gains are taxable to shareholders regardless of whether they are reinvested in additional fund shares or paid out in cash. Therefore, these dividends and capital gains need to be added into the cost basis when the investor sells the shares in the fund.

For example, suppose that an investor who had invested $10,000 in a fund two years ago and received a total of $2,000 in dividends and capital gains in the fund to date sells all the shares in the fund for $14,000. The investor's cost basis is $12,000 (not $10,000) and the gain on the sale of the shares is $2,000 ($14,000 − $12,000).

When investors sell only a part of their total fund, the procedure is different and may be tricky. This is further complicated when investors buy and sell shares actively as if it were a checking account. In fact, many mutual funds encourage investors to operate their funds like checking accounts by providing check-writing services. However, every time an investor writes a check against a bond fund, they encounter a capital gain or loss tax consequence. This does not include money market funds, which have stable share prices of $1. This action either causes a nightmare for the investor around tax time or produces extra revenue for the investor's accountant for the additional time spent calculating the gains and losses.

Keeping good records is an investor's most important responsibility in an actively traded bond mutual fund (or any mutual fund for that matter). For each fund, keep a separate folder and store all the monthly statements showing purchases and sales of shares, dividends, and capital gain distributions.

By keeping records of all transactions, investors can determine the cost basis of shares sold. This is done using one of three methods:

- The average cost method
- FIFO method
- The specific identification method

FIFO stands for "first in, first out," which means that the cost of the first shares purchased in the fund will be used first as the shares sold. Worksheet 8-6 illustrates the FIFO method of calculating capital gains or losses on the partial sale of shares in a mutual fund. The example shows that the earliest shares purchased are the first to be used in the sale of shares. After all the shares of the invested funds are sold, the basis of the dividends and capital gains shares will be used to determine any gains or losses.

Several funds provide the gains and losses on an average cost basis when investors sell shares in the funds. The *average cost method* enables shareholders to average the cost of the different purchases of shares in the fund. The two methods used are the single category method and the double category method. The former includes all the

Worksheet 8-6

Calculation of Gains/Losses on the Sale of Shares

Summary of GNMA Bond Fund

Date	Transaction	Dollar Amount	Share Price	# of Shares	Total # Shares
06/14	Invest	$10,000	$10.00	1,000	1,000
11/26	Invest	4,500	9.00	500	1,500
11/30	Redeem (sell)	13,200	11.00	(1,200)	300
12/31	Income Dividends	1,000	10.00	100	400

To Calculate Gain/Loss on a FIFO Basis

Sold 1,200 shares at $11.00 per share   **Sale Price** $13,200

Cost Basis

06/14	1,000 shares at $10.00	$10,000	
11/26	200 shares at $9.00	1,800	
	Total Cost		$11,800
	Gain		1,400

GNMA Bond Fund After Sale

Date	Transaction	Dollar Amount	Share Price	# of Shares	Total #
11/26	Invested	$2,700	$9.00	300	300
12/31	Income Dividends	1,000	10.00	100	400

shares held in the fund. The double category method involves separating the shares in the fund into short-term and long-term holdings, and calculating average prices for these two categories. Redemptions use the short-term or long-term average price. The average cost basis can get quite complex with additional sales and purchases of shares. Hence, some bond funds do not enable their shareholders to write checks against their accounts.

The *specific identification method* enables shareholders to identify the specific shares that they wish to sell. Investors can minimize their gains by choosing shares with the highest cost basis to sell first.

To minimize any potential tax hassles, investors are better off not writing checks from their bond funds for their short-term cash needs. This only creates gains or losses where the investor would have been better off investing the money needed for short-term purposes in a money market fund, which alleviates these tax problems.

Keeping good records is the solution for determining gains and losses for tax purposes. If an investor cannot determine the cost basis of their shares, an accountant can do so with good information. Without all the purchases and sales records of their shares, investors may not be able to prove their cost basis to the *Internal Revenue Service* (IRS) in the event of a tax dispute.

Purchase Plans

Besides the voluntary purchasing of shares in mutual funds, investors can use contractual accumulation and withdrawal plans for their funds.

- *Automatic Reinvestment:* Dividends and capital gains disbursements are automatically invested in new shares, instead of being paid out to shareholders.
- *Systematic Purchase Plan:* An agreement to invest a fixed amount on a regular basis for a period of time.
- *Systematic Withdrawal Plan:* An agreement to withdraw a fixed amount or number of shares on a regular basis for a period of time.

Purchase plans to periodically accumulate or withdraw funds to and from mutual funds on a regular basis have the effect of averaging the share price. By buying shares of mutual funds over a period of time at different prices, investors lessen the impact of price fluctuations. Bear in mind that if the price of the fund keeps going down, these plans will not stop investors from losing money over the short term. These methods keep investors investing in their funds when the bond market is going up or down. Several methods enable investors to average the share price. One method, dollar cost averaging, is described in the following section.

Dollar Cost Averaging

Dollar cost averaging is a method of investing the same amount of money at regular intervals over a period of time. This strategy can be used for individual bonds, stocks, and mutual funds. Generally, most investors build their portfolios over time, which means that by investing amounts at different times they avoid the risk of putting all their money into bonds or bond mutual funds at one point in time. By consistently investing the same amount in a security/fund at regular periods of time, the average cost of the security will be lower than the high price of the security for the period, and higher than the low price for the security/fund for the period. Table 8-9 shows the dollar cost averaging method when $1,000 is invested every month to purchase a bond mutual fund. The example assumes a no-load fund where no sales commissions occur.

In January, $1,000 is invested at $7 per share, resulting in 142.86 shares being purchased. The share price of the fund goes up in February to $8 per share, which means that with the same amount ($1,000), fewer shares (125.00) are bought than in January. Conversely, when the price of the fund goes down to $6.75 in May, more shares are purchased (148.15) with the same investment dollars ($1,000).

Over the 12-month period, $12,000 was invested to purchase a total of 1,467.36 shares. The average cost per share is $8.18. In this example, the investor loses money if the price falls below $8.18 and makes money when the stock price is above the average cost per share when selling. This average cost per share is $0.09 less than the average price per

Table 8-9 Dollar Cost Averaging

	Investment	Price per Share	Number of Shares Purchased
January	$1,000	$7	142.86
February	1,000	8	125.00
March	1,000	9	111.11
April	1,000	7.50	133.33
May	1,000	6.75	148.15
June	1,000	7.75	129.03
July	1,000	8	125.00
August	1,000	9	111.11
September	1,000	9.50	105.26
October	1,000	9	111.11
November	1,000	8.75	114.29
December	1,000	9	111.11

Total Invested	Average Price	Total # shares bought
$12,000	8.27	1467.36

Average Cost per Share = Total Invested/Total # Shares Bought
$$= \$12,000/1467.36$$
$$= 8.18$$

Table 8-10 Advantages and Disadvantages of Dollar Cost Averaging

Advantages	Disadvantages
1. Investors avoid having to time the market.	1. Transaction costs are high for individual bonds and when investing in load funds.
2. Investing on a regular basis over long periods of time averages the fluctuations in price.	2. Investors need to meet the minimum amounts stipulated by the fund. For individual bonds, investors need large amounts to buy bonds in round lots to lower transaction costs (buying in odd lots means higher transaction costs).
3. Using dividend reinvestment plans together with dollar cost averaging enhances the benefits over long periods of time.	3. With rising fund prices, dollar cost averaging results in higher average cost per share than if the total amount was invested at the beginning of the period.
	4. When shares in the fund are sold, the calculation of the tax basis of the shares is complicated for most investors. Records of all transactions must be kept to determine the gains and losses for tax purposes.

share during the 12-month period. Part of the reason for this is that during the months when the price per share is low, more shares are purchased for the same dollar amount. Thus, with fluctuating fund prices, the average cost per share will always be lower than the average price per share.

This does not mean that investors will always make profits by using dollar cost averaging. If the price of the fund keeps going down, the average cost per share will be lower than the average price per share, but the investor will still lose money if the shares are sold at a declining price. Table 8-10 lists the advantages and disadvantages of dollar cost averaging.

Instead of investing a fixed dollar amount, investors can also invest by buying fixed numbers of shares on a regular basis. Dollar cost averaging works better with no-load funds than load funds, where sales commissions may be higher for the smaller individual amounts invested on a regular basis.

What Are the Risks of Mutual Funds?

The major risk with bond mutual funds is the *risk of loss of funds invested* through a decline in NAV. The longer the maturity of the fund, the greater the potential decline in NAV. This is due to interest rate risk. When interest rates rise, bond prices (and NAVs of bond funds) decline. Similarly, when interest rates go down, bond prices (and the NAVs of bond funds) appreciate.

Credit risk affects those funds that invest in below investment grade bonds such as junk bonds. When nervousness arises about defaults in junk bonds, a major sell off in the junk bond market is provoked, which in the past has resulted in steep declines in junk bond prices and the NAVs of junk bond funds. However, credit risk may not be as significant for bond funds as it is for individual bonds. This is because funds are large and diversified with many different issues. Generally, the loss from the default of one or two issues would have a small, overall impact on a fund.

Some investors are naturally concerned about the *risk of insolvency* of mutual funds due to some bank failures and the shaky financial status of some savings and loan associations. Investors always run the risk that a mutual fund could go under, but the chances of this happening are small. The key distinction between banks and mutual funds is the way that mutual funds are set up, which reduces the risk of failure and loss due to fraud. Typically, mutual funds are corporations owned by shareholders. The shareholders contract a separate management company to run the fund's daily operations. The management company oversees the investments of the fund, but they do not have possession of these assets (investments). A custodian, such as a bank, holds these investments. Thus, if the management company gets into financial trouble, they do not have access to the investments of the fund.

Another safeguard is that a transfer agent maintains the shareholder's accounts. The transfer agent keeps track of the purchases and redemptions of the shareholders. In addition, management companies carry fidelity bonds, which are a form of insurance to protect the investments of the fund against malfeasance or fraud perpetrated by the employees.

Besides these safeguards, two other factors differentiate mutual funds from corporations such as banks and savings and loan associations:

- Mutual funds must be able to redeem shares on demand, which means that a portion of the investment assets must be liquid.
- Mutual funds must be able to price their investments at the end of each day known as marking to market.

Hence, mutual funds cannot hide their financial difficulties as easily as banks and savings and loans.

In addition to these checks and balances, the SEC regulates mutual funds. Thus, it is unlikely that investors in mutual funds will have to worry about losing money due to the financial collapse of a mutual fund or through fraud. However, investors should be aware that they could lose money through purchasing a fund whose investments perform poorly in the markets.

The Advantages and Disadvantages of Mutual Funds

Mutual funds have many advantages and disadvantages, which are listed in Table 8-11.

Table 8-11   Advantages and Disadvantages of Mutual Funds

Advantages	Disadvantages
1. Investors can own a fraction of a diversified bond portfolio with a small investment.	1. Professional management does not guarantee performance. Mutual funds may under-perform the markets.
2. Mutual funds are professionally managed, freeing up the investor's time.	2. When load charges and fees are included, total returns may be significantly less than if investors had bought individual bonds and held them to maturity.
3. Mutual fund companies redeem shares on demand. In the case of no-load funds, they are redeemed at NAVs.	3. Investors have no choice over the investment securities that portfolio managers make.
4. Mutual funds provide administrative and custodial duties: record keeping of all transactions, monthly statements, information for tax purposes, as well as the safekeeping of all securities.	4. Investors have no control over the distribution of hidden capital gains, which can upset very careful tax planning. Since investment companies do not pay taxes, income and capital gains are passed through to shareholders.
5. Investors have the option of reinvesting dividends and capital gains automatically for more shares in the fund or have them paid out on a monthly basis.	5. Dividend income from mutual funds fluctuates from month to month and mutual funds do not have maturity dates.
6. Mutual funds distribute dividends on a monthly basis, whereas individual bonds only pay interest on a semi-annual or annual basis.	6. Levels of risk, return, and stability of income and principal vary with the type of fund chosen.
7. Investors in a family of funds can switch from one fund to another as market conditions change. For example, when interest rates are going up, investors can switch money from their bond funds to money market funds.	
8. Many types of bond funds are available.	

Worksheet 8-7 lists the pitfalls that investors should be aware of in their choice of bond mutual funds.

Bond Mutual Funds or Individual Bonds?

Bond mutual funds have been very popular among investors, but the increasing use of the Internet, which provides more readily accessible information on individual bonds, will make it easier for investors to buy individual bonds.

The following are the advantages of bond mutual funds: professional management, diversification, the ability to invest small amounts of money, and the ease of buying and selling. For many investors, these advantages outweigh the disadvantages of mutual funds. Mutual funds may be the most practical way for investors to buy many bond types.

Worksheet 8-7

Caveats in the Choice of Mutual Funds

- Choose a mutual fund family that has a wide range of different funds, allowing greater flexibility in the switching of funds.
- Avoid funds with high sales charges, redemption fees, management, and expense ratios.
- Keep all the records of income and capital gains distributions, as well as the dates, amounts, and share prices of all purchases and redemptions of shares. This alleviates a potential nightmare at tax time.
- Avoid buying into a mutual fund towards the end of the year, which could increase the investor's tax burden. Before buying into a fund, investigate whether the fund has accumulated any capital gains distributions that have not yet been distributed to shareholders. This occurs when fund managers sell investments at higher prices than the purchase prices resulting in capital gains. These gains are passed onto shareholders at the end of the year through a capital gains distribution, even if the shareholders did not own the fund when the capital gains were incurred.

These are bonds that sell in high denominations such as certain mortgage-backed and agency bonds, and some municipal issues. Another factor in favor of mutual funds is the complexity of certain types of bonds. The complexities of mortgage-backed bonds, zero-coupon bonds, convertible issues, and derivative securities may exclude most investors from buying them as individual bonds. Through mutual funds, investors can own many different complex types of bonds.

It certainly makes sense to invest in junk bond mutual funds rather than individual junk bonds. The diversification achieved by mutual funds minimizes the impact from any unexpected defaults. Professional managers of these funds have quicker access to information about the different issues as well as greater expertise than most investors. Mutual funds also pay lower transaction fees for buying and selling bonds than individual investors.

However, in certain cases, a compelling argument arises for buying individual bonds over mutual funds. Rates of return on individual bonds are often greater from those earned from mutual funds. This is true even for no-load funds, because besides sales commissions, other fees (12 (b)-1, operating fees) exist that eat into the returns of mutual funds. By investing in individual bonds, investors avoid these fees.

The second powerful argument for individual bonds is that if they are bought and held until maturity, interest rate risk is avoided. Changes in interest rates affect the price of both individual bonds and bond mutual funds. However, if investors have a set time for which they will not need their money, they can invest in individual bonds with corresponding maturities (to their needs) and not worry about what happens to interest rates. This does not apply to bond mutual funds. If interest rates go up, a decline in the NAV of share prices of bond funds will occur. Mutual funds never mature, which means that the possibility of loss of principal is always present.

Bonds such as Treasury securities are easy to buy and by owning these individual Treasury securities, investors eliminate many of the fees that mutual funds charge, thereby increasing their returns. Moreover, when these are bought directly from the Federal Reserve Banks or branches, investors do not pay any commissions. Buying and holding Treasury securities makes more sense than investing in Treasury bond funds. However, if investors do not plan on holding the bonds through maturity, funds could be a better alternative.

Buying U.S. Treasury notes requires minimum amounts of $1,000 and $5,000 for different issues. Investors with less than these minimums are precluded from buying Treasury securities. For example, if an investor has only $4,980 to invest, individual Treasury notes are out of the question until that investor has $5,000. Similarly, if an investor has $5,950, only $5,000 could be used to buy individual Treasury notes, whereas investors could invest all of their proceeds in a U.S. government bond mutual fund. Once investors have opened a fund account, they can invest in increments of as little as $50-$100 in many funds.

Thus, bond mutual funds offer investors a convenient way to invest small amounts as well as large amounts of money. Investors could, of course, buy individual U.S. Treasury notes for the minimum amounts and invest any marginal dollars in existing bond mutual funds.

Investing in bond mutual funds is good for investors who do not have enough money to diversify their investments and who also do not have the time, expertise, or inclination to select and manage individual bonds. In addition, a wide range of different bond funds are available that offer investors the opportunity to invest in the types of bond securities that would be difficult to buy on an individual basis.

The advantages of individual bonds versus mutual funds are summarized in Table 8-12.

Investors in funds have the option of having their interest and capital gain payments paid to them in check form or having the amounts reinvested in additional shares in the fund.

Mutual funds pay no taxes on income derived from their investments. Under the Internal Revenue Code, mutual funds serve as conduits through which the income from the investments is passed to shareholders in the form of interest or dividends and capital gains or losses. With mutual funds, investors have no way of knowing the amounts of any capital gains and losses their funds might distribute, which can easily upset very careful tax planning. Individual investors pay taxes on their share of income and capital gains.

Table 8-12 Individual Bonds versus Mutual Bond Funds

	Individual Bonds versus	Mutual Funds
Loss of Principal	Not if held to Maturity	Yes, if Share Price declines
Diversification	Not unless a large number of bonds are purchased	Yes
Ease of Buying and Selling	Only for Treasury Securities	Yes
Fixed Amounts of Interest	Yes	No, amounts fluctuate
Professional Management	No	Yes
Tax Planning	Yes	No

Exercises

1. Explain the difference between open-end and closed-end funds.

2. What is the effect of a load mutual fund versus a no-load fund?

3. What is the significance of the mutual fund prospectus?

4. List the differences between the risks of bond funds and individual bonds.

End Notes

Clements, Jonathan: "The 25 Facts Every Fund Investor should Know," *The Wall Street Journal,* March 5, 1993, p.C1.

McGough, Robert: "Banks vs. Brokers: Who's Got the Best Funds?" *The Wall Street Journal,* May 7, 1993, p. C1.

Chapter 9

Managing a Bond Portfolio

The investor's objectives are the most important guidelines to managing a bond portfolio. The objectives outline the types of investments and the investor's acceptable level of risk, which ultimately determine the type of portfolio management strategy to pursue.

Knowing what investors want to accomplish from their investments enables them to manage their portfolios effectively. Buying and selling investments is relatively easy, but knowing what to buy and when to sell is more difficult. In essence, the investor's objectives and personal characteristics determine which choice of assets to hold.

The Investor's Objectives

The investor's objectives determine the purpose and time period for the investments. For instance, one investor may be saving for retirement in five years and another investor may be saving for retirement in 30 years. Although their objectives are the same (saving for retirement), the time period and elements of risk tolerance are very different.

The first step in any plan is to determine long-term, medium-term, and short-term objectives. For example, a newly wed, young family may have the following objectives:

- Short-Term
  - Set up an emergency fund (to include adequate amounts for insurance).
  - Buy a new car.
  - Buy furniture.
- Medium-Term
  - Save for a down payment on a house.
- Long-Term
  - Save for children's education.
  - Save for retirement.

Once objectives have been developed, it becomes easier to see what investors can expect from their portfolios. Before determining a strategy to achieve their objectives, investors should examine their personal circumstances, which serve as guides in the selection of their portfolio investments. Worksheet 9-1 lists the guidelines for an investor who is assembling a portfolio, as well as some of the investor's characteristics that should be considered to determine the types of investments and acceptable levels of risk.

An evaluation of these variables assists investors in the choice of investment assets and makes the level of risk that can be absorbed much clearer in the development and management of the portfolio. Personal circumstances change over time and need to be revisited on a yearly basis in order to reassess a portfolio. For example, if the breadwinner of a young couple with dependents loses his/her job and finds a temporary, lower paid job, investments in the portfolio might have to be changed from generating capital growth to income. The acceptable levels of risk

Worksheet 9-1

Guidelines for Assembling a Portfolio

1. **List objectives.**

    Short-Term Objectives

    _____

    _____

    Medium-Term Objectives

    _____

    _____

    Long-Term Objectives

    _____

    _____

2. **Evaluate personal characteristics.**

Marital Status:	single, married, widower
Family:	no children, young children, teenage children, empty nest
Age:	under 25, 25-39 years, 40-60 years, over 60
Education:	high school graduate, college degree, graduate degree
Income:	stability and level, future growth prospects
Job/Profession:	skills and expertise, ability to improve level of earnings
Net Worth/ Size of Portfolio:	level of income, assets, and net worth will determine the size of the portfolio

3. **Determine the appropriate asset allocation mix.**

Stocks	____%
Bonds	____%
Money Market Securities	____%
Total	100%

4. **Choose investments from the different asset classes.**

Stocks	Bonds	Money Market Securities
_____	_____	_____
_____	_____	_____
_____	_____	_____
_____	_____	_____

continues

---

5. At regular intervals, evaluate the asset allocation mix and rebalance if necessary.

Original Portfolio Asset Allocation   New Asset Allocation
Stocks   ____%   Stocks   _____%
Bonds   ____%   Bonds   _____%
Money Market Securities   ____%   Money Market Securities   _____%

---

for this couple determine the types of income generating investments. If they are risk averse, the investments may veer more toward capital preservation than income generation until a better paying occupation is found.

Generally, younger investors can withstand greater risk due to their longer-term outlook, but this is not always the case as pointed out in the previous example. The level and relative certainty of earned income outlines the latitude of risk that can be pursued in the investment portfolio. For example, a prosperous litigation lawyer can withstand greater risk in his portfolio by investing in growth investments due to the large amount of earned income from his occupation.

Depending on the investor's characteristics, a trade-off exists between investments generating current income versus those seeking capital appreciation. If investors opt for capital appreciation assets, they may sacrifice on current income.

A portfolio of assets is created based on the investor's characteristics and steered by the investor's objectives.

Allocation of Assets and Diversification

Asset allocation is a plan to invest in different types of securities (stocks, bonds, and money market funds) so that the capital invested is protected against adverse factors in the market. In essence, this is the opposite of the investor putting all of his/her eggs in one basket. The following example illustrates asset allocation. Imagine an investor with an amount of $200,000 to invest with the following asset allocation plan:

50 percent Common stock
35 percent Bonds
15 percent Money Market

The investor chose to invest all of the amount for common stock in Amazon, the Internet retailer of books, bought at $80 per share at the beginning of 2000, and all of the amount for bonds in the convertible debt of Amazon. The money market securities consisted of a money market mutual fund with a yield of close to six percent per annum. The value of the portfolio six months later would have declined by more than a half, as Amazon's stock, at the time of this writing, was trading in the low $30s per share. Amazon's convertible debt was also trading at depressed levels, with the only upside to the portfolio being provided by the money market securities, which grew by three percent in the six-month period.

The investor of this portfolio went only half the distance. The asset allocation plan cannot be faulted. The problem is that the investments in this portfolio were not diversified. Developing a portfolio is based generally on the idea of holding a variety of different investments in different sectors of the market rather than concentrating on investments within a single company or sector of the economy. This is done to reduce the risk of loss and even out the returns of the different investments. *Diversification* is the other balancing tool in a portfolio. The previous example illustrates a well-balanced asset allocation plan, but all the stocks and bonds were invested in the investments of one company, which did not insulate the portfolio from the risks of loss. By investing in the stocks of different companies and different types of bonds, the portfolio would have had greater insulation from the risk of loss.

This point is illustrated in Table 9-1 by an example of a portfolio with the same asset allocation as the previous example. Instead of investing the entire amount in the stocks and bonds of one company, the

Table 9-1   Diversified Portfolio

Portfolio			Total Investment
Common Stock 50%:			
200 shares Motorola	@ $35 per share	$ 7,000.00	
200 shares AOL	@ $52 per share	10,400.00	
200 shares Intel	@ $61 per share	12,200.00	
200 shares Allstate	@ $27 per share	5,400.00	
200 shares Costco	@ $32 per share	6,400.00	
200 shares Gap Inc	@ $30 per share	6,000.00	
200 shares Raytheon B	@ $23 per share	4,600.00	
200 shares Exxon-Mobil	@ $77 per share	15,400.00	
200 shares Pepsi	@ $41 per share	8,200.00	
200 shares International Paper	@ $33 per share	6,600.00	
200 shares Johnson & Johnson	@ $90 per share	18,000.00	
			$100,200
Bonds 35%			
10 Ohio Housing Finance Agency 6.85 03/01/06		$10,228.80	
10 Penn ST Higher EDL Facs Auth 5.7 05/01/08		10,200.00	
10 Harrisburg PA Auth Wtr Rev 5.0 08/15/10		10,000.00	
10 ATT 8 1/8 22		10,000.00	
10 Ford Credit 6 3/8 08		9,250.00	
10 IBM 7 1/213		10,250.00	
10 U.S. Treasury Notes 6 09		10,000.00	
			$69,928.80
Money Market Securities 15%			
29871.20 shares Money Market Mutual Fund		$29,871.20	
			$29,871.20
Total Value			**$200,000**

amount is spread into different stocks from different sectors of the economy and different types of bonds (corporate, municipal, and government). The risk of loss has been spread over a number of securities. Increasing the number of stocks and bonds held in a portfolio decreases the volatility. However, by increasing the number of stocks and bonds held in a portfolio, investors also reduce the potential performance of that portfolio. Diversification seeks a balance between the risk-return trade-off. The return on a portfolio depends on the types of investments held in the portfolio.

When classifying some of the different types of investments on a continuum of risk, common stocks are considered to be the most risky (in terms of variability in share price), followed by long-term bonds, with the shorter maturities on the low-risk end. Bear in mind that many other types of investments are available, such as commodities and futures contracts, which are riskier than common stocks. Similarly, a great variation of quality exists among common stocks. The common stocks of the well-established "blue chip" companies are considered to be less risky than the bonds of highly leveraged companies with suspect balance sheets. Table 9-2 illustrates this risk continuum.

Common stocks are considered to be the most risky due to the volatility of stock prices. However, over long periods of time where the ups and downs of the stock market can be averaged out, stocks have provided higher returns. Common stocks provide the growth in a portfolio and should be included among the investment assets to accomplish the long-term growth goals. The percentage allocated to common stocks depends on the investor's objectives and personal characteristics. As mentioned earlier, a retired widow who is dependent on the income generated from the investments in the portfolio may not have any common stocks in the portfolio. However, if the portfolio generates more than a sufficient level of income for the widow's current needs, a small portion of the portfolio could be invested in common stocks to provide some growth in the portfolio for later years.

Bonds are sought by investors primarily for their ability to generate a steady stream of income. However, an often overlooked fact is that long-term bonds (15- to 30-year maturities) also can be quite risky. Although 30-year U.S. Treasury bonds are safe investments in that the U.S. government is not liable to default on the interest and principal payments, they can be quite volatile in price due to changes in interest rates. Corporate and other types of long-term bonds will be more volatile than Treasuries due to the increased risks of default.

Table 9-2 Risk Continuum of Investments

Common Stock	Long-Term Bonds	Intermediate Bonds	Short-Term Bonds	Money Market Securities

|—————————|————————|————————|———————|—————|

High-Risk
Aggressive

Low-Risk
Conservative

Investors must weigh the advantages of taking on the greater risks of investing in other types of long-term bonds over Treasuries by examining their coupon yields. If the yields are significantly greater than those of long-term Treasuries, investors may want to contemplate purchasing these other types of long-term bonds.

The total return includes transaction costs, which are much less for Treasuries, particularly if these are bought directly through the Federal Reserve Bank or branches. If these bonds are held to maturity, no transaction costs are applied. Besides the coupon yield, the second consideration is that interest on Treasury securities is exempt from state and local taxes.

Some of the price volatility may be reduced by shortening maturities of bonds, for example, from long-term to intermediate-term. Even though returns may be diminished by shortening the length of time to maturity, intermediate-term bonds offer investors greater flexibility. For instance, if an investor's characteristics change and he/she no longer depends on current income from investments, intermediate-term securities are generally much more liquid than longer-term bonds and can be changed more easily to more growth-oriented investments.

Low-risk, low-return securities such as CDs, Treasury bills, and money market funds should account for the percentage of the investor's portfolio that will serve liquidity and emergency fund purposes. Many investors keep too large a percentage of their portfolio in these low-risk, low-return assets for various reasons.

Conservative investors who do not feel comfortable keeping only an amount equal to liquidity and emergency needs should increase the percentage. However, the returns from these low yielding investments often do not even keep pace with inflation without taking into account the effects of taxation on the interest.

No rigid formula for asset allocation exists. Rather, it is a good idea to think about the concept as a guideline when investing money. Some investors may tilt toward an aggressive portfolio, whereas others require a conservative portfolio. The mix of investment assets depends primarily on the levels of risk that investors are willing to take and their time horizons. The percentage allocated to the different types of assets can always be changed depending on circumstances. As individual circumstances change, so will the investor's objectives. For example, if the emphasis shifts to greater income generation and preservation of capital from capital growth, the percentage of the investments in the portfolio can be changed accordingly. The most important aspect of investing is having an asset allocation plan, which signifies the broad mix of assets to strive for. Once these broad categories are determined, the individual assets may be purchased. When considering the different types of securities to choose for a portfolio, investors should weigh the characteristics of the type of investments along with the risks to assist them in their overall choice.

Investors should revisit their asset allocation mix from time to time to determine whether to rebalance and realign their mix to their investment objectives. The frequency with which the asset allocation plan is rebalanced also depends on the investor's portfolio management investment style. A *passive investment style* suggests leaving the portfolio alone: in other words, buying and holding the investments without regard for factors that affect the investments in the portfolio. An *active portfolio investment style* involves changing the investment assets within the portfolio whenever external circumstances have the potential to influence performance. The management of bond portfolios is very different from the management of stock portfolios. Bonds provide regular flows of income and have fixed lives, whereas stocks do not mature, may not provide regular flows of income if the stocks do not pay dividends, and do not have maturity dates, which causes uncertainty with regard to future stock prices. This means that in the management of stock portfolios, a greater emphasis is placed on stock selection (buying those stocks that will appreciate the most). With bond portfolios, the emphasis is more on timing. This is discussed in the latter part of the chapter.

The following example in Worksheet 9-2 illustrates the need for rebalancing a portfolio. If the investor's objectives and personal characteristics have not changed one year later, the asset allocation mix should be realigned to the original mix.

Both advantages and disadvantages arise from rebalancing a portfolio. The advantages are:

- The relative weighting of the portfolio assets are aligned with the individual's objectives, personal characteristics, risk tolerance, and level of return.
- The risk of loss is reduced by selling the appreciated assets to realize capital gains.

The disadvantages of rebalancing a portfolio are:

- Rebalancing a portfolio includes costs such as the trading costs (commissions), the indirect costs of management, and advisory fees.
- Investors run the potential risk of loss that comes from selling the winners in the portfolio to buy more of the losing assets.
- Selling securities involves tax implications in taxable accounts.

Management of the Portfolio

Investors must be continually aware that not only do their objectives and individual characteristics change over time, but that their investments must be monitored due to changing financial conditions and markets. Companies change and their securities may no longer fulfill the criteria for which they were purchased. Not all investments in the portfolio will realize their projected returns, so investors managing their portfolios may need to sell and replace them with other investments. This does not mean that all or most of the investments in the portfolio should be continuously turned over. Only those investments that are unlikely to achieve the goals specified should be liquidated.

The management of bond portfolios does not require generally as much attention as stock portfolios. In fact, bonds are much more conducive to a passive management style because they pay a fixed stream of income and mature at a specified date. By selecting a convenient maturity date for the issue, the investor can wait until the issue matures to get back the principal. Not only does this strategy minimize transaction costs, but it also makes fluctuations in the value of the issue before maturity meaningless. However, should the investor need money before maturity, the current market value becomes important.

Active portfolio management strives to benefit from changes in external factors that affect the price and relative performance of the bonds under management. Table 9-3 summarizes the strategies to reduce the different types of risk facing stocks and bonds in a portfolio.

Many investors follow a more active management style than the buy-hold strategy. Such a strategy involves replacing existing bonds in the portfolio with new bonds. This is referred to as *bond swapping*. This strategy may be used for tax purposes in order to reduce capital gains taxes. At the end of the tax year, if an investor has capital gains from other transactions, the investor can sell some bonds whose prices have declined for losses to offset some or all of the capital gains. (If the bonds in the portfolio have not declined in price, this strategy cannot be used.) The proceeds from the sale of the bonds are used to buy similar type bonds (same maturity and quality). By swapping one set of bonds for another set of similar bonds, the investor has benefited by generating a tax loss, which brings about tax savings.

Table 9-3 Summary of Strategies to Manage Risk

Investment	Risk	Strategy
Common Stock	**Market Risk** **Financial Risk**	Invest for a long period of time. Diversification. Invest in companies with low leveraged balance sheets.
Bonds	**Interest Rate Risk** When market rates are declinining	Interest Rate Management Strategies Increase the maturities of the bond issues.
	When market rates are rising	Shorten maturities. Ladder maturities in the portfolio.
	Credit Risk	Invest in higher quality issues (above investment grade). Shorten maturities.
	Purchasing Power Risk	Shorten maturities. Requires active portfolio management.

Worksheet 9-2

Rebalancing a Portfolio

1. Begin with an asset allocation plan.

The investor started with the following asset allocation as illustrated in Figure 9-1.

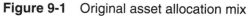

Figure 9-1 Original asset allocation mix

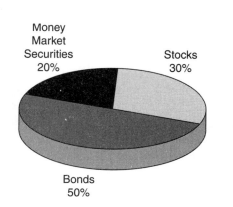

Money
Market
Securities
20%

Stocks
30%

Bonds
50%

2. Revisit the asset allocation plan after a period of time.

One year later with the rapid appreciation of the equity portfolio, the asset allocation mix has changed to the percentages shown in Figure 9-2.

Figure 9-2 Asset allocation mix one year later

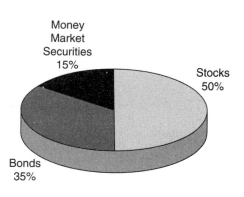

Money
Market
Securities
15%

Stocks
50%

Bonds
35%

continued

3. If necessary, rebalance the portfolio.

The investor needs to determine whether this new asset allocation mix is consistent with his/her objectives, personal circumstances, and risk tolerance. With the appreciation of the equity assets, the new equity mix is now 50 percent of the total portfolio value and the bond mix has dropped from 50 percent to 35 percent. This may be unsuitable for an investor who relies more on income generating assets than growth assets. Rebalancing requires selling off some stocks and buying more bonds with the proceeds in order to realign the asset allocation mix closer to an acceptable asset allocation mix.

4. Proposed asset allocation plan after rebalancing.

Current Asset Allocation Mix

Proposed Asset Allocation Mix

Current Asset Allocation Mix		
Money Market Securities	4	15%
Money Market Mutual Fund		$45,000
Stocks		50%
Large Cap Stocks		$150,000
Bonds		35%
Individual Bonds		$105,000
Total		$300,000
Before Tax Return		5.10%
After Tax Return		3.15%
Risk (Standard Deviation)		9.00%

Proposed Asset Allocation Mix	
Money Market Securities	15%
Money Market Mutual Funds	$45,000
Stocks	35%
Large Cap Stocks	$52,500
Mid Cap Stocks	$52,500
Bonds	50%
Intermediate Municipal Bonds	$50,000
Long-Term Treasury Bonds	$25,000
Intermediate Term Agency Bonds	$35,000
AAA Corporate Bonds	$40,000
Total	$300,000
Before Tax Return	6.15%
After Tax Return	4.5%
Risk (Standard Deviation)	7.65%

Other reasons for swapping bonds could be to improve yields (a lower yielding bond swapped for a higher yielding bond) or to take advantage of price differentials between different types of bonds, for example, selling agency bonds and replacing them with higher yielding corporate bonds. Anticipation of changes in interest rates could prompt investors to swap bonds with different maturities. If higher market rates of interest are anticipated, the investor would swap existing bonds for shorter maturities. Anticipation of lower rates of interest would lead to swapping bonds for longer maturities. Other strategies for increasing returns in a portfolio are summarized in Worksheet 9-3.

Management of Interest Rate Risk

The passive bond portfolio manager tends to buy and hold his/her investments and ignore external factors that might affect his/her investments. This is especially true for interest rates. Instead of trying to anticipate market rates of interest, investors could pursue a number of strategies that allow for changes in interest rates.

Using a *matching strategy*, an investor determines the holding period or time frame for the investments, and then selects a bond portfolio with a duration equal to the holding period. For instance, if the holding period is seven years, a bond portfolio with a duration equal to seven years is selected. Duration, which was discussed more fully in Chapter Six, "Analysis: Evaluating Bond Characteristics," is a measure of the average time that it takes for the bondholder to receive the interest and principal.

The duration value is determined by three factors:

- The maturity of the bond
- The market rates of interest
- The coupon rate

Duration has a positive correlation with maturity (the longer the maturity, the greater the duration) and a negative correlation with coupon rates and market rates of interest (the larger the coupon rate, the lower the duration). Similarly, duration moves in the opposite direction to interest rates. By matching the duration to the time period when the funds will be needed, interest rate risk is minimized. If interest rates rise, the value of the bonds in the portfolio will go down, but the interest payments received will be reinvested at higher rates of interest. Similarly, if interest rates decline, the bonds in the portfolio will increase in price, but the interest payments will be reinvested at lower interest rates. Through the use of duration, a portfolio can be protected against the changes in market rates of interest.

Active bond portfolio management involves anticipating future interest rates and using the information to position the portfolio to bene-

Worksheet 9-3

Strategies to Increase Returns

The following are strategies for increasing income received on bond investments:

- Increase the *maturities* of the bonds, particularly if the yield curve indicates that long-term rates will remain higher than intermediate-term and short-term bond rates. Bear in mind that the longer the maturity of the bond, the greater the potential volatility.
- Increase the holdings of *lower quality* bonds. Before doing so, investors should examine the spread between the yields of good quality bonds and lower quality bonds to see if the returns are worth the risks. A move from Treasuries to good quality corporate bonds with higher yields may cause less sleepless nights than a move from Treasuries to corporate junk bonds. If junk bonds are too risky, move up the spectrum to medium quality bonds. The move to lower quality bonds comes with the prerequisite that investors can tolerate the increased risks.
- Investors in the higher tax brackets should consider municipal bonds to increase their *after tax returns*. Calculate the taxable yields of municipal bonds and compare them with the equivalent taxable bond yield. This can be done by dividing the tax-free yield of a municipal bond by one minus the marginal tax rate. For example, a 4.5 percent yield on a municipal bond is equivalent to a 7.45 percent taxable yield for an investor in the 39.6 percent tax bracket. If the after tax yields are greater than what investors can get from taxable bonds, municipal bonds should be considered.

fit from the changes. One approach is to anticipate future rates and predict the future shape of the yield curve, which forms the basis for the choice of maturities for the bond portfolio.

Yield Curve Strategies

Investors can use the yield curve to make predictions about future rates. The yield curve shows the relationship between yields and maturities for each type of bond (for example, Treasuries or corporate bonds). The shape of the yield curve changes over time and investors anticipate these changes. This is illustrated in Figure 9-3, which shows three basic types of shifts in yield curves (Jones 1991, pp. 43-51). The first two diagrams in Figure 9-3 are parallel upward and downward shifts in interest rates where short-term, medium-term, and long-term rates all in-

Figure 9-3 Possible yield curve shifts

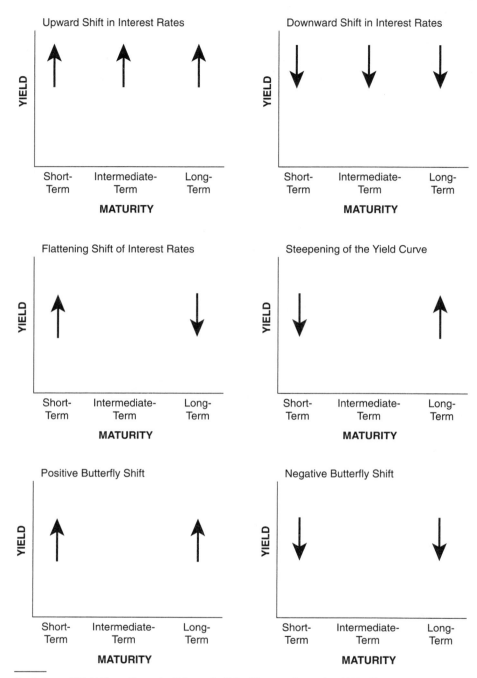

Frank Jones, "Yield Curve Strategies." *Journal of Fixed Income*, September 1991: 43-51.

crease or decrease by the same amounts. The second set of two diagrams shows the flattening and steepening of the yield curves where short-term and long-term rates go in different directions, while intermediate-term rates stay the same. The flattening of the yield curve is where the spread between short-term and long-term rates narrows and the steepening of the curve is where rate spread between short-term and long-term rates increases. The third set of two diagrams shows short-term and long-term rates rising together or falling together, causing a hump due to intermediate-term rates going in the opposite direction or remaining the same. This is referred to as the positive and negative butterfly shift.

Frank Jones (1991) studied the shifts in Treasury yield curves during the period 1979-1990 and found that the most common shifts were the parallel, flattening, and steepening Treasury yield curves. In other words, a combination of upward parallel increases in rates with a flattening of the yield curve and a downward shift in rates was combined with a steepening of the yield curve.

This discussion is relevant to investors because it indicates the different types of yield curves that require investors to first forecast the direction of future interest rates and then forecast the type of yield curve. Armed with these forecasts, investors can make decisions with regard to the maturities of the bond holdings in their portfolios.

Three yield curve strategies can be used for choosing bond maturities for a portfolio. These are:

- The ladder strategy
- The barbell strategy
- The bullet strategy

The Ladder Strategy The *ladder strategy* is another method that helps investors cope with changes in market rates of interest. It is a passive strategy that does not attempt to forecast future interest rates. Generally, long-term maturity bonds have the highest yields to maturity, but they also carry the highest interest rate risk, which means that a laddered strategy spreads the maturities uniformly over the investment period. Instead of pursuing the highest yields to maturity, a laddered strategy consists of choosing bonds with short-, medium-, and long-term maturities over a period of time. This is illustrated in Figure 9-4 with a 10-year laddered portfolio that has 10 percent of the bond issues with a maturity of one year, another 10 percent of the bond issues with a maturity of two years, and so on. When the first year's bonds mature, the investor reinvests the funds (particularly if they are not needed by the investor) in issues with a 10-year maturity to maintain the original laddering structure.

The advantages of laddering are:

- Funds become due on a yearly basis to provide for any short-term needs.
- Short-term bonds generally earn more than leaving funds in money market securities.
- The impact on the valuations of the portfolio is reduced due to fluctuations in interest rates.

Figure 9-4 Ladder Strategy

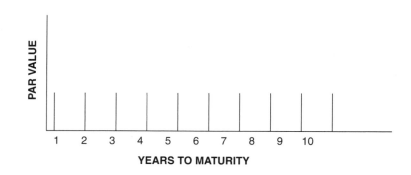

The disadvantage of laddering is that if the investor anticipates a change in interest rates, the investor would have to sell most of the bond issues in the portfolio to react fully to the anticipated changes. For instance, in the 10-year laddering example, if interest rates go up, the investor would want to replace 9/10 of the portfolio with higher coupon, shorter maturity investments. The same would be true for lower anticipated interest rates. The investor would want to replace most of the short-term maturities with longer term, higher yielding coupon issues.

The Barbell Strategy   The *barbell* or *dumbbell strategy*, shown in Figure 9-5, is used to counter the major disadvantage of laddering (having to liquidate a large percentage of the portfolio to take advantage of anticipated or actual changes in interest rates). A barbell strategy involves using only short-term and long-term bonds. Figure 9-5 shows a concentration of maturities in the fifth and fifteenth years. By eliminating intermediate-term bonds from the portfolio, the investor is better positioned to take advantage of anticipated changes in interest rates. If half the portfolio is invested in short-term bonds and lower rates are anticipated, the investor would sell the short-term bonds and reinvest in long-term bond issues. The opposite occurs when higher market rates are anticipated; the long-term bonds are swapped for short-term bonds.

The advantages of the barbell strategy are:

- By eliminating intermediate-term bonds from the portfolio, investors get increased liquidity from the short-term bonds and increased returns from holding long-term issues.
- Only half the issues need to be swapped in the event of anticipated changes in interest rates.
- If market rates of interest are correctly anticipated, investors have no need to change the portfolio.

However, the major disadvantage is that if interest rates are incorrectly anticipated, the investor could experience greater losses.

The Bullet Strategy   The *bullet strategy* has a concentration of maturities at one point on the yield curve. This is shown in Figure 9-6 where a concentration of bonds with 10-year maturities is present.

The advantage of a bullet strategy is that if cash is needed at a specific point in time in the future, a bullet strategy enables that concentration of maturities. The major disadvantage is that an adverse swing in interest rates could affect the entire portfolio.

These strategies (ladder and barbell) are attempts to eliminate the effects of interest rate risk and reinvestment risk in a portfolio. However, at best, a trade-off occurs between interest rate risk and reinvestment rate risk as shown in Table 9-4. The key ingredient for the successful management of a bond portfolio is an accurate forecast of interest rates.

Bond Indexing Strategy   Bond indexing is a passive management strategy designed to replicate the investments and performance of a bond index. Indexing has become more popular due to studies indicating that actively managed bond funds have not performed as well as indexed funds.

Figure 9-5   Barbell Strategy

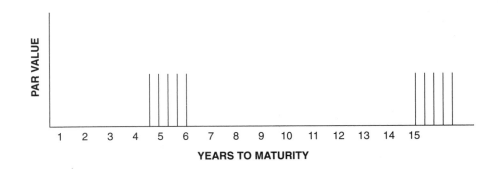

Figure 9-6   Bullet Strategy

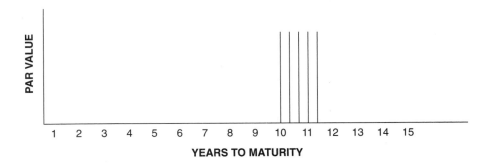

Table 9-4 Strategies to Counter Interest Rate Risk and Reinvestment Rate Risk

	Falling Interest Rates	Rising Interest Rates
Interest Rate Risk	Use Ladder Strategy	Use Barbell Strategy
Reinvestment Rate Risk	Use Ladder Strategy	Use Barbell Strategy

Conclusion

Portfolio management begins with clear objectives as to the expectations of the portfolio. With careful analysis of personal and financial characteristics, investors make an asset allocation plan of the categories of investments for the portfolio. The next step involves the choice of the individual investments and the extent of the diversification among these investments. Finally, the investment objectives guide the management of the portfolio. Managing a successful portfolio is more than selecting good investments.

The different types of investment assets can be complex. Investors should invest in only those investments that they fully understand. If the investor does not follow or fully understand the nuances of investing in individual stocks or bonds, the investor should stick with mutual funds. Besides the investments mentioned in this book, many others are available that were not discussed. However, this does not mean that they are unimportant or that they do not have a place in the investor's portfolio.

Exercises

1. Why should investors review their personal financial circumstances from time to time?

2. Why is asset allocation important?

3. List the strategies for increasing returns on a bond portfolio.

4. What are the tools of active bond portfolio management?

5. What are the tools of passive bond portfolio management?

End Notes

Jones, Frank. "Yield Curve Strategies." *Journal of Fixed Income.* September 1991: 43-51.

Chapter 10

Brokers: Investment Companies and Services

People save and invest hoping to earn significant returns. They buy and sell stocks, bonds, and mutual funds mainly as investments, although these can also be bought for speculation. Most investors buy these investment instruments hoping that they will appreciate over time. This is referred to as taking a *long position*. The opposite of the long position is the *short sale*, where investors speculate on the price of these investments going down.

The most widely used form of investing for individual investors is in the form of mutual funds, particularly with regard to bond investments. The next section discusses the classes of investment company offerings (mutual funds, closed-end funds, and unit investment trusts), and the types and need for financial help for these types of investments.

Classes of Investment Companies

The three basic classes of investment companies offer various funds with different types of investments. These classes are as follows:

- Mutual funds
- Closed-end funds
- Unit investment trusts

The extent to which investors are willing to spend time researching and analyzing the different investment company classes will determine their need for financial help.

Mutual Funds

A mutual fund invests their shareholders' money in underlying investments for which shareholders receive proportionate ownership in the form of shares in the fund. Four types of mutual funds exist: stock, bond, money market, and hybrid funds. Figure 10-1 shows the breakdown of funds invested in mutual funds for the year-end 1999 as reported by the Investment Company Institute Web site **www.ici.org**.

Mutual funds are purchased as follows:

- Directly from investment companies
- Through brokerage firms and banks
- Through supermarket family of funds

How investors purchase their funds determines their transaction costs. These costs are levied in the form of load and 12b-1 fees. Buying directly from investment companies in most cases eliminates the load fee. However, some funds within investment companies still charge load fees, even when the shares are bought directly from investment companies.

Figure 10-1 Breakdown of mutual fund investments (1999) Investment Company Institute

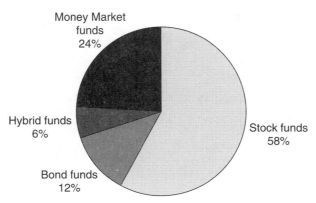

Investing in mutual funds through brokers, financial planners, and investment advisors means paying load charges. This is because brokers and many financial advisors earn their livings from fees and commissions.

A less obvious charge is levied on investors' purchases of fund shares. This happens when investors buy and sell shares in other fund families through their own investment company. Some of the large investment companies and brokers offer the purchase and sale of not only their own funds, but also those of other fund families. These investment companies and brokers are called supermarket families of funds. The compensation received is not paid directly by investors in the form of loads, but indirectly through 12b-1 fees. A 12b-1 fee is paid out of the earnings of the fund, which means that shareholders receive lower dividend amounts.

Faced with these alternatives, each investor needs to ask the question, "Do I feel comfortable choosing my own mutual funds?"

Worksheet 10-1 lists a set of nine questions to ask when investing in mutual funds, compiled by the Investment Company Institute and listed on their Web site. If investors can answer some of these questions and they know which types of funds to choose, they do not need to use brokers to buy their funds. If investors do not have any idea as to which types of mutual funds to choose, do not know which investment companies to contact for their list of mutual funds, or do not feel comfortable buying shares directly from an investment company, they should seek some financial help.

Many brokers and financial advisors justify their sales loads on mutual funds by claiming that load funds outperform no-load funds. No evidence supports this premise. In fact, studies show that due to the amounts paid for loads, load bond funds have under-performed no-load bond funds for three-, five-, and ten-year periods through 1993 (McGough, 1993). Investors are better off in the long-term by investing in no-load bond funds with low expense ratios. The same may be said for money market mutual funds especially as rates of return on these investments are at the low end of the earnings spectrum.

Worksheet 10-1

Questions to Ask before Investing in a Mutual Fund

1. What is the fund's goal?

2. What is the fund's investment strategy?

3. What are the main risks of investing in the fund?

4. What are the fund's fees and expenses?

5. Who manages the fund?

6. How are shares bought in the fund?

7. How are shares sold in the fund?

8. How are the fund's distributions made and taxed?

9. What services are available from the fund?

Source: Investment Company Institute, www.ici.org

Closed-End Funds

Closed-end mutual funds issue shares that are then traded on a stock exchange or in the over-the-counter market. Closed-end funds have a fixed number of shares outstanding, and after these are sold, the fund does not issue any new shares. The two major types of closed-end funds are stock and bond funds. These funds have professional managers who assemble and manage the investment portfolios according to the goals and objectives of the funds. These funds do not trade at their NAVs like open-end mutual funds. Instead, their share prices are based on the supply and demand for their funds, and other fundamental factors perceived to affect the value of their share prices. Consequently, they can trade at premiums or discounts to their net NAVs.

Shares of closed-end funds are bought and sold through brokers. The type of brokerage firm selected depends on the amount and level of service needed by the investor. Investors who are able to research the fundamentals of the closed-end funds, make decisions on which funds to buy or sell, and place the trades on their own can get by with a discount online brokerage firm. Investors who need advice as to which closed-end funds to invest in or a broker to supply information on these funds are better off with a full service broker or a discount broker that provides service.

Investors should be aware of the following facts with regard to the purchase of closed-end funds:

- Brokerage firms underwrite and sell newly issued shares of closed-end funds.

- The brokerage fees on these newly issued shares can be quite high, which then erodes the price of the shares when they trade on the market. For example, if a closed-end fund sells one million shares at $10 per share and has a brokerage commission of seven percent, the fund will receive $9.3 million to invest ($700,000 is deducted from the $10,000,00 proceeds). The share price will drop in value from the $10 originally paid and will trade at a discount.
- Another reason not to buy newly issued shares in a closed-end fund is that the portfolio of investments has not yet been constituted, so investors do not know what the investment assets are, and in the case of bond funds, the yields on those investments.

Unit Investment Trusts

Unit investment trusts (UITs) are registered investment companies that sell units (shares) to investors of a relatively fixed investment portfolio consisting of bonds or stocks. UITs have a stated termination date when the investments either mature or are liquidated. The proceeds are then returned to the unit-holders (shareholders). Consequently, these trusts are well-suited to bonds, with their streams of income and maturity of principal. With stock UITs, the stock is sold at the termination date and the proceeds are returned to the unit-holders. The majority of unit investment trusts sold are tax-exempt municipal bonds, followed by taxable bond trusts, and then equity (stock) trusts.

UITs can be bought through brokers who sponsor their own trusts and through brokerage firms that represent UITs. Investors who do not want to hold their trusts through maturity may sell them back to the trust sponsors. These trust sponsors are required by law to buy them back at their NAVs, which may be more or less than the amount the investor paid initially. Under certain conditions, shares of these trusts can be quite illiquid, particularly for bond trusts when interest rates are rising.

The same caveats apply for buying initial public offerings of UITs as for closed-end funds:

1. Investors do not know the composition of the portfolio's investments.
2. Investors pay sales charges or loads, which may be as much as four to five percent above the NAVs.

What Help Does the Investor Need?

Is financial help needed? If so, what kind of help? Some financial advisors evaluate investors' financial situations and then formulate financial and investment plans. Also, some stockbrokers provide investment advice as to which individual securities to invest in. Should an investor decide that he/she can do this without help, it can be easily accomplished. The investor can now administer trades without having to speak to a soul by trading online. If the investor does not want to trade online, the investor can use a broker to place his/her trades.

Financial Planners

Virtually anyone who pays a fee of $150 and registers with the SEC can be a financial advisor. (Some states require registration.) Consequently, investors should do their homework before hiring a financial planner or advisor and then evaluate his/her advice carefully.

   Credentials: Ask the planner for his/her credentials. The following are some areas of expertise:

- *Certified Financial Planner* (CFP), which means that this person has passed six, three-hour examinations given by the Certified Financial Planning Board of Standards in Denver. Investors can call the Institute of Financial Planners at the toll-free number (800-282-7526) or the National Association of Personal Financial Advisors (888-333-6659) to verify credentials. CFPs, in addition to passing the exams, must have three years of professional experience in finance and adhere to a code of ethics.
- A *Chartered Financial Analyst* (CFA) has passed three exams given by the Association for Investment Management and Research and has had three years of professional experience in the investment field. They also are required to adhere to a code of ethical behavior.
- A *Certified Public Accountant* (CPA) has passed four, three-hour exams given by the AICPA and has two years of public accounting experience. CPAs must also adhere to a strict code of ethical behavior. CPAs who work in the investment area specialize generally in providing tax advice.
- Registered Investment Advisor requires paying a registration fee of $150 to a federal government agency.

   Lawyers and insurance people also become financial planners or advisors. An awareness of the advisor's orientation is helpful. None of the degrees and certifications, however, guarantee knowledge, skills, or integrity, but they do indicate that the individual has or had a seriousness of purpose in pursuing the credentials.

   In addition to word of mouth recommendations, check up on the financial advisor's license to operate. Accountants and lawyers who give financial advice as a major part of their business must be licensed as investment advisors with securities regulators. Financial planners, advisors, and money managers must be licensed by their states, and if their businesses are large enough, with the SEC. Brokers must be licensed by their states and must register with the *National Association of Securities Dealers* (NASD) in Washington D.C. Be aware that some states allow investment advisors and planners to operate without having to demonstrate any knowledge, skills, or experience. Investors should check up on their advisor's background, previous employment, and any record of past complaints or violations. Many con artists are just waiting for trusting clients to entrust them with their money. Also, check with the SEC because advisors who oversee more than $25 million of investors' funds must register with the SEC. If they are not registered with the SEC, check with the state regulatory authorities. Investors can call the *North American Securities Administrators Association* (NASAA) in Washington D.C. at 202-737-0900 or investigate on the Internet at **www.nasaa.org**.

Even if the advisor works for a large firm, no guarantee of honesty is insured. Evaluate the information given by financial advisors and ask questions if the advice is not understood. Investors should never invest in something that they do not fully understand.

Compensation: Investors should ask their financial advisors or planners how they are being compensated. Financial planners may be compensated on a *flat fee basis*, which could be an annual fee, an hourly fee, a percentage of the total assets, or a combination of these. These vary considerably; currently, annual fees range from $1,000 to $3,000, hourly fees from $100 to $500 per hour, and percentage of assets from 0.5 percent to one percent. Some financial planners charge using a *mixture of a fee basis plus commissions* and others may charge on a *commission only basis*. Investors can never be sure if they are getting objective advice, but knowing how their advisors are compensated can help them determine the relative objectivity of that advice. Keep a tally of how much is being spent on investment advice. After a period of time, investors should evaluate whether they are getting their money's worth for the advice.

Brokerage Firms

In order to trade securities, investors need access to the market place. This comes through full service, discount, or online brokerage firms. Should an investor decide that assistance is needed in the selection of investments, a broker may be used to act as an agent. Selecting a broker/brokerage firm is a personal decision. Three basic types of brokers exist:

- Full service
- Discount brokers
- Online brokers

The amount and level of services among these basic types of brokers differ, as well as the way that the different brokers within these types of brokerage firms are compensated. The good news is that investors have many brokers and brokerage firms from which to choose. The following guidelines may be helpful.

How to Select a Broker

Services Required

Brokers charge commissions for executing trades. These commission costs vary considerably, which directly affects the investor's profits and losses. The commissions charged depend on both the number of bonds traded and the type of bonds.

Full service, national brokerage firms generally charge the highest fees and commissions, followed by *regional* service brokerage firms, which tend to be marginally cheaper. The *discount* brokerage firms discount their commissions and either charge no fees or reduced fees for miscellaneous services. Commissions are discounted even more at the *deep discount* brokerage firms. For example, the range of commissions for bonds at these discount brokerage firms varies from $2-$5 per bond with minimum amounts of $25-$50 per transaction. This range is a good yardstick for investors to determine whether the commissions charged by their full service brokerage firms are warranted. Full service brokerage firms charge more per bond transaction. Bear in mind that it is more difficult to determine the actual costs for trading unlisted bonds as the prices include the markups or markdowns.

Brokers at full service brokerage firms can be pushed to discount their commissions, particularly for clients with large accounts. Full service brokers familiarize themselves with the financial circumstances of their clients, provide opinions about specific stocks and bonds, and provide research on request from clients. Investors are paying the higher commissions for the investment advice and research available from and through the brokerage firm. In essence, a personal relationship exists that may be likened to handholding by the broker. The large, national, full service brokerage firms offer a diversified range of financial services, in addition to information, research reports, and the execution of trades.

The discount brokerage firms offer reduced commissions and in some, but not all cases, reduced services compare with the full service brokerage firms. Brokers at discount brokerage firms execute trades for clients, but they may not provide the same personal service as full service brokers. In fact, investors may not have their own personal broker. Trades may be executed by the different brokers who answer the toll-free phone number. Research may or may not be available for the asking. Some discount brokerage firms provide free research, but others may do so for an additional charge. Due to the rapid growth of online brokerage firms, pressure exists to provide free research from the same sources used by the full service brokerage firms. The trend is moving towards providing more free research and service.

The deep-discount firms offer virtually no ancillary services other than the execution of orders. However, due to competition, some deep-discount brokers offer services such as providing information and research.

Electronic trading or online brokers enable investors to place their own trades using a computer linked to the Internet. Investors can find the financial statements of all publicly traded companies on the government's Web site EDGAR (`www.edgar-online.com` and `www.freeedgar.com`). See Table 10-1 for what to look for in online trading.

Investors who do not require information and research from a broker may not need the services of a full service brokerage firm. In addition, if assistance in the selection of bonds is not needed and the investor is comfortable using a computer, an electronic brokerage firm may be suitable. On the other hand, new investors who require information and research about the market and the types of securities to buy may be more comfortable with a full service brokerage firm (or a discount firm that offers these services) and the extra transaction costs may be worthwhile.

Another consideration is the number of trades the investor makes in a year. If they only make a few trades a year, the difference in the commissions between a full service and a discount broker may not be significant. However, if an investor expects to buy and sell securities on a frequent basis, the additional commissions charged by a full service broker over an online broker will be significant. With the increased competition among brokerage firms, many full service brokers will discount their commissions if asked.

Reputation Selecting a broker or brokerage firm is a difficult decision that is similar to choosing a physician. The choice can be approached in two ways: investors can either choose a broker first, or a brokerage firm and then find a broker in that firm. Investors should be aware of many complaints of wrongdoing that have been filed against some unscrupulous brokers and brokerage firms (boiler-room operations). Bearing this in mind, even though many reputable brokers and brokerage firms are available, investors should do their homework to research their new brokers and brokerage firms thoroughly before they hand over their funds.

Both a firm's size and membership on the stock exchange affect its reputation. Large, national firms are known throughout the world. However, a small, local firm may be renowned in the local community. If a stockbrokerage firm is a member of the *New York Stock Exchange* (NYSE), its brokers have most likely passed the exam given by the NYSE and the NASD. In addition, member firms have a stricter set of rules of conduct. Investors can review their broker's employment history, where he/she is licensed, whether he/she has been disciplined, or have had any customer complaints or violations with NASD Regulation by calling 800-289-9999 or viewing the Web site `www.nasdr.com`.

Another aspect to consider is the level and area of expertise of the broker. If the investor is interested in bonds and the broker's expertise is in stocks or commodities, the investor ought to continue the search for a broker with specialized knowledge in that area.

Above all, the investor should feel comfortable both talking to the broker and with the broker's investment philosophy. Before making a final decision, find out whether any complaints have been lodged against the broker by calling the NASDs' toll-free number 800-289-9999.

Table 10-1 What to Look for in an Online Brokerage Firm

Currently, more than 100 online trading firms are available to choose from. They have different trading prices and offer a variety of services. In general, an investor wants an online brokerage firm that gives fast, reliable executions, immediate confirmations, and free real time quotes. If orders take a long time to be executed, an investor may not have the right online broker. A market order should be transacted instantaneously. Transactions should also be transacted at the best prices. An investor also wants an online firm that provides research. In addition, the choice depends on several factors:

- The type of investor
- The frequency of trades
- The services required

A long-term investor requiring help with investment decisions and wanting to trade online should look for an online brokerage firm that gives personal service. The trading costs of such a firm will probably be on the higher-end of the range, but the investor will receive investment advice.

Long-term investors who do not need any hand-holding should look for lower-end trading commissions from an online broker that provides research, free real time quotes, a Web site that is easy to use, and fast executions at the best prices.

Investors should ask about the fee structure for custodial services, account management, and transaction fees before making the final choice. See Worksheet 10-2 for some caveats of what to expect and what not to expect from brokers.

Types of Accounts at Brokerage Firms

Opening an account at a brokerage firm is as easy as opening a bank account. The investor is asked basic information, such as his/her occupation and social security number, as well as more specific information about his/her financial circumstances. Brokers are required to get to know their customers in order to use their judgement with regard to sizable transactions and whether the customers can use credit to finance their trades.

Investors will be asked how they want their securities registered. If they decide on leaving their bond certificates in the custody of the brokerage firm, they will be registered in *street name* (in the name of the brokerage firm). Interest on the securities is sent to the brokerage firms, where the payments are then credited to the customer's accounts. The main disadvantage of registering stocks and bonds in street name is that the brokerage firms may not forward all the mailings of reports and news from the companies to investors. The advantage of holding securities in street name is that when investors sell the securities, they do not need to be concerned with delivering the signed certificates within the three days before the settlement of the transactions.

If investors decide to have the securities registered in their own names, they can either keep the certificates or have the certificates stored in the broker's vaults. In the former case, investors must store

Worksheet 10-2

What to Expect and What Not to Expect from Brokers

The following are caveats as to what to expect and what not to expect from a broker:

- Most brokers make their living from commissions from trading securities. If the broker's salary is purely from commissions, as opposed to a straight salary, the broker may be biased toward encouraging the investor to make frequent changes to a portfolio. Brokers who encourage excessive trading, known as *churning,* in order to earn more commissions may be exposed to lawsuits and should be avoided, especially if the investor's investment philosophy is a buy-and-hold strategy. Keep in mind that if brokers are paid a salary, they may have to fill sales quotas in order to cover some of the fixed costs of the brokerage firm.
- Most brokers are not financial analysts and investors should not assume that they are experts in all aspects of investing. They may have an excellent feeling for and working knowledge of many companies and their relative prices. If investors need information about the stocks and bonds of companies not followed by their brokers, the brokers can obtain the relevant research information from their in-house research departments or from sources available to their brokerage firms.
- Brokers are required professionally to offer suitable investments to their clients. For example, if a broker suggests a risky, speculative security when the investor's objectives are income generation and safety of principal, the broker may be held accountable for the losses. To protect themselves, investors should state their objectives in writing and give copies to their brokers (Clareman, 1993, p. 167). Investors should never rush into investments suggested by their brokers if they are not sure about them. Ask for more information and weigh the advice or recommendations carefully before making decisions.
- Check monthly statements for accuracy. If excessive buying and selling of securities in a portfolio or any unauthorized trading occurs, put complaints in writing immediately. Do not acquiesce to any unauthorized trades even if they are profitable (it could be disadvantageous for future unauthorized trades which lose money) (Clareman, 1993, p. 168). In the case of excessive trading, the investor may be asked to sign an activity letter from the brokerage firm. Signing such a letter means that the investor approves of the excessive trading or unauthorized trades. If the investor does not approve, he/she should not sign (Clareman, 1993, p. 168).

the certificates in a safe place. It is a good idea to store stock and bond certificates in a bank safe deposit box as they are negotiable securities. If they are stolen, investors could face losses.

Three types of accounts can be used for buying and selling securities:

- Cash account
- Margin account
- Discretionary account

Cash Account With a cash account, the investor is required to pay in full for the purchase of the securities on or before the *settlement date*. The settlement date is currently three business days after the order has been executed. If a bond is bought on a Monday, the payment is due on or before the Wednesday of that week, assuming that no public holidays are within those three days. The Monday is referred to as the *trade date*. Should the investor not pay for the bonds by the settlement date, the brokerage firm can liquidate the securities. In the event of a loss, the brokerage firm can come back to the investor for the additional amounts. Generally, for online trading accounts, the money should be in the account before the trade is made.

When bonds are sold, the certificates must be delivered within three days (if securities are not held in street name) to avoid any charges. After the settlement date, the proceeds of the sale less commissions will either be mailed to the investor or deposited into a cash account with the brokerage firm. This depends on the arrangements made with the firm. It is a good idea to ask whether any fees are charged for the management of the cash and money market accounts. If fees are applied, investors should have the checks mailed directly to them. Interest rates on money market funds are currently so low (around three to four percent) that a two percent management fee could send returns after inflation and taxes into negative territory.

Margin Account A margin account enables the client of the brokerage firm to buy securities without having to pay the full cash price. The balance is borrowed from the brokerage firm. The maximum amount that the client can borrow depends on the margin requirement set by the Federal Reserve Board. For example, with a margin requirement of 50 percent, an investor buying bonds worth $20,000 would have to put up at least $10,000 in cash and would borrow the other $10,000 from the brokerage firm. The brokerage firm uses the bonds as collateral on the loan.

The brokerage firm charges interest on the amount borrowed by the margin investor. Risks are greater in margin trading because using borrowed funds to buy bonds could lead to greater losses if the bonds decline in price as well as factoring in the interest costs. However, if the price of the bonds rises significantly, the rate of return is greater for the margin investor than for the cash investor because the margin investor has invested less money.

If bond prices decline in a margin account, the brokerage firm sends the client a *margin call*. This is a notice requesting that the investor pay additional money to maintain the minimum margin requirement. If the investor does not deposit additional funds, the firm can liquidate the securities. The investor would be liable for any losses incurred by the brokerage firm.

Discretionary Account   With this type of account, the investor agrees to allow the brokerage firm to decide which securities to buy and sell as well as the amount and price to be paid for buying and selling securities. For the unethical broker, a discretionary account is the answer to all prayers!

An investor should monitor the activity in a discretionary account on a monthly basis to determine if any excessive trading by the broker for the sole purpose of earning more commissions occurs. Unless the investor knows and trusts the broker implicitly, be careful with a discretionary account.

Summary

Transaction costs include not only the brokerage commissions, but also the bid-asked spreads. Investors may be paying low commissions, but they may also not be receiving the best prices on their trades. For example, if a bond is quoted at $104 1/4 bid and $106 asked by one broker-dealer, and 104 and 105 1/4 by another broker-dealer, the bond should be purchased at $105 1/4 per bond and sold at $10 1/4 per bond. However, if the first brokerage firm is chosen, the investor will purchase at $106 and sell at $104 1/4 per bond. For 10 traded bonds, a broker's commission may range from a low of $25 at an online broker to the hundred of dollars at a full service brokerage firm. This means that if the investor needed to sell the bond (after buying at $106 per bond plus commission), the price of the bond would have to go up by at least four points to break even, assuming a $25 commission for each trade plus the one and three-quarter point spread. In other words, the bond would have to appreciate by 3.84 percent before the investor could sell it just to get back the amount paid for the investment. Bonds do not appreciate in the same way as stocks. In today's interest rate climate, a 3.84 percent appreciation in a bond would probably be more than 50 percent of the bond's coupon yield.

Spreads between bid and asked prices vary. For large, actively traded bonds, the spreads are much narrower than on thinly traded bonds. The spreads also vary with regard to the types of bonds with Treasury securities having the lowest spreads, followed by the more actively traded agency securities. Corporate and municipal bond spreads can vary significantly depending on whether the corporate bonds are listed on the exchanges or unlisted.

Sorting out the commission structure between full service brokerage firms and discount brokers can be a complex puzzle. This is because brokerage firms advertise prices that may be lower than other firms for one kind of trade, but much higher for other trades. Generally, deep-discount brokers may be cheaper than discount brokers, which may be cheaper than full service brokers. Online trading offers the lowest commissions, but investors are essentially on their own. Such investors need to be proficient in their level of knowledge on investing and the markets. Some online brokerage companies provide investment advice for their investors if needed. In addition to the fee structure, investors should consider the level of services they require.

Exercises

1. What are the criteria that investors should consider in determining whether to invest in load funds or no-load mutual funds?

2. List the major differences between a financial planner and broker.

3. What are the advantages and disadvantages of trading on margin? Use an example to quantify the advantages and disadvantages.

End Notes

Clareman, Lloyd S: "Keep Your Broker Honest," *Fortune Investor's Guide, 1994*, Fall 1993, pp. 167-168.

McGough, Robert: "Banks vs. Brokers: Who's got the Best Funds?" *The Wall Street Journal,* May 7, 1993, p. C1.

Glossary

Accrued Interest   Interest that has been earned but not yet paid.

Active Management   The portfolio manager changes the components of the portfolio frequently.

Adjustable Rate Mortgage   A mortgage with an interest rate that changes periodically to reflect the movement of a specified index of current interest rates.

Annual Report   A published report of a publicly traded company that contains audited financial statements, the auditor's report, the chairman's report, a review of the company's operations, and future prospects.

Arbitrageur   An investor/speculator who buys and sells the same security in more than one market to make risk-free profits.

Ask Price   The price at which a dealer is willing to sell a security.

Asset Allocation   Dividing investment funds among different types of investment asset classes and determining the percentage of these investment classes appropriate for a specific portfolio.

Average Cost Method   A method to account for capital gains/losses on a mutual fund by using the average cost of the shares.

Back-End Load   A fee charged by an open-end mutual fund to investors when they sell their shares back to the mutual fund.

Balance Sheet   A financial statement that indicates the wealth of a company at a point in time. The form of the balance sheet equation is: Total assets = Total liabilities + Equity.

Bankers' Acceptance   A short-term debt instrument. The acceptance is a draft drawn on a bank for approval for future payments.

Barron's Confidence Index   A ratio of Barron's average of 10 high-grade corporate bonds to the yield on the more speculative Dow Jones average of 40 bonds. It shows the yield spread between high-grade bonds and more speculative bonds.

Barbell Strategy   A bond portfolio strategy with investments concentrated in short-term and long-term maturities.

Basis Point   One basis point is equal to .01 percent. It is a measure of change on interest bearing securities.

Bid Price   The price at which a dealer is willing to purchase a security.

Bid-Ask Spread   The difference between the price at which a dealer is willing to buy a security (bid price) and the price at which a dealer is willing to sell a security (asked price).

Blue Chip Stock   The common stock of a large, established company.

Bond   The borrower of funds issues a security, which stipulates the amount of the payments to the lender.

Bond Indenture A legal document that specifies the terms and responsibilities of the bond issuer toward the lenders in the bond issue.

Bond Rating A rating is given to the bond as to the likelihood that the issuer of the bond will default on the interest and principal payments.

Bond Swap The selling of a given bond and the immediate replacement with another bond of similar characteristics to improve portfolio performance, yield, or to take advantage of tax losses.

Business Risk Refers to the nature of the company: the uncertainty about the company's sales, profits, and rate of return.

Call Premium The price above the par value that the issuer will pay bondholders for retiring their bonds when called.

Call Provision A provision in the bond indenture that enables the issuer to retire bonds before maturity.

Call Risk The uncertainty associated with the call provision of a bond.

Certificate of Deposit (CD) A time deposit issued by banks and savings and loan associations.

Closed-End Fund An investment company that issues a fund with a fixed number of shares.

Collateral Trust Bond A bond that has the backing of other financial assets.

Collateralized Mortgage Obligations A debt security based on a pool of mortgages, which pay monthly interest and principal.

Commercial Paper An unsecured IOU of large corporations.

Commodity-Backed Bonds Bonds whose coupons or maturity values are indexed to a specific commodity such as gold, silver, or oil.

Conversion Price The price that a convertible security can be exchanged for common stock.

Conversion Ratio The number of common shares received for each convertible security at conversion.

Conversion Value The value of the common stock represented by the convertible security (conversion ratio multiplied by the market price of the common stock).

Convertible Security Convertible bonds and preferred stock that can be exchanged for a specified number of common shares of the issuing company at the option of the convertible holder.

Coupon Rate The fixed rate of interest paid on a bond. The dollar amount of the interest payment is expressed as a percentage of the par value of the bond.

Credit Risk   The uncertainty associated with the financial condition of a company.

Currency Risk   The uncertainty that a particular currency may lose its value relative to another currency.

Current Yield   The dollar amount of the coupon payments divided by the market price of the bond.

Debenture   An unsecured bond.

Debt Ratio   A ratio that shows the percentage of a company's assets that is financed by debt.

Default Risk   The uncertainty that some or all of the investment will not be returned.

Derivative Security   A security whose value depends on the price of an underlying security or asset.

Diversification   Investing in different securities as opposed to concentrating on one security.

Dollar Cost Averaging   Disciplined investment approach where an investor invests a given amount at regular fixed intervals regardless of the security's market price.

Duration   The weighted average number of years that the bondholder receives interest and principal payments. It is a measure that indicates the responsiveness of the fluctuations in a bond's price to changes in interest rates.

Eurobond   An international bond denominated in a currency not native to the country in which it is issued.

Expense Ratio   The total expenses of a mutual fund as a percentage of the assets of the fund.

Face Value/Par Value   The nominal value of a bond that is repaid to bondholders at maturity.

Fed Funds Rate   The rate that banks can borrow or lend reserves.

Financial Risk   The uncertainty associated with the way the company has financed its assets.

Fiscal Policy   The government's use of taxation, spending, and debt management to attain economic goals.

Flower Bond   A particular Treasury bond that can be redeemed at face value to settle federal estate taxes.

Front-End Load   The sales charge paid to buy shares in a mutual fund.

General Obligation Bond   A municipal bond backed by the full faith, credit, and taxing power of the issuer.

Global Fund   A mutual fund that invests in both U.S. and non-U.S. securities.

Graduated Payment Mortgage A mortgage whose payments increase over the life of the loan.

Growth Fund A mutual fund whose primary objective is capital appreciation.

Growth Stock The common stock of a company that is growing faster than the norm.

High Yield Bond/Junk Bond High risk, low-rated speculative bonds.

Immunization A bond portfolio management strategy using duration, which enables an investor to meet a stream of cash outflows despite changes in interest rates.

Income Bond Debenture bond on which interest payments are made only if funds are earned.

Income Statement A financial statement that shows revenues and profits over a period of time.

Indenture A legal document that spells out the provisions of a bond issue.

Index Fund A mutual fund that seeks to match the portfolio composition of a particular index.

Inflation The increase in the prices of goods and services in an economy.

Inflation-Indexed Savings Bonds Savings bonds issued by the U.S. Treasury Department whose returns are tied to the inflation rate.

Initial Public Offering (IPO) The initial offering of shares to the public.

Interest Rate Risk The uncertainty of returns on investments due to changes in market rates of interest.

International Fund A mutual fund that invests in non-U.S. securities.

Inverse Floater A derivative security that reflects the changes in price of the underlying bonds sold with them.

Investment Companies Companies that sell shares in diversified portfolios of investments to investors.

Investment Grade Bond Bonds whose ratings are BBB and above (by Standard & Poor's).

Junk Bond Speculative bond with ratings below investment grade.

Keogh Plan A retirement pension plan that can be used to shelter self-employment income.

Ladder A technique used to construct a portfolio with different maturities over a time period.

Liquidity The ability to convert an investment into cash with a minimum capital loss.

Listed Security   A security that is traded on an organized security exchange.

Load Charge   A sales commission or fee charged by load mutual funds when investors buy or sell shares.

Load Fund   A mutual fund that charges a load fee.

Low-Load Fund   A mutual fund that charges a relatively low-load when investors buy and sell shares in the fund.

Margin   The amount of cash an investor puts up to invest in a security with the balance borrowed from the brokerage firm.

Market Risk   Uncertainty over the movement of market prices of securities.

Marketability   The ability to sell an investment quickly.

Monetary Policy   The regulation of the supply of money and credit to affect the country's economic growth, inflation, unemployment, and financial markets.

Money Market   The financial market where assets with maturities of one year or less are traded.

Money Market Funds   Mutual funds that invest in money market securities.

Mortgage-Backed Security   A debt security backed by a pool of home mortgages.

Mortgage Bond   A bond that has specific assets pledged as collateral.

Municipal Bond   A debt security issued by state, county, city, and local governments to finance public needs.

Mutual Fund   An investment company that manages the funds for the shareholders who buy shares in the funds.

Net Asset Value (NAV)   The total market value of the securities in a fund, less any liabilities, divided by the number of shares outstanding.

No-Load Fund   A mutual fund that does not charge sales commission to buy shares in the fund.

Notes   Intermediate-term debt securities with maturities between one and 10 years.

Open-End Fund   A mutual fund that has no limit on the number of shares it can issue.

Original Issue Discount Bond   A bond that is issued with a coupon below prevailing market yields and is sold at a discount.

Passive Management   The portfolio manager buys and holds securities in the fund.

Portfolio Turnover Rate   A measure of the trading activity of a fund.

Premium (Convertible Security)   The difference between the market price and the conversion value of a convertible security.

Primary Market   The market for the sale of securities for the first time by the issuer to the public.

Prospectus   A condensed version of the registration statement filed with the SEC for a new issue designed to provide information to prospective investors.

Purchasing Power Risk   The uncertainty associated with inflation.

Put Feature   A provision that enables the investor to sell the security back to the issuer at a specified price.

Recession   A decline in the Gross National Product for two consecutive quarters.

Refunding   A provision in a bond indenture that enables the issuer to call the bonds with a higher coupon rate, and pay the holders with the proceeds from a newly issued lower coupon rate bond issue.

Registered Bond   A bond whose ownership is registered with the issuer.

Reinvestment Risk   The uncertainty related to the rate that interest payments received on a bond will be reinvested.

Revenue Bond   A municipal bond that is backed solely by the revenues from a particular project, authority, or agency.

Secondary Market   The market where already existing securities are bought and sold.

Serial Bond   A bond issue with portions maturing at different dates.

Series EE Bonds   A U.S. savings bond that pays a market-based interest rate, which is a market average for five-year Treasury securities.

Series HH Bonds   A U.S. savings bond that pays semi-annual interest.

Sinking Fund   A provision in a bond that enables an issuer to allocate funds to repay the principal or purchase the bonds on the market and retire them before maturity.

Subordinated Debenture   An unsecured bond whose claims are junior to other bonds of the issuer in the event of bankruptcy.

Substitution Swap   A bond swap where an investor exchanges one bond for another bond with a higher yield.

Syndicate   A group of investment bankers who share the underwriting and distribution responsibilities in an offering of securities to the public.

Tax-Exempt Bond   A security whose income is not taxable by the federal government.

Term Bond   A bond issue in which all the bonds have the same maturity date.

Trade Deficit   An imbalance between a country's imports and exports. Imports exceed exports.

Treasury Bill   A short-term security issued by the U.S. Treasury.

Treasury Bond   A fixed income security issued by the U.S. Treasury with maturities over 10 years.

Treasury Note   A fixed income security issued by the U.S. Treasury with maturities ranging from one to 10 years.

Treasury Indexed-Inflation Securities   Treasury bonds issued by the U.S. Treasury whose returns are pegged to the rate of inflation.

Unit Investment Trust (UIT)   A type of investment company that has a finite life and raises funds from investors to purchase a portfolio of investments.

Variable Rate Note   A debt security whose coupon rate fluctuates with a specified short-term rate.

Yankee Bond   Bond issued by a foreign company or government, but sold in the U.S. and denominated in U.S. dollars.

Yield Curve   A curve showing interest rates at a particular point in time for securities with the same risk, but different maturity dates.

Yield to Call   The return on a bond if it is held from a given purchase date to the call date.

Yield to Maturity   The annualized rate of return on a bond if it is held until the maturity date.

Zero-Coupon Bond   A bond that is sold at a deep discount and pays no interest until maturity.

Answers to Exercises

Chapter 1

1. (a) Prepare a budget of expected future income and expenditures for each month, and then determine the amount that can be set aside toward savings. Write the check to the savings/investment account at the beginning of the month rather than waiting to see what is available for savings at the end of the month.
   (b) Save any additional amounts of income as opportunities arise.
   (c) Do not wait until the end of the year to save. Begin now.

2. (a) Increase the amounts saved.
   (b) Lengthen the compounding period.
   (c) Look for higher rates. This will increase future compounded amounts.

3. Stocks
   Objectives:
   - Provide capital growth to a portfolio
   - Provide growth and income to a portfolio

   Advantages:
   - Long term growth. This may reduced the amount of taxes paid.
   - Provide greater rates of return over bonds and money market investments over long periods of time.
   - Provide a store of value for investments.

   Bonds
   Objectives:
   - Provide income.

   Advantages:
   - Provide a regular stream of income.
   - Provide higher rates of return than money market securities and bank accounts.
   - Investing in municipal bonds. For investors in the higher tax brackets, this can lower the amount of Federal taxes paid.

   Money Market Securities
   Objectives:
   - Preserve capital and earn income.

   Advantages:
   - Provide safe investments with very little risk of default on principal and interest payments.
   - Provide liquidity and marketability.
   - Provide higher rates of return than bank accounts for short-term investments.

4. Money Market Securities
   Emergency fund needs
   Living expenses
   Funds needed within a one year period or less

   Bonds
   Funds needed for specific short and medium term purposes (1-7 years)

   Stocks
   Funds invested for the long term (7 + years)
   Retirement funds invested for the long term
   Education funds invested for the long term

Chapter 2

1. Real rate of return = Bond Yield minus Inflation
   $$= 5.6\% - 2.4\%$$
   $$= \underline{3.2\%}$$

2. Real rate of return $= 4.6\% - 5\%$
   $$= \underline{\text{Negative } 0.4\%}$$

3. Interest rates
   Inflation
   Unemployment
   Economic growth (or lack of it)
   Budget deficit/surplus
   Money supply
   International trade

4. • Reduce the volatility in a portfolio and even out the risks of loss.
   • Offer a steady stream of income.
   • Investors in high tax brackets may be able to reduce their federal taxes by investing in municipal bonds.

Chapter 3

1. Market rates of interest
   When rates go up, existing bond prices fall.
   When rates fall, existing bond prices rise.
   The extent to which prices rise and fall depends on the coupon rates of the bonds, the length of time to maturity, the quality of the issuer of the bonds.
   Risk assessment affects bond prices. Bonds with greater risk are more volatile in price.

2. **Dealer's Selling Price = Par minus Par (asked discount)**
   (days to maturity/ 360)
   $$= 100 - \{100\ (.0562)\ (90/360)\}$$
   $$= 100 - 1.405$$
   $$= \underline{\$98.595 \text{ or } \$985.95 \text{ per bond}}$$

   Dealer's Purchase Price = Par minus Par (bid discount)
   (days to maturity/360)
   $$= 100 - \{100\ (0.0563)\ (90/360)\}$$
   $$= 100 - 1.4075$$
   $$= \underline{\$98.5925 \text{ or } \$985.925 \text{ per bond}}$$

3. The investor loses money if the issuer calls in the bonds at the call price when the premium price is higher than the call price. If the bonds are never called in, the investor amortizes the premium paid over the life of the bond. The danger of buying bonds at a premium is that if the bonds are called soon after, the bondholder will not have held the bonds for a sufficiently long time to have received the benefits of the higher coupon yield and to have amortized the bond over a long period of time.

4. The floor price for a convertible bond is when it is valued as a straight bond. The convertible feature has no value.

   The ceiling price for a convertible bond is when the price of the equity is trading at a high price where the conversion value is the same as the convertible stock.

Chapter 4

1. Money market securities should be used for:
   - Emergency funds
   - Temporary parking places for funds.
   - Funds that are needed within a one year period.

2. - Safety of interest and principal if held to maturity.
   - Wide range of maturities available.
   - No transaction costs if bought directly through the Federal Reserve Bank.
   - Markups are the lowest of all types of bonds.
   - For some Treasury issues, investors need a minimum of only $1000.
   - Interest payments are exempt from state taxes.
   - There is an active secondary market for these securities.

3. The major advantage of inflation-indexed Treasury securities is the protection against rising inflation. Many of the advantages listed in the answers to question 2 for Treasury issues, also apply to inflation-indexed Treasury securities.

4. Agency issues offer slightly higher coupons than Treasury issues. Agency issues with de facto or de jure backing from the federal government offer relative safety of interest and principal repayments.

   Thirty-year GNMA securities are not as volatile as thirty-year Treasury securities due to the fact that principal is paid back to the bondholders on a monthly basis.

5. Convertible securities appeal to investors looking for income and the possibility of capital growth. If the convertible bond is never converted, the investor receives the regular fixed interest payments of a straight bond. If the stock price of the company exceeds the conversion price, the investor will convert the bonds into equity to share in the capital appreciation.

6. The risk of default depends on the quality of the issuer. Investors in zero-coupon bonds have more to lose than conventional bondholders in the event of a default as zero-coupon bondholders do not receive any interest payments until the bonds mature.

   Zero-coupon bonds are subject to interest rate risk and tend to be much more volatile in price than regular coupon bonds

   Call provisions of zero-coupon bonds could provide a ceiling on the price appreciation of high yielding bonds.

Chapter 5

1. Treasury bills for time periods of 1 year or less.
   For period of time longer than 1 year:
   > Treasury notes and bonds
   > Agency notes and bonds
   > AAA rated corporate bonds
   > AAA rated municipal bonds

   Bond maturities should be matched with the investor's time horizon for the use of the funds.

2. Investment grade convertible bonds
   Investment grade municipal bonds and corporate bonds

3. Compare the yield to maturity of the bonds, and in general choose the bonds with the highest yield to maturity.
   Check the reasons why the bond is trading at a premium or a discount.
   - Discount. Coupon rate is lower than the coupon rate of newly issued bonds of same risk and maturity. This is the most prevalent reason for a bond to trade at a discount. However there are other reasons which should make investors cautious:

- The bond is trading at a discount even though the coupon rate is higher than those of newly issued bonds with similar maturities. The bond may have been downgraded and has both higher credit and default risk. The bond could also be thinly traded which could further depress the bond price in the event of sale.
- Premium. If the premium priced bond looks attractive, check the call/refunding provisions before buying. Do not buy the bond if the call/refunding price is less than market price. This could result in a loss of principal in the event of call or refunding.

Chapter 6

1. Bond ratings assist investors in appraising the credit and default risks of bonds. A risk-averse investor would likely invest in top quality rated bonds whereas an investor looking for potential capital growth and higher coupon yields might choose bonds which are below investment grade quality. Checking bond ratings from time to time indicate whether the credit and default risks of a bond have remained the same, deteriorated, or improved.

2. The yields quoted below are the different measures of return on a bond.

   The *coupon yield* is the stated yield of the bond which indicates the amount of interest the bondholder receives.

   The *current yield* is the return the bond holder receives when a bond is purchased at a particular price.

   The *yield to maturity* is the annual rate of return the bond holder receives when the bond is held to maturity. This includes the assumption that the interest payments received are reinvested at the same rate as the yield to maturity.

   The *yield to call* is the annual rate of return on a bond when the bond is held to the call date.

3. *Duration* is used to manage the interest rate risk of a bond portfolio to lessen the risk of loss. This is done by matching the duration of the bonds with the time that the funds from the bonds are needed. When rates of interest change in small increments, duration provides accurate information with regard to bond pricing. However, when interest rates change in large increments, *convexity* provides more accurate information with regard to bond pricing. Convexity presents useful information in the choice of bonds by defining their relative prices to large changes in interest rates.

4. The major risks that affect bonds are discussed below:

   Interest rate risk. Interest rates and bond prices are inversely related. When interest rates in the economy decline, prices of existing bonds rise. Similarly, when market rates of interest rise, prices of existing bonds fall.

The *Risk of default* depends on the creditworthiness of the bond issuer. Bonds are rated by independent services as the ability of the bond issuers to make timely payments on interest and principal.

Reinvestment rate risk affects all bondholders who receive coupon interest payments. When market rates of interest decline, bondholders are forced to reinvest their interest received at lower yields. The opposite of this is when interest rates increase, interest receipts are reinvested at higher yields.

Purchasing power risk, also referred to as the risk of inflation, erodes the value of the bond. Bondholders receive fixed interest payments and the return of their principal at maturity. These payments do not increase with the rate of inflation, which means that there is an erosion in purchasing power.

Call risk. Bonds with a call provision may be affected by call risk. When interest rates decline by a significant amount below the coupon rate, bond issuers can call in their bonds and re-issue new bonds with lower coupon yields.

Chapter 7

1. The risk premium on a bond is based on the assessment of credit and default risk in addition to the business risk attributable to the bond. Bonds that have higher credit and default risk are assessed higher risk premiums.

2. Investors take additional risk in investments only when they expect to receive additional compensation. In other words, the greater the perceived risk in an investment, the greater the expected return.

3. The yield curve can be used by investors as a tool to forecast interest rates. With these forecasts investors can make decisions on the maturities of their bonds.

Chapter 8

1. Open-end funds issue an unlimited number of shares, whereas closed-end funds issue a fixed number of shares. With open-end funds, the shares are bought and sold at their net asset values from the investment companies sponsoring the funds. Closed-end fund shares trade at market values and are traded in the stock market. The market value of the share price depends not only on the net asset value of the closed-end fund but also on the supply and the demand for the shares. Thus, shares of closed-end funds may trade above or below their net asset values.

2. Loads are sales commissions deducted from the investors' investment funds. In other words, the load reduces the amount invested in the mutual fund. Investors in no-load funds have their entire amounts invested in the funds. This means that load funds have to produce greater returns than no-load funds to recoup the amounts paid for the loads. This is not easily achieved for bond mutual funds. Stock mutual funds may have an easier time recouping the amounts paid in loads. Investors should also check the expense ratios of the funds they are interested in. A no-load fund could have a higher expense ratio than a load fund which could negate the initial advantage. Investors should compare all the fees and expenses charged by the different funds before investing.

3. The prospectus of a mutual fund provides information on:
   • The objectives of the fund
   • The latitude of the portfolio manager for taking risks
   • The portfolio investments
   • Fees and expenses of the fund
   • Returns and an analysis of the performance of the fund
   • Investment information pertaining to the fund, such as minimum deposit amounts, withdrawal options, and the like.

4. Credit and default risk may have a greater impact on an individual's bond portfolio than on mutual funds due to the diversification and the large number of bonds held by mutual funds. The risk of loss of principal is present for both individual bondholders and mutual fund shareholders. However, individual bondholders do have some control over certain aspects of their bonds to minimize losses. Instead of selling bonds that trade at discounts, individual bondholders can hold the bonds through to maturity for a full return of their principal. Mutual funds never mature and so there is always the risk that the net asset value of the fund could be lower than the net asset value at purchase.

Chapter 9

1. Investors' personal circumstances change over time, which then can change their objectives. Different objectives require a review of the portfolio investments to realign the risk and returns to the requirements of the new objectives.

2. Asset allocation is used to protect the portfolio from losses due to adverse circumstances. By investing in different classes of investment assets, potential losses in the portfolio are evened out. For example, if the equity portion of the portfolio goes down, there is a chance that the bond and money market investments might not react the same way and reduce the effect of the losses from the equity section on the portfolio.

3. Increasing (or with an inverted yield curve decreasing) maturities. Investing in higher coupon bonds.
   Consider municipal bonds to increase after tax returns.

4. Active bond portfolio management is concerned with the factors that affect bond prices, such as interest rates, risk assessment, and yield curve. Active managers lengthen or shorten maturities to take advantage of changes in interest rates and yield curves, increase or decrease the quality of the bonds in the portfolio to increase returns, consider different types of bonds depending on the yield differential. Barbell and bullet strategies are used by active managers to manage changes in market rates of interest.

5. Passive bond portfolio managers ignore the factors that affect bond prices. Bonds are bought and held through maturity. The ladder strategy is passive in that the maturities of the bond portfolio are spread uniformly through the investment period.

Chapter 10

1. Investors who are able to choose which mutual funds they would invest in and are aware of the objectives and risks of the funds, would have no need to pay the loads for mutual funds. Investors who do not know which funds to choose should rely on the advice of a financial planner or broker, and would pay the loads to buy the funds.

2. Brokers give financial advise with regard to their client's brokerage accounts and which securities to invest in. Then, they place the trades for their clients. Financial planners have a broader scope than brokers. They evaluate investors' financial situations and formulate investment plans. Financial planners can also give advice with regard to specific investments, and if they are licensed brokers, place the trades.

3. The advantage of margin investing is the leverage that the investor obtains. When the investment appreciates, the investor receives a greater return than would an investor with a cash account. This is because the margin investor puts up a percentage of the entire investment and borrows the rest. The investment is smaller and this boosts the return. Consider the following example:

Margin Investor		**Cash Investor**	
Invests	$10,000	Invests	$20,000
Borrows	$10,000		
	$20,000		
Investment	$24,000	Investment	$24,000
Return on Investment	$4,000/10,000	Return on Investment	$4,000/20,000
	= 40%		= 20%

Leverage is a double-edged sword because this is also the greatest disadvantage of margin trading. If there is a loss of $4,000 instead of a gain in the example, the return for the margin investor is magnified to a negative 40 percent:

Return on Investment	−$4,000/10,000	Return on Investment	−$4,000/20,000
	= −40%		= −20%

The above example has not included the interest the margin investor would pay on the borrowed funds.

Index